The Art of the A

'You'll be surprised to think that my time is chiefly employed now in drawing and copying feet and hands and noses and lugs, which I am convinced is so absolutely requisite that nothing shall prevent me pursuing that study for some time, without which an architect cannot ornament a building, draw a bas-relief or a statue. Here Chambers excelled and by that means a design in itself neither immensely ingenious nor surprising may appear excessively so – and with the Lord's Will, M. Pecheux's advice and my own application a few hours every day, I will hope to outdo that formidable rival.'

Robert Adam to his sisters from Rome, 18th June 1755

'I was *not* cross only very dictatorial and impressive. They never realize that a working drawing is merely a letter to a builder telling him precisely what is required of him – and not a picture wherewith to charm an idiotic client.'

Edwin Lutyens to Lady Emily Lytton, 5 February 1897

Sponsored by Wates Construction Limited

The Art of the Architect

Treasures from the RIBA's Collections

Jill Lever & Margaret Richardson

Trefoil Books, London

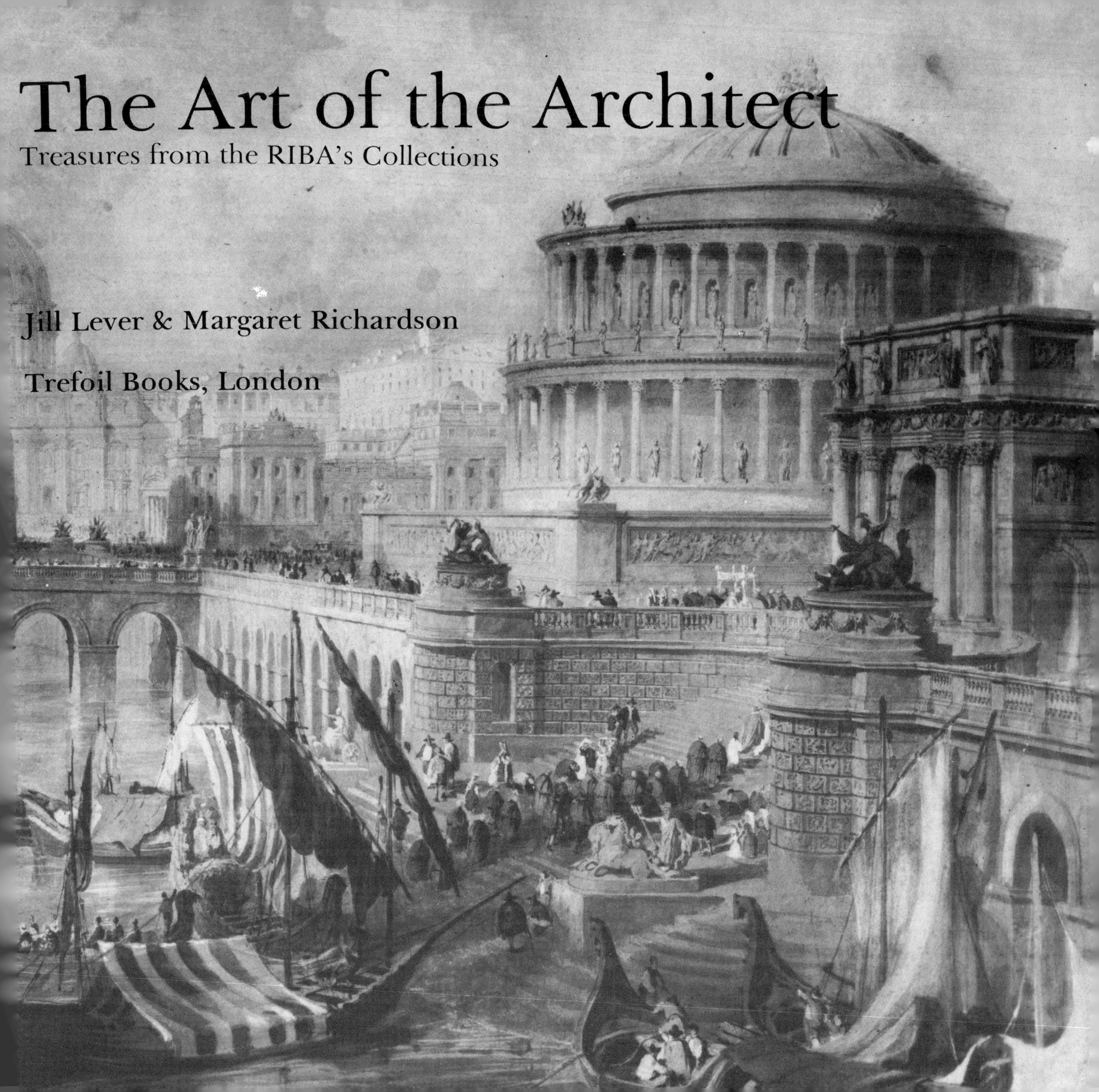

Published for the R.I.B.A. by Trefoil Books Ltd.,
7 Royal Parade, Dawes Road, London SW6

First published in 1984

ISBN 0 86294 060 5 (paperback)
ISBN 0 86294 061 3 (cloth)

Set in Baskerville by Words & Pictures Ltd., London and printed and bound by The Pitman Press, Bath

Acknowledgments

For their help with the catalogue of the exhibition we would like to warmly thank Finch Allibone and James Bettley who catalogued many of the drawings; Julia Wolton who catalogued the portraits; Angela Mace, archivist and Nicholas Savage, bibliographer.

For their help with the organisation of the exhibition we thank Anne Binney, exhibition publicist, Alex Coulter, Marilyn Mihill, Andrew Norris, Jane Preger and Charlotte Podro, paper conservator.

John Harris, Curator of the Drawings Collection and Jan van der Wateren, Director of the British Architectural Library, have been very generous with their advice and practical help.

We are most grateful for the advice and interest of many architects and scholars: Jill Allibone, John Brandenburger and James Burland of Arup Associates, Richard Chafee, Peter Cook and Christine Hawley, Charles Correa, Colin Cunningham, Michael Elkan and Josh Wilson of Richard Rogers Partnership. Lynda Fairbairn, Katy Harris of Foster Associates, Craig Hartley, Gordon Higgott, Sir Denys Lasdun, Jeremy Lever, S.N. Martoris of the Castle Museum, Nottingham, Tim Mowl, Anthony Quiney, Anthony Richardson, Eric Roberts of Mewes & Davis, Aldo Rossi, Andrew Saint, Alison and Peter Smithson, James Stirling, Charles Tarling of Adams, Holden & Pearson, Quinlan Terry, Alexandra Wedgwood and Christopher Wilson.

The exhibition was organised by Alan Irvine; the poster designed by Dennis Bailey.

Jill Lever and Margaret Richardson
RIBA Drawings Collection, 21 Portman Square, London

Foreword

John Wood
Portrait of Thomas Philip, Earl de Grey
(1781-1859)
First President of the Royal Institute of British Architects.
See page 89.

Enabling this exhibition to take place has been the most satisfying and exciting part of being President of the RIBA.

There has never before been such an extensive exhibition of the Treasures of the RIBA, and until now very few people were aware of their scale and magnificence.

There are many people to thank. Foremost are our predecessors, former members of the Institute and members of staff, whose acquisitions were so percipient. Then our benefactors, and in particular Wates Construction Ltd who have so generously sponsored this exhibition; and especially Mr Michael Wates for his personal interest. Finally, those who have worked so hard to assemble the exhibition.

MICHAEL MANSER
President, Royal Institute of British Architects

A1. **James Gibbs** (1682-1754)
Design model for St Martin-in-the-Fields, London, 1721. Made to a scale of ¼ inch to 1 foot
Pine & mahogany, the ceiling drawn (by Gibbs) in pen & wash (1130 x 610 x 1245h)
Provenance: Ordered by the Vestry of St Martin-in-the-Fields, 23 May 1721 and approved by them, 31 October 1721, the cost was £71; presented by the Vicar and Parochial Council of St Martin-in-the-Fields, 1970.
The church of St Martin-in-the-Fields is Gibbs's masterpiece and the most innovative of all eighteenth century English churches. Its influence at home and abroad (largely through the engraved plates of Gibbs's *A Book of Architecture*, 1728) was enormous. The combination of a classical temple front, Wren-ish several-storeyed steeple and Baroque interior underlines the individuality of Gibbs's architecture and his independence from Burlington's Palladianism. The model offered the members of the church vestry, a choice of treatments for the north and south sides. Their vote was for 'the Windows Expressed on the South Side of the Modell being the Rusticated Windows on a plain Ground'. Since the steeple is detachable from the model, Gibbs may well have offered alternative versions for that and, as executed, the upper stages are different. Further design decisions added an extra column either side of the portico and substituted pilasters for the engaged columns of the east end.

The design for the ceiling also changed in execution. A more ornate scheme was adopted in which domes replaced the cross-vaulting of the side aisle and coffering gave way to extravagantly decorated plasterwork panels.

The model was probably made by a cabinet-maker and one of considerable skill. For in quality the St Martin's model is second only to the Great Model for Wren's St Paul's.

Lit: T.F. Friedman, *op. cit.*; B.F.L. Clarke, *Parish churches of London*, 1966, pp. 181-2; J. Wilton Ely, 'The Architectural Model', *Architectural Review*, CXLII, 1967, pp. 26-32.

Introduction

Architectural drawings are both the graphic means to an end – the end being the building – and an end in themselves. Many great architects, like Palladio or Wren, have only produced rational and scientific drawings; but there are others, equally great, whose drawings can be compared with those made by artists. Like the critic in the *Building News* in 1884, in his review of Alfred Waterhouse's watercolours, we 'are not a little proud of an architect who can thus meet a painter on his own ground and on equal terms'.

Ever since the Renaissance architects have shown conflicting attitudes to the art of drawing. In his treatise on architecture, *De Re Aedificatoria*, 1485, Alberti advised architects against using perspective drawing because it could be inaccurate and misleading, and recommended instead the ground plan and the model. For Alberti the ground plan contained the key proportions and principal measurements of the building, and the model demonstrated the three-dimensional appearance – a view that Sir Denys Lasdun shares today. Palladio followed Alberti and only used the orthographic (straight-drawn) method of plan, elevation and section; he was followed by Inigo Jones, Wren, Hawksmoor, Lord Burlington, and, in the twentieth century, by the architects of the Modern Movement, who also revived the only accurate pictorial method of drawing – the axonometric. A.C. Pugin preached the dubious principle that architects should think not in terms of space, mass, surface or light and shade, but of abstract arrangements of pure lines, and Norman Shaw reacted against the artistic and coloured perspectives of his time by producing cold and literal drawings 'without figures or hansom cabs'. William Butterfield went further; he had a horror of self-advertisement and did not exhibit or publish any drawings in the architectural press. His own were 'small and highly unattractive' and he never signed or dated them.

On the other hand there are architects who have always had an innate 'genius for drawing'. There are many, like Thomas Harrison in the eighteenth century, who are 'very clear and ready in explaining with their pencils', or who, like Robert Adam, remind themselves to take to Scotland their 'books of sketches, and colours in the ivory case'.

We have tried to reflect these paradoxes in making a selection of drawings for this exhibition, choosing drawings made for many different purposes. The architect is drawing inventive diagrams for making buildings and his drawings must be judged within the conventions of his practice. But the danger is that the layman is often excluded; we have attempted, therefore, to explain the different purposes of architectural drawings and to trace the development of their graphic conventions.

The 1970s marked the beginning of a new appreciation of architectural drawing as an art form in its own right. The public exhibition of such work was no longer confined to the Architecture Room at the Royal Academy.

The starting point was the opening in 1972 of the RIBA's Heinz Gallery with an exhibtion of some of its greatest historical drawings, to be followed by Eileen Gray in 1973, James Stirling's drawings in 1974, R. Norman Shaw's in 1976, *London 1900* in 1978 and many others. In 1973 the Victoria and Albert Museum brought to notice the high quality of Victorian architectural drawings in its exhibition *Marble Halls*; in 1975 the Museum of Modern Art in New York did the same for Beaux Arts drawings. The Architectural Association opened its own gallery in 1979, and by alternating exhibitions of student work with shows of historical and modern masters, raised the standard of student draughtsmanship. The Viollet le Duc exhibition in Paris in 1979 and the Lutyens exhibition in London in 1981 presented many different types of architectural drawings as exhibitable items. The recent exhibition in Paris this year, *Images et Imaginaires d'Architecture* at the Centre Pompidou, has shown that architectural drawings can have enormous popular appeal. Even the commercial galleries have begun to see architectural drawings as marketable collectors' items.

We are still only on the brink of exploring an uncharted area of artistic invention. Architectural drawings are difficult to appreciate, and, understandably, perspectives have predominated in most exhibitions and publications. Once conventions and purposes have been understood we can begin to enjoy the particular pleasures they offer. The best of them have sure perspective and fine line, vigorous or sensitive penmanship, delicate monochrome washes or the quiet rendering of planes by colour. An added bonus is the more literal pleasure from the innumerable bizarre or worthy schemes that only survive as buildings on paper.

Purposes of drawing

Architectural drawings are most often thought of as the means to an end, part of the process that goes into making a building. The commission and the client's brief come first, then follows the architect's first designs, often rough, explanatory sketches, what Inigo Jones called the 'first scitzo' or 'first draught'. Some architects, though, (Halsey Ricardo was one) claim that they begin with ruled drawings made to scale. But Palladio's sheet of studies and record drawings (5), Inigo Jones's chimneypiece design with its figure studies in the margins (14), Charles Garnier's designs for the Paris Opéra (94) and Mendelsohn's sketchy designs for the Bexhill Pavilion (116) are all examples of spontaneous, freehand drawings that show the design at its earliest stage and yet have the essentials of the final design. The next stage is a more fully drawn-out design, freehand or ruled, but to a scale. It is at this stage that the patron will probably be brought in and that further revisions, reductions or enlargements will be made: thus Prince Bezbarotko asked for something smaller when he saw Quarenghi's design for a palace (43) while Gibbs's memorial for the Duke of Newcastle (23) became larger and more magnificent. Agreement reached, the 'approved' scheme is drawn – a formal set of plans, elevations and possibly sections (drawn in that sequence until well into the nineteenth century). Plans and elevations of the principal features, like the stair or portico, may be drawn to a larger scale. The drawings are 'finished' with shading and washes and when perspectives became acceptable, these would be drawn too. The totality and reality of a fully worked out scheme, such as Talman's Trianon design (18) replace the suggestion and experiment of the first designs.

'Presentation' drawings, that is, highly finished drawings made to explain a design to a patron and to persuade and impress as well, have a long history but were not (and are not) used by all architects. Nor is it possible without the evidence of, say, the committee minutes relating to Horace Jones's bascule bridge design (91) to be certain that a drawing was specifically made for presentation. Competition drawings are certainly made for presentation though their potential allure is often restricted in scope by the competition's rules so that, for instance, perspectives (if allowed at all) may have to be monochrome (66, 80, 95).

When final agreement is reached, the architect prepares the drawings for the builder, providing enough information for the translation of his design into the building itself. It is difficult to generalise about the nature of working drawings over a period of five hundred years since, as with all kinds of architectural drawings, there is only the evidence of what has survived. And though Palladio, for example, is known to have made full-size details, none exist now. The earliest working drawing in the RIBA Collection is the late Gothic plan and elevation, with cut-away section, for a niche (8). This is dimensioned on a grid that allowed the mason to make full-size bench drawings and cut out templates of the repeated elements of, for example, pendant arch or finial. The Smythson design for a rose window (11) gives exact information to the mason on the setting out of the parts of the window while in many of Inigo Jones's designs for windows and doorways, the masonry courses, imposts, voussoirs and keystones are drawn with great precision, and there are occasional details drawn to a larger scale. John Webb, in 1665, made very detailed drawings for King Charles's apartments at Greenwich; fully dimensioned and drawn to a quarter full-size. The first complete set of working drawings (at the RIBA) with full-size details for mason, joiner and plasterer are for Onslow House and are dated 1780. From that date, surviving sets of working drawings become increasingly larger and more detailed with, for instance, 188 for James Wyatt's Ashridge Park, 1807-13. The Houses of Parliament required a vast number of drawings; the drawing for floor tiles (71) were made in the sub-contractor's shop from Pugin's rapidly drawn but sufficient designs. Norman Shaw's full-size drawing for a weathervane (99) indicates the architect's concern with craft and detail while Foster's ten times full-size detail (123) illustrates, together with the Rogers's drawing for a crane ((129) one of over 10,000 drawings prepared for the Lloyd's building) the minute attention to detail required for today's technologically inventive buildings.

The need for detailed drawings hinges on several factors. The introduction of a new style, say, of Palladianism to Gothic-trained masons, may be one; another may be a new approach to architecture, for example, so intimately concerned with craftsmanship was an architect like Philip Webb, that leaving nothing to chance, he wrote lengthy instructions on already comprehensively detailed drawings for the carver or stuccoist. Or, it may be the employment of new methods of construction, as with Fowler's advanced use of cast-iron and laminated tiles for Hungerford Market (63), or the use of new building materials on an extensive scale, such as the terracotta chosen by Waterhouse for the Natural History Museum (82).

Changes within the building industry also contributed to the multiplicity of working drawings. While competitive tendering was already a long-established system, it reached a new intensity in the 1850s and '60s and estimators (and, later, quantity surveyors) became an essential part of the building team. Since they required very full working drawings and specifications, architectural offices became larger, and new, more efficient methods of copying drawings, involving commercially-manufactured tracing paper, tracing cloth, and anastatic and 'blue' printing processes, were developed.

The process of design and construction completed, the architect may make a record of the building, for himself, as with Quinlan Terry's drawing of a summerhouse (128) or Denys Lasdun's model of the National Theatre (A5). Or, the client might perhaps receive a beautifully-bound album of highly finished drawings: George Steuart's drawing for the library at Stoke Park (44) was one of eight presented to his client, Mr Joshua Smith; Humphry Repton's Red Books (53, 54) are another kind of record. Or the new owner might commission an artist to make a portrait of his house: Buckler made ten watercolours of Ashridge Park for the Earl of Bridgewater (57) and Thomas Hope commissioned John Britton to write a description of the Deepdene with watercolours made by W.H. Bartlett (59). Another kind of record drawing is the measured drawing of an existing building (2) or a survey drawing, of which Hawksmoor's dashing sketch of a choir stall canopy at Westminster Abbey (22) is a particularly pleasing example.

Not all designs depend upon a commission and nineteen of the drawings shown here relate to competitions. The earliest competition design in the RIBA Collection is Scamozzi's design for the Rialto bridge in Venice, made in 1587. Regular competitions were not held in Great Britain until the last part of the eighteenth century and the Bank of England competition, won by Soane in 1788, is among the earliest and most important. Grellier, Barry, Brodrick, Waterhouse, Jackson, Garnier, Belcher, Rickards, Mendelsohn, the Smithsons, Spence and Stirling are among those architects represented here by competition designs or designs made for a building won in competition. Not all were successful for an architect cannot hope to build all of his designs. But those unbuilt designs are a legitimate part of an architect's work and the 'paper architecture' of Boullée, Sant'Elia and other visionary architects has been enormously influential.

Summerson wrote that 'architecture is a chained and fettered art . . . but when once we remove architecture from the arena of the solid and material . . . we are free at last to *depict* those things which architecture might do in certain circumstances – circumstances bounded only by the remotest confines of possibility. Here is the sphere of the maker of architectural fantasies'. (fn i) And of theoretical and ideal schemes, caprices, imaginative compositions and archaeological reconstructions as well as of the merely eccentric. The theoretical reconstructions of the Temple of Solomon by C. Stanley Peach or of Palestrina by George Hadfield suggest why it was the ancient and classical world that most often stimulated architectural imagination. The earliest drawings for fantastic architecture, setting aside the 'conceits' of the Elizabethan architect, Robert Smythson, date from the seventeenth and eighteenth centuries, that is, from the Baroque period.

Stage design is an area where imagination is limited only by the capacity of stage carpenter and scene painter and it is often difficult (as with Galli-Bibiena's drawing (24)) to distinguish between the 'theatre of illusion' and imaginative architectural compositions. G.B. Piranesi's views of Roman ruins and reconstructions of ancient Rome are intensely dramatic (D5); engraved or etched, they reached a wide audience captivated by their visionary and artistic qualities. It is hardly possible to overstate how

2. **Andrea Palladio** (1508-1580)
Measured drawings of a capital, architrave, frieze, cornice and pedestal from the Temple of Augustus at Pola, Yugoslavia, *c.* 1540
Brown & black pen (420 x 280)
Provenance: Burlington-Devonshire Collection (Palladio VIII/4 verso), as given for no. 1.
Palladio never drew in perspective himself, preferring the more accurate methods of plan, elevation and section. It is, therefore, very likely that in this case he copied a drawing by the Veronese painter-architect, Giovanni Maria Falconetto (?-1535), who is known to have made surveys of the Roman antiquities in Pola, and whose drawings Palladio would have seen in the collection of Cardinal Ridolfi in Verona after Falconetto's death in 1535.

It seems clear that Palladio made the copy *before* visiting Pola, and when he did so he added in many new measurements (in a darker ink), and even drew in more accurate outline mouldings, in elevation, on the pedestal on the right and on the three stepped fascia of the architrave. He later included this building in his survey of 'Ancient temples' in *Quattro Libri*, 1570, Chapter 27, plates 78-80, and his precision and interest in the subtleties of classical architecture are shown in the care he took over detail. For example, in describing the architrave, he is at pains to point out that its 'first fascia is large, the second less and the third under the cimacium is also less. These fascia project forward in the lower part; which was done that the architrave might have but little projection, and thus might not obstruct the letters which are in the frieze in the front'. Falconetto has drawn this detail incorrectly by reversing the heights of the three fascia.
Lit: Giangiorgio Zorzi, *I Disegni delle Antichità di Andrea Palladio*, 1958, pp. 36, 81, fig 189 (attributed to Falconetto).

10. **Robert Smythson** (*c.* 1535-1614)
Design for a Screene To be Builte at Worsope Manner.
Scale: drawn to a scale of 17/12 inches to 1 foot.
Brown pen wash, with pink, yellow red washes, added red pen inscription with some incised lines (260 x 330)
Provenance: Robert Smythson and subsequently as given for no. 8
Smythson's two-storey, arcaded, stone screen was intended for the hall of Worksop Manor, Nottinghamshire (built 1585 and destroyed by fire in 1761). However the evidence of other drawings in the Smythson Collection suggests that the screen was built to another design, also by Robert Smythson.

By the 1580s, the idea of the hall as the focus of life in the country house, shared by family, servants and visitors, had receded. And the hall screen with a gallery above and openings below (leading to the kitchen, pantry and buttery), was fast becoming outmoded. Smythson's design though medieval in function, was modern in design for it shows his sympathy for the restraint and balance of Italian Renaissance architecture. The adaptation of the three-part Serlian motif for the lower storey suggests Sebastiano Serlio's *L'Architettura* as one possible source for the design. The woodcut illustrations from that book may also have contributed to his manner of drawing. For instance, the hatching, cross-hatching and

broken lines that the block-maker used to give depth to Serlio's architecture have been used by Smythson in his drawing. His use, though, of brown wash is misjudged and he would have done better without it. Its use behind the balustrade is not only incorrect but serves to emphasise the over-wide spacing of the balusters that resulted from centring them between the triglyphs of the frieze.

Lit: M. Girouard, 'The Smythson Collection of the Royal Institute of British Architects', *Architectural History*, V, 1962, pp. 39,91,; M. Girouard, *Robert Smythson and the Architecture of the Elizabethan Era*, 1966, p. 101, pl. 55.

34. **Edward Stevens** (*c.* 1744-1775)
Design for a 'London house, fit for a person of distinction', 1763
Pen & watercolour within a wash border
(470 x 610)
Provenance: purchased in 1933.
Edward Stevens was apprenticed to Sir William Chambers from 1760-1766. He was much thought of by Chambers, who was always anxious to advance his brighter pupils, and allowed a fair measure of responsibility and independence. He drew several of Chambers's presentation designs but exhibited this design at the Free Society of Artists under his own name –even though he was in the Chambers office at the time. (Three other sheets in the set, the front elevation, plan and transverse section are also at the RIBA.)

The section, showing the full decoration of a house, was an established architectural convention by the 1760s; what is unusual in this drawing is that the interior decoration should be shown in colour. Chambers himself was the first to show a complete scheme for the interior decoration of a house in colour in his unexecuted design for York House, Pall Mall, of 1759 (also at the RIBA), a drawing which much influenced Stevens's method of presentation.

Lit: J. Harris, *Sir William Chambers*, 1970, *passim*.

37. **Charles Joachim Benard** (1750-?)
Design for a triumphal arch, commemorating the freedom of the seas, 1784
Pen & watercolour on a blue mount with ruled border & band of gold leaf (370 x 520)
Provenance: presented by Sir John Drummond Stewart, 1838-9

In 1742 the French architect Legeay returned to Paris from Rome, where he had worked with Piranesi, and brought with him a new approach to architectural drawing. He encouraged his pupils to make greater use of perspective, render shadows and include details. Among these pupils was Benard's own master, Moreaux-Desproux. Of Benard himself very little is known: he was born in Paris and studied at the Académie d'Architecture from 1774 to 1776; his only recorded work was the theatre at Marseille (now destroyed) for which he won the competition. He appears to have been in Italy in 1784, where he made measured drawings of Hadrian's Villa for the Académie.

This unexecuted design – with its wealth of references to the architecture of Imperial Rome – celebrates the Treaty of Versailles of 1783, and may have been the 'composition' that had also to be sent to the Académie in Paris. Triumphal arches were popular commemorative monuments as they had obvious antique antecedents.

Lit: *Procès Verbaux de l' Académie Royale d'Architecture*, VIII, 1924, *passim*; L. Hautecoeur, *Histoire de l'Architecture Classique en France*, IV, 1952 pp. 42, 152, 162; *Piranèse et les Français*, catalogue of an exhibition, French Academy in Rome, 1976 *passim*.

45. **Joseph Bonomi** (1739-1808)
Design for Rosneath, Dumbartonshire for the 5th Duke of Argyll, 1806
Pen & watercolour with ruled & wash border (625 x 980)
Provenance: as for no. 42.

Rosneath, Bonomi's most important work, was built to replace an earlier house burnt to the ground in 1802, and was itself gutted by fire in 1943 and demolished soon after. Fortunately the RIBA has many of the working drawings and thus the evidence for Bonomi's design is fairly complete. The perspective (exhibited at the Royal Academy in 1806) shows the north front with its five-column entrance portico. The unconventional, almost unique, arrangement of an odd number of columns (echoed in the three detached columns fronting the wings) is explained by the portico being a porch for carriage traffic (porte-cochère); the use of a central column in front of the door emphasises that access is from each side of the portico. The Ionic columns were thirty feet high and the roof crowned by a 23 foot high drum containing a bedroom that must have offered superb views of the Firth of Clyde. The kitchen and other offices were in a sunken basement with open courts at each end, entered via a subterranean street, 156 feet long and nearly twelve foot wide. Wide enough, that is, for the horse and cart that can be seen at the entrance to the 'street' (on the left hand side of the drawing).

Bonomi's draughtsmanship, like his architecture, was brave and dignified; his work merits more attention.

52. **Alexander Carse** (*fl. c.* 1794-1838)
View of the 'Willow Cathedral'
See page 75.

76. **Robert Lewis Roumieu** (1814-1877)
Design for a house in an Italianate style, *c.* 1860
Pen & watercolour over pencil with brown pen & ink & gouache added (495 x 675)
Provenance: as for no. 75.
Since Roumieu's architecture has so often been judged as deplorable, it is difficult to approach it without some prejudice. H.-R. Hitchcock considered that his works were 'wild fantasies', Goodhart-Rendel described him as an architectural rake, Summerson wrote of Milner

Square, Islington (now carefully restored) as 'an unhappy dream' and Ian Nairn (of 33-35 Eastcheap) as 'truly demonaic ... the scream that you wake on at the end of a nightmare'. But no matter how eccentric his buildings, Roumieu always depicts them most engagingly.

In the perspective shown here, blue skies (though rather turbulent), pretty trees and flower beds, the gently coloured gradations of stonework, a flock of fashionably dressed ladies – all contribute to a delightful picture of *nouveau riche* life in the Home Counties.

Roumieu's detailing is always inventive. He takes as his theme here, brackets: bracketed copings for chimneys, paired brackets to support the eaves and that re-appear under the cornice, windows are supported on brackets and have bracket-like keystones, the porch has clever bracket capitals and, like the garden walls and piers, has buttresses in the form of brackets. As a contrast, the brackets under the projecting drawing room window take the shape of wantonly nude female figures.

The location of the house is not known though Roumieu is said to have designed several in the Harrow Weald.

Lit: J. Summerson, *Georgian London*, 1945, p 268; H.S. Goodhart-Rendel, 'Rogue architects of the Victorian era', *RIBA Journal*, LVI, 1949, p. 255; H.-R. Hitchcock, *Early Victorian Architecture*, 1954, p. 158; I. Nairn, *Nairn's London*, 1966, p. 34.

82. **Alfred Waterhouse** (1830-1905)
Design for the door of the Natural History Museum, London, *c.* 1872
Pen & watercolour (950 x 590)
Provenance: presented by David Waterhouse (architect great-grandson), 1970.
The Natural History Museum, South Kensington, is in many ways an exceptional building. It has, for instance, no back or sides because Waterhouse designed it in two stages and the second stage was never built. It was also the first building in Britain (possibly in the world) to be faced entirely with terracotta. Waterhouse appreciated the durable, washable qualities of that material and liked 'those beautiful accidental tints' that firing gives to it. He chose to emphasise those accidental variations of colour when he made this drawing for the principal door to the Museum. Drawn to a scale of half-an-inch to a foot with plans at two levels, it is certainly the most beautiful large scale working drawing in the RIBA Drawings Collection. Following what was by now his established practice, Waterhouse got an assistant to draw with a fine pen, straight edge and compasses, the outlines of the design. Waterhouse then drew the freehand detail including the animal and foliage decoration that illustrate the subject of the Natural History Museum and the Romanesque ornament that expresses the architectural style of that building; then he added the glowing watercolour. It is astonishing that at a period when he was running seventeen substantial jobs (including Manchester Town Hall, Eaton Hall and a large house for himself) that Waterhouse could find time to design and draw so many of the details for the Museum. Yet two volumes of his drawings for decoration (at the Natural History Museum) and the two hundred or so surviving working drawings, many bearing the evidence of his hand (at the RIBA), show his intense involvement with every aspect of his architecture.
Lit: Survey of London, *The Museums Area of South Kensington and Westminster*, XXXVIII, 1975, Ch XIII; M. Girouard, *Alfred Waterhouse and the Natural History Museum*, 1981, *passim*.

profound and lasting his influence has been. Sir William Chambers said that 'the effect of his compositions on paper has seldom been equalled'. Both Chambers and Robert Adam, Charles Michel-Ange Challe (25) and the chief practitioners of French Neo-Classicism took over Piranesi's vision of Antiquity and many of his drawing conventions. A single image, for example, his triumphal bridge published in *Opere Varie* in 1750, was the source for Sandby's Bridge of Magnificence (51), Soane's Triumphal Bridge, and Thomas Harrison's design for a Military and Naval Monument (47). Piranesi's influence was also profoundly felt by J.M. Gandy whose drawings (60, 61) are on the two themes, Death and 'Marble Halls' that characterise most architectural fantasies. Gandy's 'dreams' were those of a man unable to cope with the demands of architectural practice while Robert Adam's poetical landscape fantasies (38) were an escape from the grind of one of the largest and busiest offices in England. Philip Tilden thought 'it essential for every artist, as he works at his own problem at hand, to occupy himself also with some scheme of magnitude. It matters not whether his castle or cathedral be on paper, and never reach . . . realization. . . . He will be building up his own character and ideals in the process' (fn ii). Tilden found a client, Gordon Selfridge, for his extravaganzas: a gigantic castle in Hampshire and a colossal tower for the department store (111). Yet another kind of 'architect's dream' is the caprice where, as in Allom's 'View of Rome', real buildings, some 'improved', are re-composed into an ideal townscape.

There is a difference between the fantastic and the ideal for though both tend towards the grandiose, ideal designs are more plausible and more coolly drawn. They come, unsolicited, from public-spirited architects responding to national sentiment. Those concerned with re-housing the monarch or parliament or parliament's servants, and these are generally sited in Whitehall, almost never get built but may lead to a commission of more modest scope for some other architect. Designs for national monuments (37, 47), once the costs are considered, remain as paper architecture. The River Thames has been particularly favoured by idealists: Sandby's 'Bridge of Magnicence' is only one of many examples but so large is the drawing (5.230 metres long) that no space could be found here for Walcot's scheme (4.540 metres long) for straightening the Thames (RIBA).

William Walcot was the most successful fantasist and draughtsman of the early twentieth century and his romantic archaeological reconstructions (114) prove the continuing fascination of the Antique world. Like Piranesi, he built little and earned his living from his drawings and etchings. It is only very recently that practising architects have turned to making drawings for sale as objects of art and where 'it is the process rather than the product, that is being enshrined'. (fn iii)

Publication was the purpose of some of the drawings shown here, for instance, Ramelli's design for a siege machine (7) was published as a woodblock illustration while Webb's design for King Charles's bedchamber (16) and Gerbier's coronation arch for the same monarch (17) were engraved. Stuart's view of the Tower of the Winds (31) became the engraved headpiece to Chapter 3 of the first volume of *The Antiquities of Athens* (1762). Other of the drawings shown here, formed the basis for published plates; some of Thomas Hope's economical sketches (49) were redrawn more formally and to a larger scale for his *Historical Essays* . . . (1835). Self-advertisement was as much a spur to publication as scholarship and Colen Campbell, James Gibbs and, most notably, Robert Adam, all produced books that illustrated their work. Adam employed the very finest draughstmen and engravers for his publications and Clérisseau's subtle and accurate drawing (33) was published in Adam's *Ruins of the Palace of the Emperor Diocletian* . . ., while Zucchi's architectural allegory (39) was the frontispiece to *Works in Architecture* that has been, a book *of Robert and James Adam* described as the most magnificent practice brochure ever published, at any rate until 1910 when Wasmuth published a folio of Frank Lloyd Wright's drawings that included his design for the Francis Apartment Buildings shown here (106). For architects generally, the scope for publishing their designs was hugely increased by the advent, from the 1840s, of the illustrated architectural journal.

Another outlet for discreet self-advertisement and one that generates yet another kind of drawing is the architectural exhibition. Of these the major one, despite recurring complaints from architects, is still the Architecture Room at the Royal Academy's annual summer exhibition in London. No less than twenty-three of the drawings shown here have been exhibited at the RA, from Bonomi's drawing room design (42) exhibited in 1783 to Quinlan Terry's design for a summerhouse (128) exhibited two hundred years later. The Royal Academy has attempted at various times to impose restrictions on what architects may exhibit. At a period when there was some friction between the RA and the RIBA, the Institute's Council's report (1874) noted that 'the novel and somewhat suddenly issued notice that . . . preference of place would be given to those architectural drawings which were the actual handiwork of the exhibitors, has taken many members of the profession by surprise. However desirable . . . an architect, in full practice [cannot] always be expected to devote sufficient time to a work which, after all, only illustrates, and is not in itself a substantial specimen of the art which he follows'.

There is not room here to show or discuss one of the most interesting of all kinds of architectural drawings, those made as part of an architect's training. These include drawings from casts, drawings from life, sciagraphic exercises and measured drawings as well as design drawings. There are, though, some examples of sketches made by student architects. George Stanley Repton's sketch and record book (55) begun when he was sixteen and articled to John Nash shows diligence and careful draughtsmanship. And Robert Smirke's journals and sketches (B2, B3, 46) are a record of a Grand Tour that furnished him with the essentials of his Greek Revival architecture. Drawing other architects' buildings is not just a youthful exercise: Palladio looked to Rome as his hunting ground for architectural precedents, the 'Gothic Revivalists scoured Europe for Gothic ammunition' (fn iv) and the Eclecticists discovered their sources in Bruges and Nuremburg, Holland and Spain. Some of the earliest and most important drawings in the RIBA Collection are not drawings *for* buildings but drawings *of* buildings. Though it is not of the greatest relevance in a discussion on the purpose of drawings, it would be interesting to know when sketchbooks first became part of the architect's equipment. 'Sketchbook' can be rather a misleading term since it implies freehand drawings of buildings (or other subjects) made with pencil, pen, watercolour or any other medium that can be carried in the pocket (29, 97). But they are as often record books with freehand or ruled drawings made to scale, or design sketchbooks (30, 103) or a combination of everything with notes as well (49, 55, 85). The earliest sketchbooks were made to order but at some time in the late eighteenth century, it was possible to buy them ready-made from artists' merchants.

Conventions in drawing

People who have no specialist knowledge of architecture often find it difficult to appreciate architectural drawings as they do not understand the different conventions – even though they may be perfectly at ease with an ordnance survey map. Plans, elevations, sections and axonometrics have to be understood: their language is abstract and diagrammatic. The perspective, however, seems to belong to the reassuring world of naturalistic painting. It has been suggested that as the architects of this century have turned increasingly to axonometrics, elevations and sections to present their schemes, the gap in understanding between the profession and its public has become more marked. But in studying the different conventions in use since the Renaissance to the present day, what emerges is a pattern of continuity; it may, then, be useful briefly to define the drawing conventions most used by architects.

Plans

Plans, which are diagrams of buildings made by projection on a flat surface, are the most common of all architectural drawings and have changed little from the Renaissance to the present day. They were called 'plattes', 'plots' or 'platforms' in the sixteenth century (11); the term 'plan' was first used, in a printed source, in 1678, although Inigo Jones used the word earlier in labelling his designs.

Although mostly drawn on separate sheets, they are often placed below an elevation to add information to the design (3, 10, 15). In the English late Gothic design for a canopied niche (8), which is essentially a working drawing, the plan shows three stages of the canopy and the crown, nestling inside one another like Chinese boxes. With added colour, and if read like a map, the plan can be the most informative of all the conventions as is seen in Cook and Hawley's competition design for Trondheim City Library (124).

Elevations

An elevation is a directly frontal view of a building made in projection on a vertical plane. As a term it was not used in England in the sixteenth and seventeenth centuries, the current words then being 'upright' and 'front'. Like plans and sections, elevations are accurate – in Palladio's sense – and are essential drawings made by architects to study the geometric proportions of a design, but misleading and difficult for the layman in that they do not convey recession and projection unless read with a plan (15).

There have been many occasions, however, in the past and present, when the client has been sophisticated enough to 'read' and appreciate a design in elevation. Palladio used no other graphic means to present a scheme and even used the more complicated method of 'alternative elevations' in drawing up two very different options for the Palazzo da Porto Festa (4). Similarly, both James Wyatt's and Robert Mylne's clients must have been able to respond to the abstract qualities of 'fastidious restraint' in the spartan elevations of Badger Hall (41) and Wormleybury (40), particularly as they are unlikely to have been offered perspectives for these schemes. In 1950 the Smithsons were not required to submit perspectives or models for the Hunstanton competition. Their elevations are hard to read but do convey better than any other kind of drawing the Miesian qualities of their design (120).

Sections

A section (either 'cross' or 'longitudinal') is a drawing representing a building as it would appear if cut through on a plane at right angles to the line of sight. The English word was first used in a printed source in 1669 (and given current expression in W. Halfpenny's *The Art of Sound Building*, 1725), although it was one of the earliest orthographic conventions in architectural drawing. It was much used by Palladio, but was not in common use in England until the second half of the seventeenth century. Wren, like many twentieth century architects, often used the section for practical purposes – for example to study the effect of a transeptal crossing in the Church of St Magnus the Martyr (19). However, one of the most frequent uses of the section from the late seventeenth century onwards was the opportunity it gave the architect to show different schemes for interior decoration, making it one of the most delightful of architectural conventions for the layman. John Webb showed his design for King Charles II's bedchamber in section in 1665 (16), and Colen Campbell's section through Mereworth Castle (26) is one of four specifically made to show the complete scheme of decoration for the interior; the sections published in *Vitruvius Britannicus* did much to popularize the use of the section in England. Sir William Chambers took it a stage further. He not only popularized the convention that shows the section of a new design in ruins as if it were an existing building (32), but also was the first to show an interior in colour – a method that was copied by his pupil Edward Stevens in his design for a London Town house (34).

Since the Renaissance, the section has often been combined with one-point perspective to produce a 'sectional perspective', or with an elevation to produce a 'sectional elevation'. The 'sectional elevation' produced by Arup Associates in 1981 (126) is little different from Wren's half-long section, half-elevation of Trinity College Library of 1677 (All Souls, Oxford).

Perspectives

The art and science of drawing in perspective was developed in Italy in the fifteenth century. Leon Battista Alberti, if not as worthy as Brunelleschi to claim the invention of linear perspective, was the first to codify, in his treatise *Della Pittura* 1436, a sound practical method of effecting it. But, as we have seen, his advice to architects against using perspective drawings had a far reaching influence and led to two parallel methods in architectural representation: the orthogonal method in presenting a design in plan, elevation and section, and the pictorial method in presenting buildings in perspective. The two systems descended on the one hand from Alberti to Palladio, and then to Inigo Jones, Wren, Hawksmoor, Burlington (and into modern times), and on the other from Leonardo and Bramante to Peruzzi, Giuliano SanGallo to Jacques du Cerceau in France, who by 1576 had established a style of formal perspective drawing, chiefly of elaborate views of great chateaux and axially planned gardens. These influenced English topographical engravers in the seventeenth century, who in turn determined the development of the architectural perspective in the late eighteenth century.

The convention of the perspective was particularly slow to cross the English Channel. It does occasionally occur in the late fifteenth and sixteenth centuries in a few minor touches to explain projections in 'uprights' – for example in the English late Gothic design for a canopied niche (8). There is an early tentative use of one-point perspective in the RIBA's design for Burghley House of 1585, and a fairly accomplished use of parallel and bird's eye perspective in John Thorpe's design for his own house, 1600 (Soane Museum). But although Vredeman de Vries's *Perspective – The Most Famous Art of Eyesight* appeared in 1604, architectural drawing in England was dominated by Inigo Jones's orthogonal designs, which were based not only on his own collection of original drawings by Andrea Palladio but on Palladio's own enormously influential publication, *I Quattro Libri dell'Architettura*, published in 1570.

In the seventeenth century, the French topographical engravers, the Le Pautres, the Marots and the Perelles, moved the sight lines high up, producing 'bird's-eye' perspectives. These, together with Wenceslaus Hollar's views of London, David Logan's bird's-eye perspectives of Oxford and Cambridge (1675 and 1688) and Jan Kip's and Leonard Knyff's three volume *Nouveau Théâtre de la Grande Bretagne*, 1700, had a great effect on draughtsmanship. William Talman, for example, adopted the elevated, bird's-eye method of perspective when he wanted to convey the totality of a *design* – rather than a view *of* a house – as can be seen in his design for his Hampton Court Trianon of 1699 (18).

The most influential of the seventeenth century textbooks on perspective was Andrea Pozzo's *Perspectiva Pictorum et Architectorum* of 1693. The 1707 London edition bore an 'approbation' by Wren, Hawksmoor and Vanbrugh, which is odd as none of them generally drew their designs in perspective. Wren had been much influenced by Jules Mansard in Paris and favoured the more austere orthogonal method of draughtsmanship. The only perspectives published in the *Wren Society* volumes (1924-43) are presentation engravings by topographical artists of his finished works. Hawksmoor, too, generally did not draw in perspective, although he did occasionally make vigorous sketch perspectives in pen with applied grey wash, as in his survey sketch of a canopy in Westminster Abbey (22). His expert exercise in one-point perspective of Castle Howard (21) is based on similar design perspectives engraved by William Talman.

In the early eighteenth century, textbooks were becoming plentiful: Brook Taylor's *Principles of Linear Perspective* of 1715 was the first manual in English and became the standard source for students for over a century. William Halfpenny's twenty books on building included one on perspective in 1731. It was not until the 1770s, however, that English architects made much use of the perspective convention, and when they did it had evolved into a particularly English phenomenon – the watercolour perspective set in a pictorial landscape. A number of distinct sources came together to produce this convention.

The first was the influence of architectural draughtsmanship in Paris and at the French Academy in Rome, where both William Chambers and Robert Adam were influenced by C.L. Clérisseau (33) and G.B. Piranesi (D5). The second was the influence of perspective geometry from the Italian stage designers, the Bibiena family (24), who had invented the *scena per angola* in which the perspective, instead of being designed along a central axis, was constructed on one or more diagonals. Then there was William Kent, who consistently set his own designs in perspective in landscape settings; and, finally, the influence of the topographical painters, Canaletto, William Marlow, Thomas Malton and Paul Sandby.

In 1768 the Royal Academy was founded, and it is probably no coincidence that the last thirty years of the eighteenth century saw the development of the 'design' perspective set in a landscape; there can be little doubt that these perspectives were especially prepared for exhibition at the RA to hold their own with oil and watercolour paintings. Several – for example Bonomi's design for Rosneath (45) are even drawn with watercolour *tromple d'oeil* mounts. The Bonomi, or Nash (56) drawings could very well be topographical paintings, and this convention is continued right through the nineteenth and well into the twentieth century. Many architects employed established topographical artists to make their perspectives. Sir Charles Barry used Thomas Allom (73); Anthony Salvin, James Deason and George Arthur Fripp (74) and Colonel Sir Robert Edis, George Nattress (93). But other architects made their own: C.R. Cockerell, Sir Matthew Digby Wyatt, Alfred Waterhouse and Sir Ernest George could rival the best. The nineteenth century also saw the rise of the perspective artist, who was often an architect by training. J.M. Gandy (60, 61), Axel Haig (86), Howard Gaye (87), William Walcot (114), Cyril Farey, and R. Myerscough-Walker (119) were the most celebrated, but their enormous success redoubled the constant criticism both of the perspective as an architectural convention, and particularly of its use in competitions, and of its over-riding presence in the RA Architecture Room. By the 1920s perspectives had virtually disappeared from competitions but it was not until the early 1970s that they were gradually replaced by simple line drawings and models at the RA. In the same way, since the 1930s, architects have chosen to present their unrealized schemes in the technical and architectural press, in plan, elevation, section and axonometric.

Perspectives, however, are still made, either by the architect, his office or by a professional perspective artist. They are produced for competitions, (where they are occasionally still allowed), for exhibition or for the client, and although they have often been superseded by the model, remain the most easily comprehensible of all architectural drawings.

Axonometrics

'Axonometry' literally means the 'measurement of axes', and as a term was not used until 1865. It is really a generic term used to include all forms of parallel projection – for example the isometric projection, where the two vertical planes are drawn at 60° to the horizontal plane, but has come to be specifically used to describe the method where the plan is drawn to true shape and scale, and the plan form then tilted at 45° to provide the third dimension, height, which is drawn to the same scale as the plan. It is consequently the most accurate method of projection and the most informative in that it represents the true proportions of both plan and volume.

The axonometric is not new, having been used in France in the eighteenth century; but was taken up in the early nineteenth century by engineers and by the compilers of textbooks on building construction. Joseph Gwilt used the convention in his *Encyclopaedia of Architecture*, 1842 to show a projected view of roofs and chimneys: he did not call it by that name – simply using the term 'drawing projection'. It came to a much wider audience in the textbooks produced by Antonin Choisy, *L'Art de Bâtir chez les Romains* 1873 and the two volume *Histoire de l'Architecture* 1899. Choisy went further and drew up-tilted axonometrics, principally to convey informative diagrams of roofs and vaulting. These were revived by James Stirling for his 'up-views' of buildings at Sheffield University and Queen's College, Oxford.

The axonometric was one of the few pictorial drawing conventions adopted by the architects of the Modern Movement, who rarely made perspectives. It was used by Le Corbusier and aptly suited his phrase 'the plan is the generator'; it was used with applied colour by the architects of the De Stijl Movement, who influenced Raymond McGrath (113), and, in line, by all the architects of the Modern Movement from the early 1920s to the present day.

Other drawing conventions

There are many other conventions in architectural drawing. One that is not shown in this exhibition, but which was much used in the eighteenth century, is the *laid-out wall elevation*. It is thought to have been invented by William Kent in 1735 to explain his design for a new House of Lords (RIBA), and took the form of a plan with elevations projected outwards in four directions, like a cut-out model.

Humphry Repton invented the slide (or flier or overlay) to help demonstrate 'before and after', a method delightfully used not only in his Red Books (53, 54) but also by his sons G.S. and J.A. Repton in their architectural designs.

The concept of the *trompe l'oeil* added 'sheet', which can be seen in Sir Thomas Graham Jackson's design for the new Examination Schools, Oxford (90), was originally popularized by Piranesi in *Le Magnificenze di Roma* 1751, and was rediscovered by architectural draughtsmen for line drawings in the second half of the nineteenth century.

Realism and pictorialism in drawing

For a drawing to be easily read by a non-architect some degree of 'naturalism' is essential. Even for the builder, the use (from the eighteenth century) of coloured washes made a working drawing more legible. R. Phené Spiers writing on the subject of colour washes for contract and working drawings (fn v) considered that 'the colour employed should be in harmony with the colour of the material indicated'. His 'list of colours which seem to be generally accepted in most architects' offices' included: stone, represented by raw umber; terracotta – burnt umber; concrete – mottled grey and raw umber, and so on. It is interesting that in the most technical of drawings, naturalism in the choice of colour washes was considered very important. An early (and rather endearing) use of colour to add realism to a drawing can be found in Robert Smythson's design for a large window (9) while other drawings of his at the RIBA have smoking chimneys or coals and flames in a fireplace design, (by John Smythson) painted in pink and grey washes.

Except for large, important buildings for which models might be made, Palladio's patrons were shown plans, elevations and sections. To make them more intelligible, Palladio shaded many of his elevations to give an illusion of depth and washed, in a darker tone, the voids of windows and doors; sections were washed in graduated tones so as to make the curved form of a dome or vaulted hall more apparent. Extra realism might be given to the elevation of a palazzo (4) by indicating the texture of rusticated masonry but Palladio did not, as his contemporary Ramelli did, use figures to give scale or explain purpose (7) nor did he use the realistic finish of Gentili's design for a torchbearer (6). Inigo Jones kept closely to Palladio's drawing conventions and so did the Palladians of the eighteenth century, except that they introduced shadow to explain, for example, a portico (27) that if shaded and not shadowed looks as though the columns are in relief rather than freestanding. Without a plan, Inigo Jones's porticoed brewhouse elevation (15) would be easily mis-read. The Neo-Palladians' freer use of shadow was derived from the Baroque draughtsmanship that Gibbs (23) had learnt in Italy and Hawksmoor (21) had seen in engravings. Campbell's drawings for *Vitruvius Britannicus*, like his drawing for Mereworth (26), were shaded and shadowed in a suavely regulated fashion but 'had no sense of atmosphere, movement or light'. (fn vi)

Semi-pictorial architectural draughtsmanship, where sky and colour and such romantic conceits as 'ruinization' co-existed with ruled and compass-drawn elevations and sections, was introduced into England by William Chambers (32) who had learnt it in the studios of Paris and Rome. Chambers's semi-pictorialism gained currency through such followers as Edward Stevens (34) and John Yenn and via the exhibition of his drawings at the Society of Arts (from 1761) and later at the Royal Academy, as well as through Thomas Wright's *Six Original Designs for Arbours*, 1755, the first published architectural designs to show buildings in natural settings. For Chambers, realism stopped with the addition of landscape and of rain-streaked masonry; his designs, unlike Humphry Repton's (53, 54) could never be mistaken for topographical views.

The introduction of figures into architectural drawings may have come from eighteenth-century Italian stage designs reinforced by the influence of Piranesi's published works. There are, though, earlier precedents: John Harvey has described a design for King's College Chapel of *c.*1508 as the earliest known English architectural drawing with figures (dressed in academic garb) (fn vii). Talman's bird's eye view for a Trianon (18) has an 'entourage' of people, horses, cattle and coaches but this is an unorthodox drawing based on cartographic conventions. And William Kent is always the exception to every rule: he conceived his designs as pictures, setting them in landscape perspectives, with figures. But his designs always have the appearance of 'sketches'. Bonomi's more formally set up interior perspective of a drawing room (42), made in 1782, is one of the earliest English designs of the eighteenth century, to have figures in it. And he uses mirrors, windows, open doors and reflective floor surfaces to give a three-dimensional sense of reality and of space beyond space. Fantasy designs (38, 60, 61) lend themselves particularly well to a full pictorialism where ruled outlines have no place. Drawn freehand, they are true pictorial architectural designs. Most of the drawings made in the 1830s, shown here, are semi-pictorial but in a new kind of way. They use landscape, boats, people and horses to indicate scale, purpose, environment, volume, space and distance, and are increasingly anecdotal. Architects now felt free to do what they wished about the 'pictorial accompaniments' in drawings where 'rectilinear outlines were ruled in as neatly as they would have been in an elevation, only the texture of materials and the trimmings, mineral, vegetable, and atmospheric, provided by landscape and sky, being drawn freehand' (fn viii). Devey was an exception, though, (96) and by the 1890s, the Edwardian Baroque architects Belcher (95), Pite (101), Wilson (103) and Rickards (110) were drawing or painting their competition and other designs without a ruler or compass in sight. Though the architects of the Modern Movement were uninterested in pictorialism in its fullest sense they did not ignore the usefulness of 'trimmings' or the intimacy of freehand drawing (D6). Highly accomplished perspectivists such as Myerscough-Walker (119) went for something different, an almost photographic realism which despite its modernity is still in the early and mid-Victorian tradition of semi-pictorialism; as is Basil Spence's perspective of Coventry Cathedral, drawn in 1957 and with the graphic mannerisms of that period.

The Architect as Artist

From the beginning of the twentieth century, architects received their training in architectural schools. Before that, those that called themselves architects had usually been grounded in some other art or discipline, particularly before the eighteenth century, when the system of apprenticeship provided an established training. While Wren was a Professor of Astronomy, Balthazar Gerbier a courtier and diplomat, Vanbrugh a soldier and playright, Colen Campbell a lawyer and Barry a surveyor, there were also many, who like Gibbs, turned to architecture because they 'had a great genius to drawing'. Throughout the eighteenth and nineteenth centuries, architects took lessons in painting and drawing, as well as studying the principal monuments of antiquity on the Grand Tour; some were apprenticed to painters or craftsmen; others, like William Kent, were painters.

Inigo Jones is first recorded as a 'picture maker' in 1603 and it was as a painter and decorative artist rather than as an architect that he first established himself. He brought a fluent wash rendering to England and his technique of pen and cross hatching with wash added has a painterly quality; he must possibly be judged as an artist rather than an architect, and was, incidentally, the first architect to sign his designs (15). Nicholas Hawksmoor trained in Wren's office and became a precise and expert draughtsman; but he also had a very personal and informal manner of sketching and his pen and wash designs can easily be recognized among the Wren office drawings.

Sir William Chambers and Robert Adam had Clérisseau as a drawing master in Rome in the 1750s – both of them wanting to acquire the ability to draw buildings in watercolour in a 'free manner'. Chambers had also trained in Paris under J.F. Blondel and then came under Piranesi's influence in Rome. He introduced many new ideas to Britain and made his architectural drawings into artistic productions. Robert Adam produced a series of Picturesque landscape fantasies which he never exhibited but which were the recreation of his leisure hours (38); these were influenced by Alexander Cozens and William Gilpin and take their place in the English watercolour tradition.

James Stuart trained as a fan painter and used a thick gouache technique for his views of Greek antiquities (31); Quarenghi studied as a painter in Bergamo and Rome and his perspectives are often more painterly than architectural – his figures do more than just suggest scale (43). Thomas Sandby was also a topographical watercolourist, and as Professor of Architecture at the Royal Academy taught his students to apply a 'soft and agreeable' watercolour technique to architectural drawings. Thomas Harrison, although 'plain in person and manners' was 'very clear and ready in explaining with his pencil' and as a draughtsman is the most elegant of all the English Neo-Classicists. Joseph Bonomi, who had been employed in the Adam office for many years to make many of the more decorative drawings, did more than any other architect to give the design perspective the status of a topographical watercolour that could hold its own at the RA.

In the nineteenth century, C.R. Cockerell stands out as one of the greatest artist-architects. Although he had begun his training in his father's office, he later spent several years on the Grand Tour, and was reluctant to abandon his pursuit as an archaeologist and artist and return to the 'drudgery' of an architect's office. He was one of the first architects to make and value the design *sketch*, and his few perspectives also have great quality as works of art in their own right. Several of the leading nineteenth century architects made their own perspectives, but it was unusual to do so in an era when most either employed topographical artists or perspectivists. Sir Matthew Digby Wyatt, Sir Ernest George and Alfred Waterhouse stand out as the best. They all three exhibited topographical watercolours as well as their own perspectives, and had the standing as artists, as Sir Hugh Casson does today. (121)

George Devey had been taught by J.S. Cotman before he became an architect and was an excellent watercolourist. Many of his designs give the appearance of being off-the-cuff topographical sketches, and he often drew spontaneously for clients when explaining a scheme. Lutyens did the same; his father, Charles Lutyens, had been an established animal painter and his god-father was Landseer. His designs occasionally took the form of artistic watercolour sketches (103) and he continued all his life to sketch his designs in pencil and crayon and to make marvellously inventive doodles.

In the late 1890s and early 1900s, in an era of brilliant pen draughtsmanship, Beresford Pite and E.A. Rickards stand out as having especial 'bravura'. It is always possible to recognize the thick agitated line and hatched skies of Pite's highly personal drawing style; similarly the vigour and excitement of a Rickards drawing were always admired by other architects.

Several of the architects of the Modern Movement have shared the same vision as some of the cubist and abstract painters. Le Corbusier and Amedée Ozenfant initiated the painting movement known as 'Purism' in 1918, and the group of artists who after the First World War became associated under the title 'De Stijl' included several architects. It is sometimes possible to be uncertain whether one is looking at an abstract painting by Mondrian or a plan by J.J.P. Oud. This painterly De Stijl influence can be seen in the McGrath axonometric (113).

Sir Basil Spence and Sir Hugh Casson both have the standing of 'artists' in the recent past and present. Spence's spontaneous drawings in chalk have much in common with John Piper's topographical landscapes, and Casson's sensitive pen and wash sketches can be compared with contemporary book illustration in the Forties and Fifties, and particularly with the work of Edward Ardizzone.

The Treasures of the Royal Institute of British Architects

'The survival over a period of 500 years of objects as frail as drawings can only be attributable to a whole series of fortunate circumstances. In the first place the artist who drew them must exhibit . . . a justified conviction of the importance of his achievements . . . [and] there is another less obvious prerequisite for their preservation in any quantity: that is a passion for hoarding on the part of the artist'. (fn ix) Architects have always been collectors; the earliest English drawings in the RIBA Collection dating from around 1500, were in the collection of Robert Symthson (*c.*1535-1614) 'Gent[leman], Architect & Surveyor' who gave them with his own drawings to his son John, who gave them with his own drawings to his son Huntingdon, from whom they went to John the Younger (1640-1717) after which they were preserved by the Byron family who sold them in 1778 to the Reverend D'Ewes Coke, from whose descendants the drawings were bought by the RIBA in 1927. A fascinating story but an even more marvellous one, because of their influence on English architecture, is the account of how Andrea Palladio's drawings came to this country. Palladio died in 1580 and it seems that he left his drawings to his son Silla from whom Inigo Jones, on his second journey to Italy (1613-14) bought a large number. Those with Jones's own drawings were left to his pupil John Webb (1611-1672) who bequeathed them, with his own drawings, to his son William with strict instructions that they should not be dispersed. But William dying young, the collection was sold by his widow and came into the possession of John Oliver, Surveyor to the City of London, from whom William Talman acquired them after his death in 1701. From William they passed to his son John Talman, one of the greatest English collectors of his time. John Talman's own drawings were made on 'paper as strong as paste-board' and so large 'that the Vast Volume in wch they are conteined are Four feet high & require 2 men to open & shutt them'. (fn x) The Talmans (like other collectors from the seventeenth century onwards) gave the drawings they acquired a distinctive mark of ownership, an inscribed triple T. John Talman had his drawings bound into about two hundred volumes, classified by subject. A 'library' method of preserving drawings that continued into the nineteenth century, though the alternative of separately mounting drawings, giving them ruled and washed (or gold) borders and storing them in portfolios, portfolio stands or cabinets was another system adopted by collectors. In 1721, John Talman was persuaded by Lord Burlington to sell him a 'Book of Designs & Planns &c by Inigo Jones' and a 'Parcel of Architectonicall Designs and Drawings by Palladio'. Three years before, Burlington had found at the Villa Maser Palladio's drawings of the Roman Baths and had brought them back to England. When Burlington died in 1753 his collection (each drawing bearing a triple red-ruled border of ownership on its mount) passed to his daughter Charlotte who had married the 4th Duke of Devonshire and in 1894 the 8th Duke gave to the RIBA most of the Palladio drawings and those of Jones and of Webb, now in its Collection.

One of the reasons why Palladio's drawings have survived for four hundred years, cherished by successive generations of architects, is because they were exemplars. Together with his buildings and his book *I Quattro Libri dell'Architettura* (D3), they provided the framework of an architectural system, Palladianism, that is influential even today. Among other reasons why architectural drawings are collected are that they provide an insight into the imagination of the architect and present his ideas in their purest form. They record buildings that no longer exist in that form or were never built.

When the Institute of British Architects was founded in 1834, drawings were collected either for their scholarly or antiquarian interest. But shortly afterwards the 1839 Report of the Institute's Council, after discussing the hoped-for acquisition of one of Charles Percier's drawings (he had recently died), stated that 'this application arose from the conviction of its being extremely important that the Institute should, if possible, possess some autograph specimen of the talents of every distinguished architect, as they may hereafter enable those, who may write on the history of the arts or the biography of architects, to refer to authentic records'. Thus the acquisition of drawings was now seen as a resource for future historians. During the 1870s, there were repeated pleas from the Council for members to present their designs to the Collection so that 'in this manner the progress of contemporary Architecture may be illustrated by records which will be useful to the student and interesting to posterity'. Here, drawings are viewed as a teaching aid as well as future records. In 1878 the Secretary (C.L. Eastlake, later Keeper of the National Gallery) reported that 'the nucleus of a Collection of Drawings [of] buildings recently restored . . . has been formed by the contributions of Messrs Carpenter, Hugall, Seddon and Withers, Fellows and by Messrs Fulford and Tarver, Associates'. These were designs for the restoration of medieval churches and included survey and measured drawings. More drawings of this kind were added to the Collection and reflect the Institute's concern with the preservation and sensitive restoration of ancient buildings. Design drawings from contemporary architects were also still sought. But by 1912 when C. Harrison Townsend read a paper on some of the drawings at the RIBA (fn xi) it was obvious that most members were quite unaware of what the Collection held. The *cognoscenti* though, were concerned about the decision of the Victoria and Albert Museum, urged on by architect R. Phené Spiers, to collect architectural drawings on a major scale. Nor could they have been reassured by the offensive tone of Assistant Keeper E.F. Strange's vote of thanks when he said that 'we can do for you in the matter of architectural drawings far more than you would be able to do for yourselves, even if you were to spend as much money on your collection as we do on ours . . . and although I am only a guest, I hope I may be forgiven if I say that your collection would be very much more important and valuable if that had been realised earlier. . . . The opportunities of collecting old drawings of architecture and ornament are very quickly passing away, and within a few years it will be almost impossible . . . to go into the market and buy them. I do not suppose the Institute will be able to compete with us in a matter of that kind'. Strange also pointed out that at his museum 'we have a staff . . . we have accommodation . . . [and] our drawings are catalogued' adding that, as an outsider 'I sincerely hope it will be possible for the Institute to afford some facilities to students'. Harsh words but just, for clearly in 1912 the RIBA had become moribund. Drawings were still given by its members and even, occasionally, bought, but the last printed catalogue had been published in 1871, there were no specialist staff, there was no space and the drawings were inaccessible to all save the most determined. Things improved a little after the Institute moved to Portland Place in 1934 and drawings were disinterred and decently housed within the Library. Later, in early 1959, the drawings separated from the Library and had their own room, albeit a small one, in 68 Portland Place.

The next development in the collecting of drawings by the RIBA, from the 1960s onwards, has come from changes in the way that architectural history is studied. For more than a century, the papers read at the Institute and the articles published in its *Journal* on architectural drawings and drawing had come from architects, whose view of the subject was coloured by practical experience. But architectural history has become now the province of professional architectural historians, few of whom have worked at a drawing board. Howard Colvin, in a speech at the inaugural meeting of the Society of Architectural Historians of Great Britain in 1958, spoke of the discipline of architectural history and described architectural drawings as 'documents . . . [that] throw light on the history of a structure, on the mind of an architect, or on the building practice of an age'. (fn xii) This has always been the case but 'the rise of architectural history' has meant that every kind of drawing, the details as well as the perspectives, has to be collected; comprehensiveness must be the aim and much has been achieved in the last decade by the acquisition by the RIBA of the collections of, for example, Alfred Waterhouse, Oliver Hill, Sir Edward Maufe and Ernö Goldfinger. Since 1971, the Drawings Collection with its 300,000 drawings and Heinz exhibition gallery has been housed at 21 Portman Square, London.

The most important architect-collector of the nineteenth century was Sir John Soane. His collections of antiquities, architectural fragments, medals, casts, manuscripts, paintings, models and architectural drawings were established as a museum in April 1833. That museum, and more important, his professional rectitude, were significant influences upon the founding members of the Institute of British Architects. Their first Address included among their aims 'the foundation of a library of printed books of every species connected with architecture . . . manuscripts of a similar description . . . drawings illustrative practically and theoretically of the art in its widest application . . . a Museum of antiquities, models, casts, specimens of materials used in building, and of all such other objects as may tend to the illustration of the Arts and Sciences in their application to design and construction'. A year later, the by now eighty members of the infant Institute were, additionally, asked to donate or bequeath, sculptures, pictures and instruments. The response was liberal, so much so that, in May 1836, the Council reported 'that our rooms are scarcely sufficient to receive them, and some steps must be taken in order to obtain more space', a problem that is still with us.

The choice of objects that were collected seems, now, rather curious. Some, like the hundreds and hundreds of stone and marble and other specimens were the equivalent of today's architects' samples. While the casts and sculptures and medals were a reflection of current architectural taste. The first honorary secretary of the Institute was Thomas Leverton Donaldson, a numismatist, as well as architect, who wrote the first complete book on architectural medals, gave many examples to the Collection and designed the Institute's first medal. Their importance for him lay in the fact that they were more permanent than the buildings they commemorated so that, for instance, the coins and medals of Antiquity are often the only illustrations of some of the most important buildings of Greece and Rome. Plaster casts of architectural ornament might have been found in many architects' offices in the nineteenth century for 'even if an architect can spare time for frequently travelling from one monument of ancient Art to another . . . he still needs, when at home, the aid of casts to recall the richer portions of the details to his memory' (fn xiii). Early gifts to the Institute included a 'cast of the Capitals of the Column and Pilaster of the Erectheum at Athens' from Philip Hardwick and 'six dozen casts [of] specimens of Gothic Architecture taken from Winchester Cathedral' given by R. Wallace. The founding of the Architectural Museum in 1851 (fn xiv) and its acquisition of several thousand (almost entirely Gothic) casts encouraged the RIBA to pass its own collection (of chiefly classical casts) into the Museum's safekeeping (1869-70). In 1903 they became the property of the Architectural Association when it took over the defunct Museum's premises in Tufton Street and in 1916, all the extant casts (about 4,000) were given to the Victoria and Albert Museum.

Portraits

The founders of the Institute, concerned as they were with the social status and respectability of their newly constituted union of '*bonâ fide* Architects' sought to give tone to the rented rooms in Covent Garden, that were the first headquarters, by hanging portraits 'of all the most distinguished Architects who have preceded us'. The request for such was generously received and portraits of Sir Robert Taylor, Nicholas Revett, James Wyatt (C9) and Sir John Soane as well as a fine statuette of Inigo Jones (C2) and a bust of Sir Christopher Wren, soon adorned the Institute's rooms. The long presidency (from 1835 to 1859) of Earl de Grey, 'an amateur of considerable cultivation and artistic taste' was acknowledged by a portrait (C11) that begun the tradition of each past president having his portrait painted or sculpted. Probably because of the intimacy that often exists between artists and architects, the sixty or so paintings and busts that commemorate past presidents of the RIBA are often of exceptional quality.

Drawing instruments

The drawing instruments in the Collection of the RIBA have recently been exhibited and published (fn xv). The early gift of an apomecometer ('an instrument for ascertaining the vertical heights of towers, spires &c'), a cympagraph ('an instrument for copying, at full size, the profile of mouldings'), a teleiconographe ('an instrument for sketching at long distance') or a goniameter ('used to obtain a correct representation of natural objects') presented by their respective inventors, though ingenious were too complicated to be taken up for general use. But the more simple pens, compasses, dividers, sectors, rules and so on, some of them dating from as early as 1600, offer a fascinating insight into architectural drawing practice. Drawing instruments are still collected by the Institute and a recent acquisition is the drawing table and stool designed and used by Sir Ernest George.

Manuscripts

The first manuscripts collected by the Institute were the texts of lectures given at its meetings and of essays submitted for student prizes. Symptomatic of a passing phase of taste was the effort from 1839 to acquire autograph letters that was stimulated by W.C. Mylne's gift of letters written by Piranesi and others. Gradually, an assortment of diaries, account books, unpublished treatises and other papers were accumulated, the most precious of them the heirloom copy of Wren's *Parentalia* (B1). There has been a shift of direction in the last ten years with the realisation that, where possible, the whole of an architect's output, correspondence and scrapbooks as well as drawings, should be preserved, and with the skilled care of an archivist, this has brought a new vitality to the Manuscripts Collection. The importance of the RIBA's own archives is also becoming increasingly apparent.

Photographs

In 1855, the Institute's Council reported that 'the facility with which the most exact representation of buildings . . . can now be obtained by means of photography, affords students a fund of information, unenjoyed by those who had preceded them'. Despite the rather sour-grapes tone of this pronouncement, the novelty and potential of photography were irresistible and photographs were now added to the Collection. Some of the most treasured of the 80,000 prints, negatives, postcards, lantern slides and videotapes that now make up the Photograph Collection, are the two hundred rare photographs of American buildings taken in the 1860s and 1870s.

The Library

The first books in the library of the Institute of British Architects (there were 108 by May 1836) were given from the shelves of such founding members as T.L. Donaldson, P.F. Robinson, John Goldicutt, H.E. Kendall and James Noble, from well-disposed publishers and booksellers like John Weale and Ackermann & Co., and from the prolific author, John Britton. Many of the books were the practical ones that any architect might have by his drawing board, dealing with ventilation and warming, prevention of dry rot, the law of dilapidations and the construction of chimneys, together with published specifications, books on perspective and isometric drawing, and geometry, as well as pattern books, books of the orders and books on Gothic architecture and ornament. The published exemplars of classical architecture by Vitruvius, Palladio, Fréart, Blondel and Gibbs, essential for generations of practising architects, were to be found in the twin bookcases designed by J.B. Papworth and were to be supplemented by many others. There were also a few books on contemporary architecture and a greater number dealing with archaeological discoveries – a subject of particular interest to the founding members of the Institute.

In 1845, the Institute moved to 'the more aristocratic neighbourhood of Grosvenor Street, where at No. 16 it occupied rooms for many years afterwards', though by 1848 when the lease was renewed, the 'want of space . . . for the due arrangement of the [rapidly growing] library and collection' was becoming obvious. However, the move in 1858 to 'more commodious and becoming rooms' in Conduit Street meant that, for a while, space was not a problem and, encouraged, the Library Committee under Wyatt Papworth issued, in the 1860s, lists of '*Libri Desiderati*' to the Institute's members. Coupled with a special library subscription opened in 1870, this was so successful that by 1876 the Council reported once again that because of 'the constantly increasing number of works and drawings, the want of proper accommodation in the library . . . is now urgently felt'. A Premises Improvement Fund was established and by 1880, the Conduit Street rooms, including the library, had been enlarged and added to so that the libraries bequeathed by Philip Hardwick, T.L. Donaldson and James Fergusson, as well as purchases from the sale of the libraries of Sir William Tite, Professor Robert Willis, William Dyce RA, Owen Jones, M.D. Wyatt and A.J. Beresford Hope, could be housed.

The RIBA stayed at Conduit Street until 1934 when it moved to Portland Place. The attics and cellars of the old premises yielded up books and objects long forgotten and, sadly, it must have been then that those curiosities not already dispersed finally disappeared: the 'Model of the Temple at Edfon, as restored by Napoleon . . . executed by Mr Deighton in his most exquisite manner' (donated in 1836), 'Two portions of Wood Dowels from One of the Pylons of the Temple Palace at Carma' (1849), the 'colossal plaster bust of Canova' (1858), and much more. The RIBA still has, though, a fragment of wood said to be from the coffin of Sir Christopher Wren given by a verger of St Paul's Cathedral to George Adam Burn in 1851 and by Burn's son to the Institute in 1940.

The first exhibition of the RIBA's treasures was held in 1935 to mark (one year late) its hundredth anniversary. This, only the second such exhibition in the Institute's history, is a personal choice from the ever-growing Collection, selected to show how architects draw and have drawn in the past; what emerges are unexpected pleasures and a pattern of continuity. We hope the exhibition will offer an agreeable introduction to the purposes and conventions of architectural drawing.

Jill Lever and Margaret Richardson,
RIBA Drawings Collection, 21 Portman Square, London.

89. **George Aitchison** (1825-1910)
Design for the decoration of the *Front Drawing Room* at No. 15 Berkeley Square, London, for Frederick Lehmann, 1873
Watercolour & gold paint (530 x 725)
Provenance: presented to the RIBA by George Aitchison's executors, 1910
Aitchison is best known for the house he designed and decorated for Lord Leighton in Holland Park Road, Kensington in 1864-66, which led to a number of commissions from wealthy clients and established him as a master of decoration and ornament. Frederick Lehmann's house was one of his finest schemes and was singled out by M.D. Conway in his *Travels in South Kensington* of 1882. This design shows one wall of the Red Drawing Room. The sliding doors had frames of ebonized wood, foliated with gold, and long central panels of amboyna wood inset with ovals of olive-coloured Wedgwood ware presenting classical figures. The walls were plain pink, edged with decorative bands, and provided an elegant background for Mr Lehmann's collection of paintings which included several watercolours by Turner. The frieze of peacocks was painted on canvas by Albert Moore. No wallpapers or stencils were used throughout the house: the decorative schemes were designed by Aitchison and hand-painted by Frederick Smallfield or painted on canvas by Albert Moore. Aitchison's significance lies chiefly in his patronage of decorative painting and craft by the leading artists of his day – for example Lord Leighton, Thomas Armstrong and W.E.F. Britten all worked on his interiors – and it was often remarkable that he managed to persuade artists of this calibre to undertake work of this kind. Sadly, with the exception of Leighton House, none of Aitchison's decorative work survives today and can only be studied in the collection of designs at the RIBA.
Lit: M.D. Conway, *Travels in South Kensington*, 1882 pp. 159-65; M. Richardson, 'George Aitchison: Lord Leighton's architect', *RIBA Journal*, LXXX, 1980, pp. 37-40.

96. **George Devey** (1820-1886)
Design for a model farm in Silesia (now Poland), *c.* 1868
Pencil & watercolour (180 x 325)
Provenance: presented on indefinite loan by W. Emil Godfrey, successor to the Devey office, 1968.
Devey's father disapproved of his ambition to become a painter and made him an architect as a compromise (he trained in the office of Thomas Little). He was nevertheless an excellent water-colourist who handled wash with the ease of an expert; it comes as no surprise to learn that his art-master at Kings College School had been none other than J.S. Cotman. Devey had copied many of his teacher's works and acquired through these a feel for the picturesque cottage. It was Cotman, therefore, who inspired his pioneering study of vernacular buildings as a source for his own designs.

By the 1860s Devey had a flourishing country house practice. He worked for many branches of the Rothschild family, and this unexecuted design shows a Wealden farmhouse transported to the Baron Ferdinand's estates in Silesia. He has presented it in aerial perspective, which allowed him to include views of all the buildings in the scheme and to give an idea of their layout.
Lit: W.H. Godfrey, 'George Devey FRIBA, a biographical essay', *RIBA Journal*, XIII, 1906, pp. 501-525.

04. Charles Francis Annesley Voysey
857-1941)
esign for a Clock Case to be Made in Wood & Painted
Oil Colour, 1895. Drawn full size
encil, gouache & gold paint (785 x 565)
rovenance: as no. 102.
'oysey designed this clock for himself. It stood
n the hall chimneypiece of his house 'The
)rchards' in Chorleywood, Hertfordshire (and is
ow in the Victoria & Albert Museum). Keenly
nterested in symbolism, Voysey chose 'Time &
'ide Wait for No Man' as his theme and
llustrated it with a scene of sailing boats (Hope)
gainst a sunset sky with swallows (Spring),
ypresses (Death) and flowers (Spring). The roses
Love) and coiled serpents (Evil) were omitted.
The shallow, spiked dome and splayed pilasters,
ppear in other Voysey designs for textiles,
vallpapers, tiles and bookplates. While the
eart-shape used for the hour hand of the clock
s virtually a Voysey trademark.

The painting of the clock case (made in softwood by F. Coote for £1.10) was carried out by Voysey himself. And so the full size details of decoration, shown here, are at the same time a working out of the design and a practice run for its execution. Voysey kept the drawing as a record drawing, and used it again for a clock manufactured in aluminium (without painted decoration).

Lit: J. Brandon-Jones & others, *C.F.A. Voysey: Architect and Designer 1857-1941*, exhibition catalogue, Brighton, 1978, pp. 75, 81;
J. Symonds, *C.F.A. Voysey, Catalogue of the Drawings Collection of the Royal Institute of British Architects*, 1976, p. 54.

103. **Edwin Lutyens** (1869-1944)
The 'Munstead Wood' sketchbook
See page 117.

105. **Henry Wilson** (1864-1934)
Design for the staircase for the Chapel-Library wing, Welbeck Abbey, Nottinghamshire, for the 6th Duke of Portland, 1897
Coloured chalk & watercolour (1155 x 735)
Provenance: presented by the Victoria & Albert Museum, 1955.
The Chapel and Library at Welbeck Abbey were designed by J.D. Sedding in 1889. But he died in 1891 before work started and Henry Wilson, his most brilliant pupil, took on fitting the rooms into the South block of the Smythson wing and was responsible for all the details. Work was completed by 1896 and then partly destroyed by fire.

This drawing is one of the best examples of Wilson's style: free Arts and Crafts Baroque with much imaginative 'Art Nouveau' metalwork and carving. Wilson had been devoted to Sedding and after his death completed all his jobs well into the late 1890s before giving up architecture and becoming a metalworker, sculptor and designer. He was one of the most original Arts and Crafts architects (although the extent of his influence is yet to be established) and produced drawings which are consistently the most dramatically presented of the Movement, and the largest. He drew vigorously and loosely in charcoal or coloured chalks on grey or blue sugar paper, not white cartridge. His perspectives were drawn for publication or exhibition, but even his working drawings were roughly sketched in pencil or charcoal – illustrating his theory that drawings should be diagrams, 'skeletons on which the craftsman builds' and not finely executed documents inhibiting the development of the workman's mind. This drawing was exhibited at the RA in 1897 and the *Builder* commented that it was a 'splendid piece of colour effect' but that it did not convey 'the actual nature of the work; it is not very easy to tell, for instance, whether the figure work and ornament shown in balustrades and other portions is carving in relief in coloured marbles, or painted or inlaid colour decoration. A French drawing would leave us in no doubt as to this, though it might not have the vigour and freedom of Mr Wilson's watercolour work'.
Lit: *Builder*, LXXII, 1897, pp. 391, 393, 437, 477, 529; G. Stamp, *The Great Perspectivists*, 1982, pl. 91; M. Richardson, *Architects of the Arts and Crafts Movement*, 1983, pp. 72-73.

113. **Raymond McGrath** (1903-1977)
Design for the Dance and Chamber Music Studio, British Broadcasting Corporation, Portland Place, London, 1929.
Gouache (695 x 520)
Provenance: presented by the architect in 1974.
The exteriors of Broadcasting House in Portland Place, by Val Myer, 1929-32, were predictably a compromise, but for the interiors the Studio Design Committee set out to express the new technology in a more stylish way. They chose the young Raymond McGrath (who already had something of a reputation with his experimental use of glass at 'Finella' in Cambridge) to be the Decoration Consultant in charge of studio design. For his colleagues he appointed Serge Chermayeff, Wells Coates, Edward Maufe and Philip Trotter, but, sadly, none of the interiors have survived in their original state. As well as this studio, 'Studio BB', designed for the recording of dance bands, octets and chamber music, McGrath also designed the Vaudeville Studio.

The axonometric perspective, which is the most common method of presentation used by architects today, was not invented in the twentieth century. It had been much used in France in the eighteenth century and later, and most notably, by Antonin Choisy to illustrate his *Histoire de l'Architecture* in 1899. It was taken up again and used extensively by the architects of the Modern Movement; Le Corbusier used the axonometric to present his design of 'Ateliers d' artistes' in as early as 1910. The axonometric has the advantage of representing both plan and volume and of being constant in measurement; it was therefore seen as a more honest form of projection and representation.

McGrath's axonometric, with its brilliant and opaque primary colours and quality of painterly abstraction, was probably influenced not so much by Le Corbusier as by the Dutch De Stijl Movement. Theo van Doesburg, van Eesteren and Rietveld issued a Manifesto in 1923, *Vers une Construction Collective*, which was accompanied by a page of designs for a house shown in axonometric. It was published in *De Stijl*, VI, in 1924. They also published a design for an 'hotel particulier' dated 1922, in axonometric with applied primary colours, in *Architecture Vivante*, 1925 (Autumn issue), one of the most influential journals of the Modern Movement which regularly published original drawings, including coloured plates, from 1923 onwards.
Lit: British Broadcasting Corporation, *Broadcasting House*, 1932; R. Banham *Theory and Design in the First Machine Age*, 1960; David Dean, *The Thirties Recalling the English Architectural Scene*, 1983, fig 60.

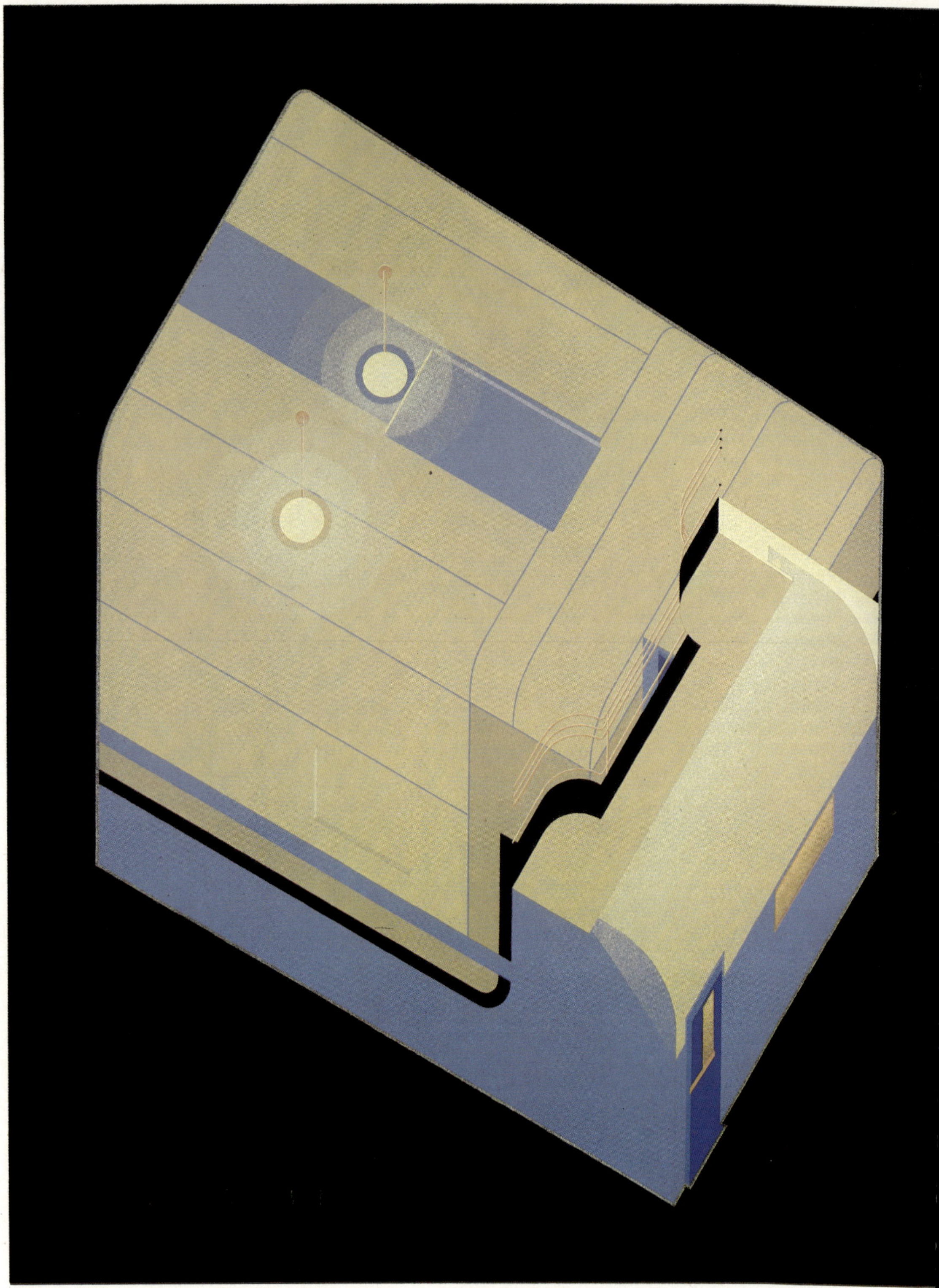

109. **Charles Frederic Mewès** (1860-1914)
Design for a small swimming pool, *c.* 1910-1914
Pen, pencil, gouache, indian ink, chinese white & gold paint with a gold-leaf border (400 x 575)
Provenance: purchased at Sotheby's, 25 June 1981, lot 54.
This drawing was previously thought to be a design for a ceiling in the Ritz Hotel, London, which was designed by Mewès and Davis in 1903-06. No rooms, however, of this shape and size, with six columns, exist in the hotel and as the original mount was inscribed with Mewès's name alone and with a French scale (*Mr Mewès Archte/No 1932 99B/Echelle: OM 05mm*), it seems likely that this design is for a small swimming pool or plunge-pool.

Mewès and the Englishman, Arthur J. Davis, had both been trained at the Ecole des Beaux-Arts in the 1880s. Mewès designed the Ritz in Paris in 1896 and made Davis his London partner in 1900; together they designed both the London Ritz and the Royal Automobile Club in Pall Mall in 1908-11. Mewès's office in Paris designed many other hotels and between 1900 and 1914 undertook the design for all the interiors of the trans-Atlantic passenger ships of the Hamburg-Amerika line.

In its colouring, perspective and use of a gold-leaf border the drawing reflects the training Mewès had at the Beaux-Arts. The use of stippling, however, and the 'deco' nature of the painted water give the drawing almost a Parisian air of the Twenties, although it must be dated to *c.* 1910-1914 as Mewès died in 1914.
Lit: R. Chaffee, unpublished PhD thesis, London University 'The Influence of the École des Beaux-Arts on British Architects', 1983.

115. **Corbett, Harrison & MacMurray, Hood & Fouilhoux, and C. Howard Crane**
Design for the *Grand Foyer*
See page 125.

Venezia analoga

Illustrations

The drawings reproduced here are all from the Drawings Collection of the R.I.B.A., except nos A5, 124, 125, 126, 128, 129 which are lent by the architects.

The sizes of drawings are given in millimetres: height precedes width.

KEY TO CATALOGUE ENTRIES

1 – 130 Drawings
A1 – A5 Models
B1 – B5 Manuscripts
C1 – C19 Portraits
D1 – D6 Published works

1. Unidentified Italian draughtsman,
c. 1510-1550
Perspective view of the Palazzo Caprini (usually known as the 'House of Raphael'), Rome, with a detail of the lower storey rustication and the outline of a Doric capital
Brown ink over pencil with grey wash (275 x 380)
Provenance: Burlington-Devonshire Collection (Palladio XIV/II). ? Silla, son of Palladio; 1613-15, Inigo Jones (1573-1652); Jones's assistant, John Webb (1611-1672); William, son of John Webb, who died prematurely; *c.* 1681, John Oliver (*c.* 1616-1701); William Talman (1650-1719); John, son of William Talman (1677-1753); Charlotte, daughter of Lord Burlington and wife of the 4th Duke of Devonshire; in 1894 presented to the RIBA by the 8th Duke of Devonshire.

One of the most famous drawings in the Collection, it records Bramante's Palazzo Caprini of *c.* 1501-10, where Raphael lived from 1517-20. The palace was later destroyed so this drawing, together with Antonio Lafreri's engraving of 1549, is of great importance – particularly as only the drawing shows how Bramante coped with the junction of two façades by a grouping of three columns. The palace became a 'modern classic' with its new formula for a rusticated lower storey with a Doric 'piano nobile' above, and was imitated by many architects including Palladio at the Palazzo Porto.

The drawing was attributed to Palladio until the 1970s, but Howard Burns has concluded that there can be no basis for this attribution. Palladio never made topographical or design drawings in perspective as he followed Alberti in his view that: 'Between the Design of the Painter and that of the Architect there is this difference, that the Painter by the Exactness of his Shades, Lines and Angles, endeavours to make the parts seem to rise from the Canvas, whereas the Architect ... would have his Work valued not by the apparent Perspective but by the real Compartments founded upon Reason' (L. B. Alberti *De Re Aedificatoria*, 1485, Leoni's translation, 1726).

Palladio was a neat and precise draughtsman and in all his measured drawings of the Roman baths and antique remains preferred to record buildings orthographically in plan, elevation and section with accurate measurements which told him not how the building looked but how it actually was. He did collect drawings by other artists of ancient and modern buildings and it is easy to see how exciting this particular sketch must have seemed in conveying a new building by Bramante, especially if he had access to it before his first visit to Rome in 1541.

Lit: H. Burns, L. Fairbairn & B Boucher, *Andrea Palladio, 1508-1580*, exhibition catalogue, Arts Council, London, 1975, no 407, p. 231; D. Lewis, *The Drawings of Andrea Palladio*, exhibition catalogue, International Exhibitions Foundation, Washington, 1981-2, no. 28, p. 52.

2. **Andrea Palladio** (1508-1580)
Measured drawings of a capital, architrave, frieze, cornice and pedestal from the Temple of Augustus at Pola, *c.* 1540
See colour plate page 9.

3. **Andrea Palladio** (1508-1580)
Preliminary design for the Villa Valmarana, Vigardolo, near Vicenza, Italy, *c.* 1541
Brown pen & wash within a single-ruled red line border (380 x 235)
Provenance: Burlington-Devonshire Collection (Palladio XVII/1recto), as given for no. 1.
This project for a centrally planned villa, with a square salone lit from above by four thermal windows, is related to Palladio's design for the Villa Valmarana (RIBA, Palladio XVII/2), which was the first villa he designed after his return from Rome in 1541. The doubling-up of two independent suites of rooms may also suggest that the design was for two brothers or for the cousins Giuseppe and Antonio Valmarana.

Palladio's study of the Roman baths in Rome can be seen in his use of the 'thermal' or 'Diocletian' window, the cross vaults (indicated by the crossed lines on the plan) and in the most common of all Palladian features, the 'Serlian' entrance – antique references that may have seemed too strange and unfamiliar for the client, which may account for the fact that this particular project was never executed.

The drawing is a presentation design – made for the client or as a record for himself – and shows Palladio's method of work when producing neat, scale drawings. He has first incised the main elements with a stylus and compasses without ink, and then drawn in ink with an ordinary quill pen over these lines, finally adding the sepia wash. The red line framing the design was added by Lord Burlington in the 18th century.
Lit: H. Burns, L. Fairbairn & B Boucher, *op. cit.*, *passim*; D. Lewis, *op. cit.* no. 43, pp. 77-8.

4. **Andrea Palladio** (1508-1580)
Alternative designs for the Palazzo da Porto Festa, Vicenza, *c.* 1549
Pencil, sepia pen & wash (280 x 405)
Provenance: Burlington Devonshire Collection (Palladio XVII/9 recto), as given for no. 1.
The drawing is a presentation design for the client, Giuseppe Porto, offering him a choice of two alternative and quite different solutions. On the left is a concern for texture and volume: a rusticated ground storey – where rougher blocks around the entrance and at the corners are contrasted with smooth – is surmounted by Ionic half-columns, heavy entablature and attic floor. On the right is a smoother and lighter design: a rusticated base supports a piano nobile where the attic floor is contained within tall Corinthian pilasters. The left hand design was essentially the one selected, although the ground floor followed the solution offered by Bramante's design for the House of Raphael (no. 1) which Palladio must have seen in Rome in the 1540s.

The drawing is doubly interesting in not only presenting the alternative proposals but in showing us how aware a Renaissance client must have been of all the more intellectual subtleties of a classical design.
Lit: H. Burns, L Fairbairn & B Boucher, *op. cit.*, pp. 232-4.

5. **Andrea Palladio** (1508-1580)
Record sketch of Lodovico Beretta's project for the Palazzo Municipale at Brescia, preliminary design for the Villa Barbaro Nymphaeum at Maser and sketch projects for palace façades, 1550-1554
Brown pen, with pencil upper right (430 x 280)
Provenance: Burlington-Devonshire Collection (Palladio X/15 recto), as given for no. 1.
This is a fascinating drawing as it gives us an insight into Palladio's method of work showing how he sketched, invented, and recorded buildings and projects in a spontaneous freehand with quill pen.

The earliest visual note on the sheet is the large part-elevation at the centre which records Lodovico Beretta's preliminary design for the Palazzo Municipale at Brescia between 9 September and 15 November 1550. He may then have returned to the sheet four years later in about June 1554 to tack on Jacopo Sansovino's later recommended design for the Palazzo Municipale at Brescia (top left), and at the same time added his own alternative design for the top storey at Brescia (lower left), and then probably continued to play on the same theme in two sketches for elaborate palace façades on the right and in the preliminary design for the Villa Barbaro Nymphaeum which is related to them (top right). The doodle at the bottom is probably of his own left hand.
Lit: H. Burns, L. Fairbairn & B. Boucher, *op. cit.*, no. 426, p. 239; D. Lewis, *op. cit.*, no. 100, p. 170.

C1. **Attributed to John Cheere** (1709-1787)
Lead bust of Andrea Palladio (1508-1580)
(420h, excluding base)
Provenance: unknown; included in 1871 catalogue.
John Cheere is known to have copied the statue of Inigo Jones by Rysbrack at Chiswick, and it is possible that this bust, generally taken to be a representation of Palladio, was loosely based on the bust of Palladio which Rysbrack also made for Lord Burlington, which was based, ultimately, on a portrait by Palladio's contemporary, Veronese; the fact that there is no totally reliable depiction of Palladio helps one to overlook differences between the two busts. Opinion about the appearance of Palladio differs; he is usually shown either as in this bust, or as bearded and lean and hungry.
Lit: R. Gunnis, *Dictionary of British Sculptors 1660-1851* 1953; T. Friedman, *The Man at Hyde Park Corner*, exhibition catalogue, Leeds and London, 1974; M.I. Webb, *Michael Rysbrack Sculptor*, 1954.

6. **Antonio Gentili da Faenza** (1519-1609)
Design for a metal torchbearer for the Chapel of the Most Holy Sacrament, St Peter's, Rome, *c.* 1581.
Brown pen wash, heightened with white (500 x 155)
Provenance: the drawing was described in 1912 as being one of 120 sheets by miscellaneous draughtsmen bound in a volume; it may have belonged to the French architect Henri Marlet in the late eighteenth century in Rome.

Antonio Gentili – goldsmith and engraver – is practically unknown today, yet was a highly regarded artist in sixteenth century Rome. Thirty five years after his death, Baglione included Gentili's biography in his *Le Vite de' Pittori*; in it he praised his work and described the pair of torchbearers for which this is a design. Gentili was not averse to copying and was influenced by both Cellini and Michelangelo (of whose work he is known to have had casts in his studio). Volbach argues convincingly that the torchbearers are not all his own work: the stem dates from the early *cinquecento* and can be attributed to the Venetian School, while Gentili was responsible for the Baroque additions. The drawing itself is of great quality and may have been a 'presentation' drawing, to be shown to the patron. Cellini provides ample evidence of this practice in his autobiography.
Lit: G. Baglione, *Le Vite de' Pittori*, 1733 p. 103; W.F. Volbach, 'Antonio Gentili da Faenza and the Large Candlesticks in the Treasury at St Peter's', *Burlington Magazine*, XC, 1948, pp. 281-286.

D1. **Leon Battista Alberti,** (1404-1472)
De Re Aedificatoria. Florence, 1485
Editio princeps of the first and most intellectually ambitious of the great Renaissance treatises on the art of building well. Probably composed between 1444 and 1452 the treatise, like many others by Alberti on subjects ranging from painting and sculpture to the life of his dog and the common fly, addressed learned patrons of a small circle of literati centred on the brilliant court of Lorenzo de'Medici. Himself a prominent patrician within this highly cultivated circle Alberti was able to elucidate the rational and universal validity of Brunelleschi's new architecture and to draw a fundamental distinction between the intellectual process of design and the physical task of construction that has served to define the function of an architect ever since.
Exhib: Fol. c5^{a}. Roman letter (BMC VI, pp. 630-31).
Provenance: Purchased at Chatsworth duplicate sale, 1882; presented by Arthur Cates, 1896.
Eighteenth century red morocco, gilt.

7. **Agostino Ramelli** (1531-1600?)
Design for a siege machine, *c.* 1588
Brown pen & wash on vellum (215 x 330)
Provenance: one of five drawings by Ramelli found in a collection of drawings by William Newton. Presented by Andrew Oliver, via Wyatt Papworth, 1891.
Ramelli was a military engineer. Born at Ponte della Tresia, he served under the Count of Marignano in the war against Siena, was summoned to France by Henry III and is known to have been wounded, then captured at the siege of La Rochelle in 1573.

This drawing is an illustration for a book of his inventions – *Le Diverse e Artificiose Machine* (fig. CXLII) dedicated to Henry III and published in Paris in 1588 and in Leipzig in 1620. In many learned circles of the High Renaissance, mathematics was considered the superior science; Ramelli classed engineering as a subsidiary branch of this subject and of almost equal importance. His descriptions are detailed, as they were to be put to practical use, and he sought purity of line in his drawings. The machine is shown in perspective from above, and details are inset or drawn in cut away section, to better reveal how it operates. Figures – crudely drawn – do the same and add naturalism, as does his attempt to place his invention within a setting.

D2. **Vitruvius** (*c.*84-14 BC)
De Architectura libri decem traducti. Como, 1521
The first printing in the vernacular, Cesare Cesariano's edition was also the first to include a commentary. The unique authority of Vitruvius as the author of the only work on architecture to survive from antiquity led, in the first decades of the sixteenth century, to an intense effort by humanist scholar-architects in all the various growth points of Renaissance Italy to render his Latin intelligible, his meaning visual, and his message relevant to current needs and aspirations. Nowhere did this effort find more beautiful and idiosyncratic expression than in the woodcuts, ornaments and typography of the 'Como Vitruvius', a masterpiece of Lombard Renaissance graphic art and, for all its faults of scholarship and interpretation, a precious reflection of ideas about proportion and beauty current in the Milan of Bramante and Leonardo.
Exhib: Fol. XV^{b}. Elevation of Milan Cathedral. Woodcut (415 x 290mm)
Provenance: T.L. Donaldson's copy. eighteenth century mottled calf, re-backed.

D3. **Andrea Palladio,** (1508-1580)
I Quattro Libri dell'Architettura. Venice, 1570
First edition of possibly the single most influential architectural book ever written. Exemplifying the essential teachings of Alberti – and through him Vitruvius – by constant reference to and illustration of his own experience, method, and proven solutions, Palladio offered in a clearly arranged form and in the directest possible language, precisely the information and instruction that was of most help and concern to the practising architect. Only later, after his deification in England by the neo-Palladians, did his *Quattro libri* assume the character of a sacred text, and his models and proportions the prescriptiveness of a canon.
Exhib: Title-page. Letterpress in woodcut architectural frame.
Provenance: With Burlington's autograph dated 'Jan 7, 171[9?]'; presented by Burlington to the Earl of Bessborough, July 1740; purchased at the Bessborough sale, April 1848, by J.J. Scoles (lot 1029) and presented by his widow, 18 January 1864. eighteenth century English panelled calf, re-backed.

D4. **Andrea Palladio,** (1508-1580)
Fabbriche antiche ... date in luce da Riccardo Conte di Burlington. London, 1730.
Celebrated by Pope in the *Epistle to ... Burlington* (April 1731) this facsimile of Palladio's reconstructions of the Baths of ancient Rome was originally intended by Burlington to form the first part of an ambitious publishing programme to include all the most treasured Palladio drawings in his collection. Though nothing more came of the project the *Fabbriche antiche* nonetheless illustrate perfectly the deep faith that Burlington had in the power of such drawings to communicate the essential lessons that Palladio had learnt from antique architecture. So unconcerned was he with the actual buildings they were intended to represent that he omitted to identify some of the plans properly and even failed to transcribe the explanatory notes that Palladio had himself written on the drawings.
Provenance: Bookplate of A. Russell Pollock dated 21 April 1860. Modern binding.

8. **English late Gothic master**
Design for a canopied niche for a statue, *c.* 1500-1530
Brown pen with grey & brown washes, with red chalk under-drawing on vellum (495 x 130)
Provenance: ?; Robert Smythson (1535-1614); John Smythson (died 1634); Huntingdon Smythson (died 1648); John Smythson the Younger (1640-1717); ?; sold by the 5th Lord Byron at Newstead Abbey, Nottinghamshire, June 1778, lot 344; bought there by the Rev. D'Ewes Coke of Broke-hill Hall, Derbyshire; by descent to Mrs S. Coke of Broke-hill Hall from whom the drawing with others was purchased by the RIBA in 1927.
English architectural drawings of the medieval period are exceedingly rare. There are three (including the design shown here) dating from about 1500 in the RIBA Drawings Collection. All are from the collection of Robert Smythson, a mason-trained architect of the Elizabethan period who probably acquired them by family or 'office' descent.

Dr Christopher Wilson has suggested that the canopied niche could have been one of a pair flanking an altar set in front of an East window but that, on the other hand, the plan suggests that the niche was freestanding and not surrounded by plain wall. Certainly, no surviving canopied niche corresponding to this design has yet been identified.

The drawing, much of it freehand, is most delicately done. The design is complex, with buttresses, miniature rib vault, cusped arches, crocketed finials, cresting, crenellations, mouldings and virtually all the decorative vocabulary of late medieval architecture. The superimposed plan shows three stages and the crown; the elevation is shaded and is cut away at the bottom left hand side to show the profile of the mouldings. Essentially, it is a working drawing and a poignant reminder of those many other early architectural drawings that, sadly, have not survived.
Lit: M. Girouard, 'The Three Gothic Drawings in the Smythson Collection', *RIBA Journal*, LXIV, 1956, pp. 35-6.

9. **Robert Smythson** (*c.* 1535-1614)
Design for a two-storey bay window, *c.* 1568-1572
Brown pen & brown & green washes, with some incised lines (360 x 180)
Provenance: Robert Smythson; and subsequently as given for no. 8.
The earliest surviving drawing made by Robert Smythson, this design is associated with Longleat House, Wiltshire where Smythson worked from 1568 as chief mason for Sir John Thynne.

The elevation is drawn on paper with a watermark that suggests it was imported from France; very little paper was manufactured in England at this time. A blank stylus was used to incise guide lines and a quill or reed pen with ink to draw-in the design. A green wash gives a realistic impression of the window glass while hatching and cross-hatching, added with a brush, suggests the lattice patterning of leaded lights. Finer pen hatching is also used and was perhaps derived from the woodcut plates of architectural books. Another bookish idea is the aeolipyles used here as ball-shaped finials. Vitruvius described them as 'hollow bronze balls, with a very small opening through which water is poured into them. Set before a fire, not a breath issues from them before they get warm, but as soon as they begin to boil, out comes a strong blast due to the fire'. The adaptation of a scientific instrument as an architectural ornament was owed, no doubt, to the attractive woodcut illustrations of the 1511 and 1521 editions of Vitruvius's *De Architectura*. In Book IV of Serlio's *L'Architettura* (1537) aeolipyles decorate the openings of chimneypieces and, indeed, placed on a fire such contrivances did help to prevent the chimney from smoking. But Serlio also uses aeolipyles to crown pediments and pilasters, and this must be where Smythson borrowed them from.
Lit: M. Girouard, 'The Smythson Collection of the Royal Institute of British Architects', *Architectural History*, V, 1962, pp. 34, 77; M. Girouard, *Robert Smythson and the Architecture of the Elizabethan Era*, 1966, pp. 69-70, pl. 21.

10. **Robert Smythson** (*c.* 1535-1614)
Design for a Screene to be builte at Worsope Manor
See colour plate page 10.

11. **Robert Smythson** (*c.* 1535-1614)
A: Draughte: For the Platte of a Rounde: Window, 1599
Brown pen with some incised lines (495 x 195)
Provenance: Robert Smythson and subsequently as given for no. 8.
'Platte' or 'plot' or 'platform', 'upright' or 'front' are the terms used by Elizabethan architects for plan and elevation. This virtuoso exercise in the setting out of the *munnells* (mullions), transoms, *vausers* (voussoirs) and springers of a rose window is a reminder of Smythson's Gothic stone-masonry background, and of his versatility too. Another drawing in pen and wash of the same window emphasises its lovely spinning lines and was made, perhaps, for Smythson's own delight or else to persuade a possible client. But here, the carefully drawn scale (7/12inch to 1 foot), setting-out lines and *Poyntes to Fynde the Ovalle Sirkelle* (ellipse) are directed to the mason.
Lit: M. Girouard, 'The Smythson Collection of the Royal Institute of British Architects', *Architectural History*, V, 1962, pp. 46,119 ; M. Girouard, *Robert Smythson and the Architecture of the Elizabethan Era*, 1966, p. 129, pl. 90.

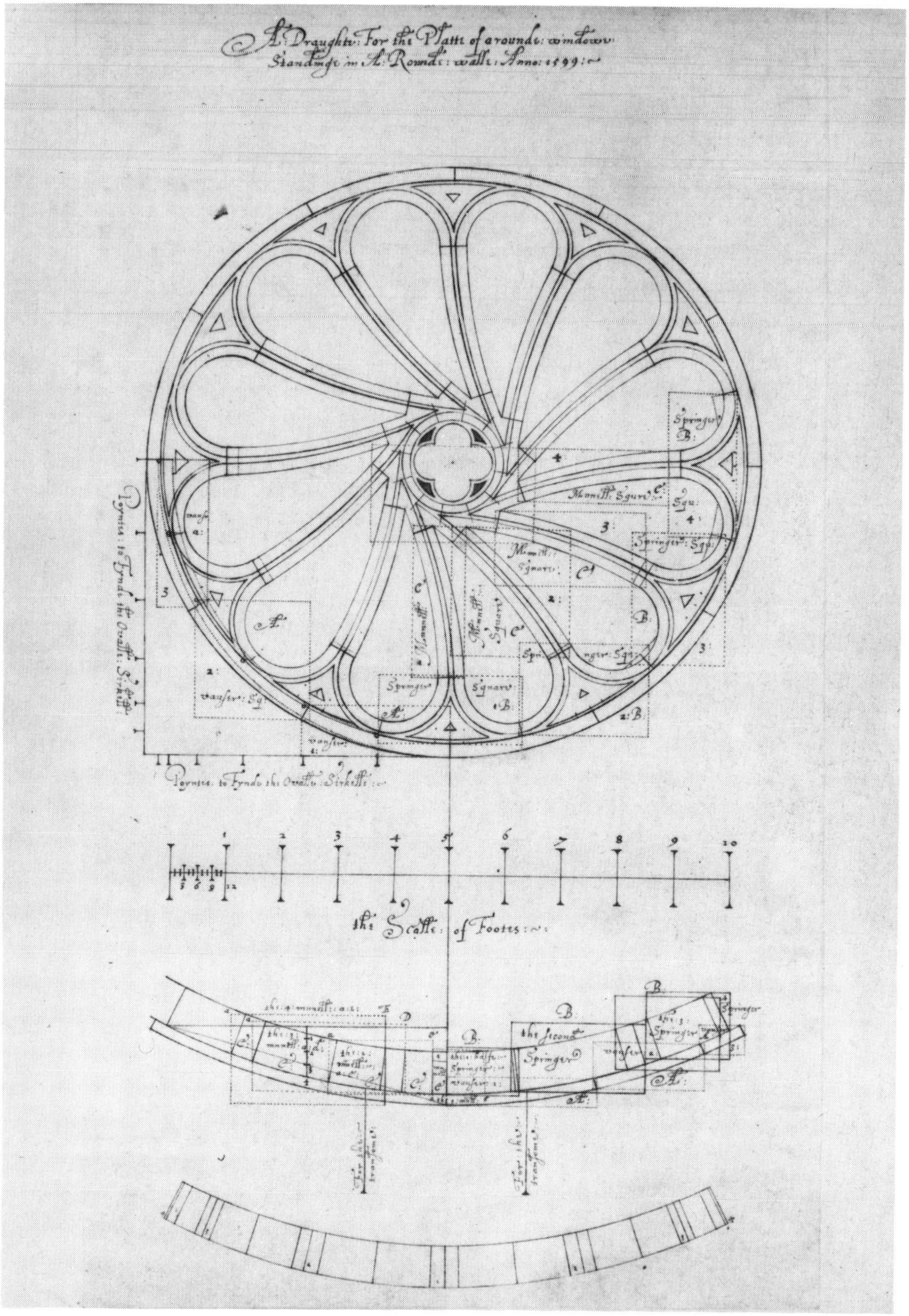

12. **Inigo Jones** (1573-1652)
Self-portrait, *c.* 1620, attached to a design for a cartouche
Brown pen (300 x 140, two sheets joined)
Provenance: Inigo Jones and subsequently as given for no. 1
Inigo Jones is first recorded (in 1603) as a 'picture maker' and it was as a painter and decorative artist rather than as an architect that he first established himself. His earliest surviving drawings (*c.* 1605) are for masque costume designs, prettily done in pen and watercolour but unremarkable. During the next few years, Jones taught himself to draw: first in a painterly free wash technique then, as his interest in architecture increased, in a disciplined pen and wash manner (no. 15). He also used a vivid pen technique, often with hatching, that conveyed the sculptural qualities of a design (nos 13 & 14).

For the hundreds of studies of heads that Jones drew (most are at Chatsworth House, Derbyshire), he used a pen (sometimes fine, sometimes coarse) with hatching and cross-hatching. Four self-portraits survive; one is (unusually) in red chalk but the others, made between about 1615 and the 1630s, are in pen. Drawn from the same viewpoint, each shows Jones a little older, a little more melancholy than the last.
Lit: J. Harris, S. Orgel and R. Strong, *The King's Arcadia*, exhibition catalogue, London, 1973, pp. 58-9, 210-211.

13. **Inigo Jones** (1573-1652)
Design for the *Great Doure* of the Banqueting House, Whitehall, London, 1619
Brown pen & some pencil (550 x 355, two sheets joined)
Provenance: Inigo Jones and subsequently as given for no. 1
The rebuilding of the Banqueting House, destroyed by fire on 12 January 1619, fell to Inigo Jones, Surveyor-General of the King's Works. The design and building programme was very rapid: by April 19th, the designs and estimates were ready, the building accounts were opened on June 1st and were closed, on the completion of the building, on March 31st, 1622. The accounts do not mention the Great Door and thus it may not have been executed or, if it was, it did not survive for very long.

Jones's *scizo* (Italian, schizzo, that is, sketch) of the Great Door was made in the bold pen and cross-hatched technique that was used for his most significant architectural designs; the large size of the sheet seems, too, to stress the importance of this particular design. The vigorous pen lines, of which only a few are ruled, and the energetic hatching and cross-hatching that emphasise the Mannerist sculptural qualities of the open-pedimented, tabernacle frame, indicate the furious pace at which Jones worked out his successive series of design solutions in the three months before the final design was presented.
Lit: P. Palme, *The Triumph of Peace*, 1957, pp. 227-8.

14. **Inigo Jones** (1573-1652)
Design for chimneypiece and overmantel for the Queen's House, Greenwich, for Queen Henrietta Maria, *c.* 1633-5.
Pen, some wash & pencil (190 x 290).
Provenance: Inigo Jones and subsequently as given for no. 1.
The Queen's House was originally built for Anne of Denmark, wife of James I, and remained unfinished after her death in 1619. Between 1630 and 1635 the work of completing it was carried out for Henrietta Maria of France, wife of Charles I.

The drawing for a chimneypiece with its studies of figures in the margins is of great interest. As John Harris has pointed out, its design source lies in plates 14 and 9 of Jean Barbet's *Livre d'Architecture d'Autels, et de Cheminées* (published 1633) from which Jones extracted the mannered use of a broken and scrolled pediment as well as the urns that stand on the slopes of the triangular pediment. The use of a French exemplar is explained by the fact that Italian treatises offered few or no chimneypiece designs and also because the Queen, not unnaturally, favoured French fashions.

Jones's architectural designs almost never have 'doodles' on them, and the studies of figures in the margin of this design are probably explained by a train of thought stimulated by the winged *putti* of the chimneypiece.
Lit: J. Harris, 'Inigo Jones and his French sources', *Metropolitan Museum of Art Bulletin*, XIX, 1961, pp. 256-64.

15. **Inigo Jones** (1573-1652)
Design for a brew-house, 1638 or later
Brown pen & grey wash over incised lines with pencil dimensions added by John Webb
(385 x 220, three sheets joined)
Provenance: Inigo Jones and subsequently as given for no.
Inigo Jones's design for a brew-house has long been attributed to the one built at Newmarket in 1616-17 for Charles, Prince of Wales and demolished during the Interregnum. However, Gordon Higgott's close study of Jones's undated architectural drawings offers fresh evidence. Working on the facts established by the drawing itself and covering such points as the use of the ruler, type of scoring implement, style of outline drawing and of wash, method of presentation, inscribing hand (which here belongs to John Webb, Jones's assistant), signature and so on, Mr Higgot's conclusion is that the brew-house drawing was made in 1638 or later. Thus it belongs to the very last stage of Jones's architectural career and such a date tallies very well with the stylistic evidence, in particular, the use of very reduced Tuscan detail.

To the non-specialist, accepting the fact that the draughtsmanship does indicate a mature hand, it is puzzling that the structural design is so assured. The square pyramidial roof would not have fitted the rectangular (about 36 x 46 feet) space below. Four of the windows of the side elevation are placed too close to the corners which is structurally (and aesthetically) poor practice. And the middle windows are skewed into the partition wall, presumably so as to centre them on elevation.

The patron and site for the brew-house are not known.
Lit: G. Higgott, Ph.D, 1985.

C2. **John Michael Rysbrack** (1694-1770)
Terracotta statuette of Inigo Jones (1573-1652)
(505h, including base)
Provenance: presented by Sir Jeffry Wyatville, *c.* 1836.
In about 1725 Rysbrack was commissioned by Lord Burlington to carve busts of his two heroes, Palladio and Inigo Jones, and not long after this Burlington commissioned two full-length statues of the same subjects, to adorn the exterior of his new house at Chiswick; these were probably in place by 1730. This statuette of Jones is no doubt a preliminary model for the statue. Jones is resting his arm on a rough version of his design for Whitehall Palace, for which there were a number of schemes; the one shown here is based on a drawing in Burlington's own collection.
Lit: *RIBA Journal*, XXXVIII, 1931, pp. 220-221.

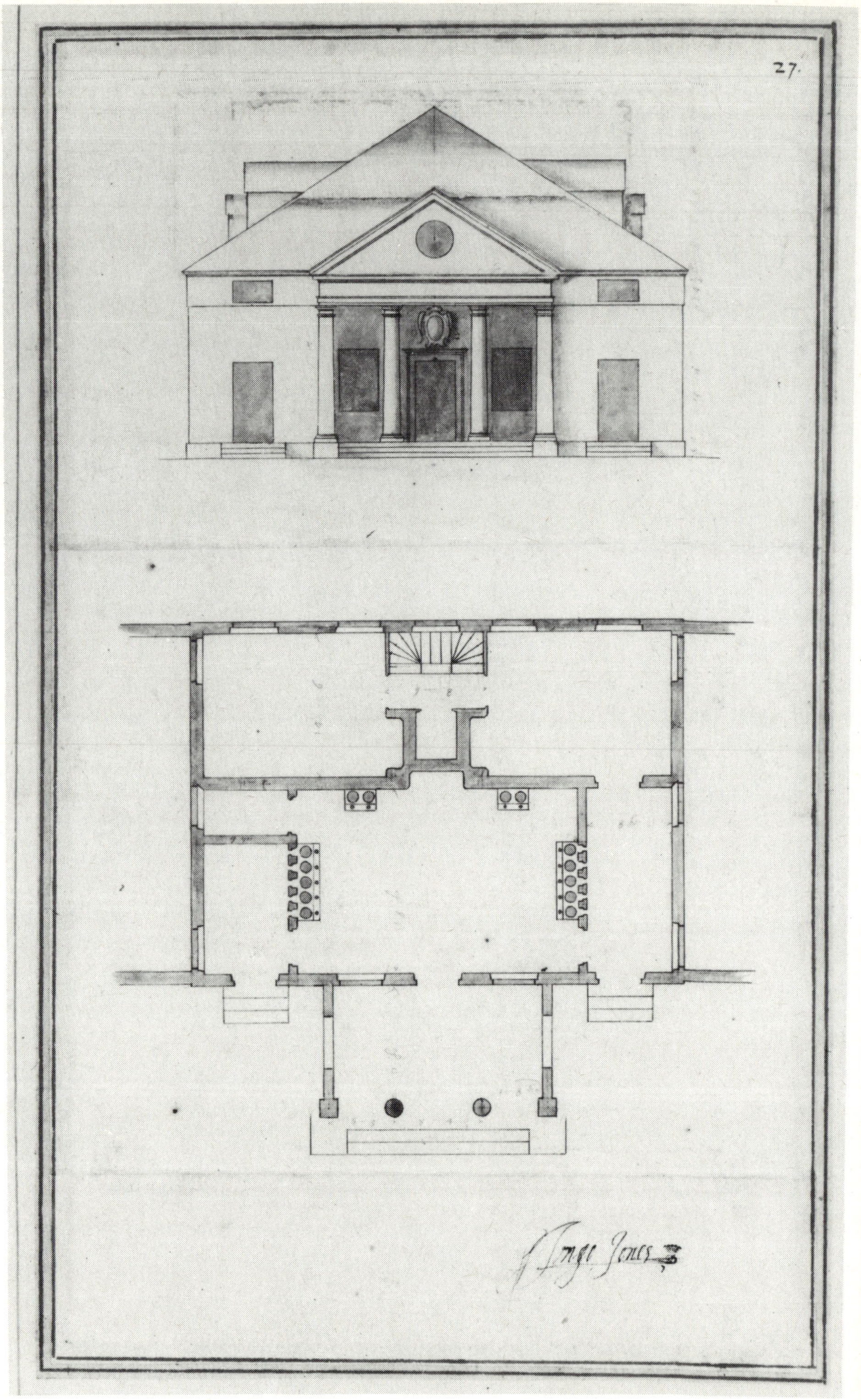

16. **John Webb** (1611-1672)
Unexecuted design for the bedchamber of Charles II at Greenwich Palace, 1665
Pen (290 x 445)
Provenance: John Webb and subsequently as given for no. 1.
Webb's designs for the decoration of the King's apartments at Greenwich Palace were not (except for some chimneypieces) carried out. Thirty-five of the drawings have survived and though several are details, simply drawn, many are as carefully drawn-out as teh section shown here, and share the same rather finicky system of hatching and cross-hatching. Webb had been Inigo Jones's pupil and life-long assistant and though he never achieved the elegant ease of his master's drawing style, he was a competent draughtsman. The range of techniques found in his drawings may be explained, perhaps, by the search for a personal idiom. The Greenwich decorative drawings form a distinctive group and it could be that Webb had some idea of publishing them. He did not do so himself but, in 1744, John Vardy published an engraved plate of the bedchamber section together with three of the Greenwich chimneypiece designs, attributing them to Inigo Jones.
Engraved: J. Vardy, *Some Designs of Mr Inigo Jones...*, 1744, pl. 4.
Lit: J. Lever, *Architects' Designs for Furniture*, 1982, p. 39.

17. Sir Balthazar Gerbier (1592-1663)and **Peter Mills** (1598-1670)
Design for a temporary triumphal arch for the Coronation of Charles II, 1661, erected near the Royal Exchange, City of London
Brown pen & grey wash (465 x 275).
Provenance: ?; Lord Burlington (1694-1753); Charlotte, daughter of Lord Burlington and wife of 4th Duke of Devonshire; in 1894 presented to the RIBA by 8th Duke of Devonshire.
In John Ogilby's *The Relation of His Majestie's entertainment passing through the City of London to his coronation with a description of the triumphal arches and solemnity* (1661, 2nd ed. 1662), it was stated that 'the architectural part was by Peter Mills, Surveyor of the City, and another person who desires to have his name concealed'. This last was almost certainly Sir Balthazar Gerbier, whose disloyalty during the Interregnum resulted in his banishment from Court after the Restoration.

The triumphal arch shown here (one of four) has a naval theme. The drawing has been 'pricked for transfer', that is, pinholes were made through the leading parts of the design to allow a copy (presumably for the engraver) to be made. There are some differences though between the preliminary design shown in the drawing and the executed design that was engraved. The naval symbolism of astrolabes, Mars and Neptune, the Four Continents, Atlas and so on was clarified and, in order to reduce costs, the figures were either painted on the arch or were live representations, so that, for instance, the niches within the arch had 'living figures representing Arithmetick, Geometry, Astronomy, and Navigation'.
Lit: J. Ogilby, *op.cit.*

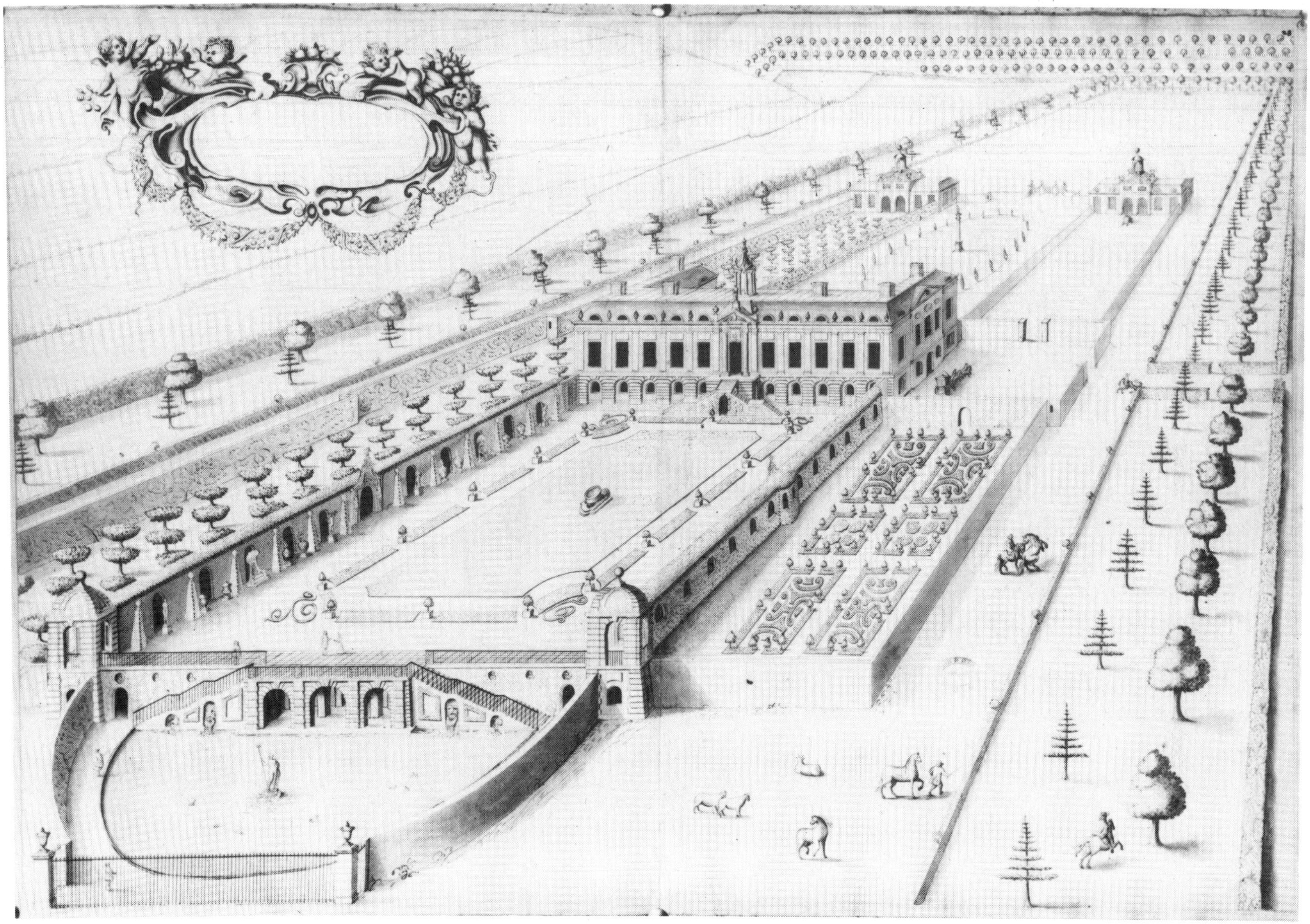

18. **William Talman** (1650-1719)
Design for a Trianon, near Hampton Court Palace, *c.* 1699
Pen & wash with some brown pen, within (faded) double-ruled, red pen border (515 x 735)
Provenance: John Talman ; Lord Burlington (on the evidence of the red pen border); presented by J.W. Hiort to the RIBA, 6 July 1835
Talman made this design for a 'Trianon' (an informal retreat from the rigid etiquette of court life) in, or just before, 1699 when he was Comptroller of Works to King William III. However, the King died in 1702, Talman lost his post, and the Trianon was never built.

The design was a comprehensive one with gardens (perhaps designed with George London, Deputy Superintendent of Royal Gardens) that were, in effect, a series of outdoor rooms. Talman, wanting to convey the totality of the design, adopted an elevated perspective method generally called a bird's eye view. Until now, these had been used only by topographical artists to make views of country seats ('estate portraits') and the like. Among Talman's vast collection of books, prints and drawings there would have been many engraved versions of such views. His unconventional and innovative use of the bird's eye view for architectural design was an important step in the development of architectural draughtsmanship, though one not fully taken up until the nineteenth century.
Lit: J. Harris, *William Talman, Maverick Architect*, 1982, passim.

19. **Sir Christopher Wren** (1632-1723)
Cross-section and detail of window for the Church of St Magnus the Martyr, City of London, *c.* 1670-71.
Brown pen & pencil (260 x 415)
Provenance: sale of the Marquess of Bute's Collection, Sotheby's, 23 May 1951, lot 14/52; purchased by the National Art Collections Fund, with other Wren drawings subsequently presented or re-sold to the RIBA.
Wren might well have remained a professional astronomer and amateur architect, had it not been for the Great Fire of London, which gave him a unique opportunity to demonstrate his talents. Thwarted in his desire to redesign the whole plan of the City, he had to content himself with the details – those being, principally, St Paul's Cathedral and no less than fifty-two City churches. Few drawings in Wren's own hand have survived, as most of the drawings for his buildings were made by draughtsmen (such as Nicholas Hawksmoor) working in his office. Wren's style of draughtmanship is distinct and personal, and this is a good example of it; unlike other drawings for the same building which are the product of the office, and are more finished works in pen and grey wash, this is plain and unfinished but nonetheless scientifically precise. The decorative detail is hardly more than indicated, the whole not a work of art but a means to an end. St Magnus was one of the first batch of City churches, designed in 1670 or 1671, when Wren must still have been grappling with the problem of the modern town church; other drawings for St Magnus demonstrate that this one marks an important stage in the design, introducing a kind of transeptal crossing on the north-south axis, which produced the lunette under the vaulted ceiling that is sketched in the top left-hand corner.
Lit: J. Summerson, 'Drawings for the London City Churches', *RIBA Journal*, LIX, 1952, pp. 126-129, and 'Drawings of London churches in the Bute Collection: a catalogue', *Architectural History*, XIII, 1970, pp. 30-42.

20. **Nicholas Hawksmoor** (1661-1736)
Record book of views of towns or individual buildings in Nottingham, Coventry, Warwick, Bath, Bristol, Oxford and Northampton, 1680-83
55 pp; bound in brown leather, brown pen, some with pencil, some with brown wash, some shaded & hatched (195 x 165)
Provenance: presented by R.J. Wilson in 1935.
This leather-bound volume has always been referred to as Hawksmoor's 'topographical sketchbook', but is more likely to be an early record book, drawn and compiled from about 1680-1683 when he was Wren's personal assistant. It contains amateurish drawings of towns or individual buildings and appears to be a scholarly attempt to record them – perhaps even with an eye to publication, as many of the pages carry figure numbers.

Hawksmoor probably sketched some of the buildings on the spot, prior to making the drawings for this book, but also looked at contemporary engravings or had access to original drawings of unexecuted projects. For example, in preparing fig. 2 on f. 7, the view of Nottingham, he must have made a preparatory sketch on the spot but he must also have seen Richard Hall's engravings of the same subject which were published in Robert Thoroton's *Antiquities of Nottinghamshire*, 1677. The title cartouche is very close to Hall's, and it seems odd that Hawksmoor should include Belvoir Castle, which can only be seen on the clearest of days, unless he was copying Hall. Similarly, on f. 53, Hawksmoor has drawn *All Hallowes* (All Saints) Church, Northampton, *with* a Corinthian portico. The portico was not added until 1701, and when it was it had Ionic capitals. Perhaps he had access to the original designs, or he could have designed his own portico to complete the building.
Lit: K. Downes, *Hawksmoor*, 1959, p. 2, no. 1

B1. **Sir Christopher Wren** (1632-1723)
Heirloom copy of *Parentalia: or Memoirs of the Family of the Wrens*, 1750
Pen, pencil (365 x 240)
Provenance: presented by Lawrence Weaver on behalf of a group of subscribers, 1911.
This volume, bound in gilt-tooled red leather, was specially made up for Margaret Wren, daughter of Stephen Wren who was a grandson of Sir Christopher Wren. It contains a copy of *Parentalia: or Memoirs of the Family of the Wrens* compiled by Christopher Wren, son of Sir Christopher, published by Stephen Wren in 1750, and 34 Wren family manuscripts dating from 1634 to *c.* 1720 and 140 prints of engravings interleaved. It remained in the Wren family until 1911 when it was bought by a group of subscribers from Mrs Piggott née Catherine Wren-Hoskyns, the last surviving direct descendant of Sir Christopher Wren, and given to the RIBA Library. This unique volume is an important source of biographical information and includes manuscripts by Matthew Wren (1585-1667), successively Dean of Windsor and Bishop of Hereford, Norwich and Ely, uncle of Sir Christopher; Christopher Wren (1591-1658), Dean of Windsor, father of Sir Christopher, and Sir Christopher Wren himself.

The present exhibit shows a letter (interleaved between pp. 194 and 195) by the young Wren to Faith Coghill whom he married in 1669. Returning to her a repaired watch he says 'But have a care of it, for I have put such a spell into it that every beating of the ballance will tell you 'tis the pulse of my heart which labours as much to serve you and more truly than the watch'. The photograph shows instructions by Wren for learning a sign language. Wren's interest in this was probably due to the fact that his tutor in mathematics, Dr. William Holder, was an expert in communicating with the deaf and dumb.

Other Wren manuscripts in the British Architectural Library's collection include the contract documents for Winchester Palace and the Royal Naval College, Greenwich.

Lit: Weaver, Lawrence, 'The interleaved copy of Wren's "Parentalia" with manuscript insertions' in *RIBA Journal* Vol 18 1911 Jun 30 pp. 569-585. Weaver, Sir Lawrence, *Sir Christopher Wren*, London, George Newnes Ltd, 1923. Introduction pp. vii-x.

C3. **Eighteenth century copy after Edward Pearce** (*c.*1630-1695)
Marble bust of Sir Christopher Wren (1632-1723) (700h, including socle)
Provenance: unknown; not included in 1871 catalogue.
The original bust by Pearce (or Pierce), in the Ashmolean Museum, Oxford, was, according to Wren's son, carved in 1673, the year in which Wren was appointed architect to the new St Paul's cathedral. The only significant difference between this copy and the original is that Wren's eyes, in the latter, have pupils; their omission by the eighteenth century copyist was perhaps an attempt to give the subject that touch of classical heroism which blank eyes are thought to convey. Pearce, who was possibly apprenticed to Edward Bird, an artist employed by Wren to execute painted decoration in the City churches, worked for Wren on a number of projects as both mason and woodcarver; he was, for example, the master mason for St Clement Danes (1680-81), and one of the 'mason-contractors' for St Paul's, although Pearce and a fellow mason, Jasper Latham, later fell out with Wren over their contracts. Apart from the bust of Wren (of which there is another copy, of plaster, at All Soul's College, Oxford), Pearce's best-known works are his busts of John Milton (*c.*1656) and Oliver Cromwell (1672).
Lit: R. Gunnis, *Dictionary of British sculptors 1660-1851*, 1953; H.M. Colvin (ed.), *The History of the King's Works*, V: 1660-1782, 1976, p. 34; K. Downes, *Sir Christopher Wren* exhibition catalogue, Whitechapel Art Gallery, London, 1982.

C4. **Attributed to Grinling Gibbons**
Boxwood relief of Sir Christopher Wren (185 x 145)
Provenance: collection of James Wyatt, PRA (1746-1813); presented by Thomas Willoughby, FRIBA, 1861.
Gibbons was born in Rotterdam, and came to England at the age of about nineteen. The credit for his 'discovery' is given to the diarist, John Evelyn, who took Gibbons to London in 1761 and introduced him first to the King, and then to Hugh May and Wren; the result of which was that he was employed at Windsor to carve a chimney piece. He was appointed Master Carver in Wood to the Crown by Charles II, a post he held until the reign of George I. He is best known for his wood carving, and his works include the altar piece for St Mary Abchurch, built by Wren in 1681-86, and decorative work at St Paul's Cathedral between 1689 and 1695; but he was also responsible for a number of church monuments and statues, including that of James II outside the National Gallery.
Lit: R. Gunnis, *Dictionary of British sculptors 1660-1851*,1953; K. Downes, *Sir Christopher Wren* exhibition catalogue, Whitechapel Art Gallery, London, 1982.

C5. **Attributed to Johnathan Richardson** (1665-1745), second quarter of eighteenth century
Portrait of Sir John Vanbrugh (1664-1726)
Oil on canvas (1500 x 1260)
Provenance: unknown, not included in 1871 catalogue.
Due to the influence of the Earl of Carlisle, for whom he had built Castle Howard, Vanbrugh was created Clarenceux King of Arms in March, 1704. Clearly he was proud of this post for in this portrait and in an identical one at the College of Arms, signed by Richardson and dated 1725, as well as in Kneller's Kit Kat portrait (*c.*1705), he is wearing his badge of office. His election, however, was not a popular one because he knew nothing of heraldry or genealogy, both of which he had ridiculed in his plays. Vanbrugh is holding a plan inscribed 'Blenheim' which he began designing in 1704.

Johnathan Richardson was the leading native portrait painter of the first 40 years of the eighteenth century and he helped Kneller found the St Martin's Lane Academy in 1714. His portraits were always good likenesses but Vanbrugh's rather cool detached gaze betrays nothing of his wit and conviviality.
Lit: E. Waterhouse, *Painters in Britain, 1530-1790*, 1978; P. and L. Murray, *A Dictionary of Art and Artists*, 1977.

21. **Sir John Vanbrugh** (1664-1726) and **Nicholas Hawksmoor** (1661-1736)
Preliminary design for the entrance front of Castle Howard, Yorkshire, 1699
Inscribed: (verso): by Margaret, Duchess of Newcastle: *Mr Vanbrooks draft of a great house* (the word *great* being inserted)
Brown pen & grey wash (360 x 1060)
Provenance: Duke of Newcastle, to whom Vanbrugh sent the design as an advertisement in 1703; presented to the RIBA on indefinite loan by Lady Anne Bentinck, Welbeck Abbey, 1978.
Sir John Vanbrugh, the playwright, first met Nicholas Hawksmoor in the spring of 1699. Vanbrugh had just 'turn'd to architecture' but had little or no idea of how to put his ideas into practice or onto paper. Hawksmoor was then the best trained architect of his day with a personality well suited for the role of right-hand man to the master. This drawing encapsulates their relationship.

It represents Vanbrugh's earliest idea for Castle Howard, but is in Hawksmoor's hand, expertly drawn in one-point perspective, a method of presentation taken from architectural engravings of the time and one much used by Vanbrugh's rival, William Talman. It is likely that Vanbrugh had already engaged Hawksmoor as his 'organizer, draughtsman and designer' by at least 26 June 1699, as this design corresponds to the measurements given in a letter of that date from Thomas Worsley to Lord Carlisle, describing plans for the house at that stage.

It is an imposing but obviously experimental design: the wings are a long way from the body of the house and the connecting passages appear to be ten-bay open arcades; the body of the house is small in comparison with its final form; the elevation of the main block is top heavy and the small cupola was later changed into a much larger dome.

Lit: K. Downes, *Hawksmoor*, 1959, p. 284, no. 525; second edition 1979, p. 274; K. Downes, *Vanbrugh*, 1977, *passim* (fig 18).

22. **Nicholas Hawksmoor** (1661-1736)
Survey sketch of a choir stall canopy in Henry VII's Chapel, Westminster Abbey, London, 1725
Pencil, brown pen & grey wash (735 x 200, two sheets joined, the lower 250 mm blank & folded)
Provenance: purchased, 1963.
After the death of Wren in 1723, Hawksmoor succeeded him as Surveyor to Westminster Abbey. This survey sketch of one of the existing sixteenth century canopies in Henry VII's Chapel was made by Hawksmoor in about 1725 when the stalls in the chapel were extended by one bay eastwards. At that date the chapel was enlarged to form the headquarters of the Most Honourable Order of the Bath which George I had revived. Although the stalls themselves were new in the east bay, the canopies were old, having been obtained by removing the back half (facing the aisle) of the canopies to the back row of the south side – a solution which Jocelyn Perkins has called 'a policy of hopeless vandalism'.

Hawksmoor's drawing is a good example of his spontaneous free-hand sketching style. It shows his ability to convey structure and volume by the use of flickering penwork, cross hatching and fluent wash shading, a characteristic of all his informal design drawings.

Lit: Royal Commission on Historical Monuments, *London*, I, *Westminster Abbey*, 1924, p. 69; J. Perkins, *Westminster Abbey, Its Worship and Ornaments*, II, 1940, pp. 170-173; K. Downes, *Hawksmoor*, 1979, p. 285.

23. **James Gibbs** (1682-1754)
Design for a monument to John Holles, 1st Duke of Newcastle, drawn to a scale of 1 1/5 inches to 1 foot, *c.* 1713-14.
Pen & wash within a double ruled border (715 x 510)
Provenance: by descent to Lady Anne Bentinck, by whom presented on indefinite loan, 1978.
Though Gibbs is said to have been the first British architect to make a practice of designing monuments, other earlier architects had occasionally done so. There are, for instance, Elizabethan designs for monuments among the Smythson drawings at the RIBA, and what is thought to be Inigo Jones's first design for a structure was for a monument, of about 1606, to Lady Cotton (also at the RIBA).

Gibbs had a training unique among British architects: he was the pupil of Carlo Fontana, the leading architect of Rome and master of the later, classicizing phase of Baroque. The design for a monument to the Duke of Newcastle (died 1711) shown here, is the 'second' design, the 'first' and 'third' designs are in the Soane Museum. As executed, the monument (in the north transept of Westminster Abbey) is both larger and more elaborate. The 'second' design, because it was made early in Gibbs's career, shows inevitably the influence of his master, Fontana, both in its design and draughtsmanship: so that, for instance, the broken pediment with festoon is a Fontana motif while the naturalistic shadows are a Fontana mannerism.
Lit: F.T. Friedman, James Gibbs 1682-1754...., PhD thesis, London University, 1971, pp. 67-75.

24. **Giuseppe Galli-Bibiena** (1695-1757)
Design for a stage set, after 1723.
Pen & wash with some brown pen & wash within, quadruple-ruled & wash border (330 x 485)
Provenance: presented by Sir John Drummond Stewart, 1838-9
The Galli-Bibiena family dominated theatre design from the 1680s to the 1780s and their work influenced many English architects travelling abroad. Giuseppe was trained by his father, Ferdinando, who had developed the type of scenery illustrated in this drawing. Perspective in the Renaissance stage set had been calculated along a central axis; in Ferdinando's 'scena per angola' it was arranged along diagonals to greater effect. Both designs and the finished scenery were usually monochromatic, and contrasting masses of light and shade added to the drama. The shadow that envelops the central building in this composition owes little to natural light sources and, as a result, deprives the scene of any real sense of depth. Giuseppe has inscribed the drawing *Primarus Archt.*, which suggests he had already inherited his father's post of Theatrical Engineer to the Imperial Court in Vienna. He travelled widely, designing temporary theatres, firework displays for various celebrations, and catafalques.

Lit: W. Jeudwine, *Stage Designs*, 1968, p. 19; A. Hyatt Mayor, *The Bibiena Family*, 1945; *Four Centuries of Scenic Invention – Drawings from the Collection of Donald Oenslager*, exhibition catalogue, 1974-75, *passim*.

25. **Charles Michel-Ange Challe** (1718-1778)
Procession within the Temple of Minerva,
c. 1743-49.
Brown pen & washes & watercolour (circular, 310 diameter)
Provenance: presented by Sir John Drummond Stewart, 1838-9
Challe abandoned the study of architecture after a few years and devoted himself to painting. He worked in the studios of Lemoyne and Boucher, who encouraged him to try for the 'Grand Prix'. This he won in 1741. He stayed in Rome from 1742-49 and while in Italy visited Roman sites, sketched ruins and composed – as did many of his fellow students – numerous architectural fantasies, of which this is one. Challe was greatly influenced by Piranesi, an influence seen here in the monumental architecture, dramatic lighting and convincing impression of space. Although 'correct' perspective plays a fundamental role in the success of the drawing, it has not been calculated. Architectural details are suggested by light strokes of the pen.

Upon his return to Paris he attempted to make his name as a history painter, with little critical success. In 1765 he was made 'Dessinateur du Cabinet du Roi' and as such designed stage sets and decors for court festivities.

Lit: *Piranése et les Français 1740-1790*, exhibition catalogue, French Academy in Rome, 1976, pp. 69-82; A.P. Wunder, 'Charles Michel-Ange Challe, a study of his Life and Work', *Apollo*, LXXXVII, 1968, pp. 22-33

26. **Colen Campbell** (1676-1729)
Design for Mereworth Castle, Kent, for Colonel John Fane, *c.* 1722
Pen & washes within a triple-ruled border (335 x 470)
Provenance: in 1966 a large collection of Colen Campbell's drawings were found in two Yorkshire country houses – Newby Hall and Studley Royal. These were bought for the RIBA by the Wates Foundation.
Mereworth was the first of four houses in England that have as their source Palladio's Villa Almerico (La Rotonda). Although the closest to the original, Mereworth is not a slavish copy and there are important differences; so that, for instance, the dome is steeper and thus Baroque rather than Palladian. Campbell drew at least four sections for Mereworth, each showing different structural solutions for the dome and each offering a different scheme of decoration. These are the only surviving essays by Campbell in that field and the first demonstration of a Neo-Palladian interior. Not, though, an entirely successful one, for the motifs are a rag-bag assortment and often ill-placed.

As a draughtsman, Campbell must have been extremely active. Though his earlier drawings (of, say, 1712) are awkwardly done, the drawing programme required for his own practice and for many of the 300 plates of *Vitruvius Britannicus* (1715, 1717, 1725) soon made him proficient. The Mereworth section shows Campbell's draughtsmanship at its best, though perhaps a little flawed by the inelegantly drawn freehand details.
Lit: J. Harris, *Colen Campbell*, *Catalogue of the Drawings Collection of the Royal Institute of British Architects*, 1973, *passim*.

27. **Richard Boyle, 3rd Earl of Burlington** (1694-1753)
Design for Chiswick House, London, (elevation of the entrance front, drawn to scale of 1in to 6 feet, by Henry Flitcroft) *c.* 1723
Pen & wash (310 x 370)
Provenance: ?; stamped *Architectural Society* (the drawing must have been acquired by the Society which, founded in 1831, was united to the Royal Institute of British Architects in 1842).
Chiswick Villa (now House) was designed by Lord Burlington for his own use. Based loosely on the Villa Rotonda, its sources lie also in the drawings by Palladio and Inigo Jones that Burlington owned. He had acquired them as part of his 'mission ... to reinstate in England the canons of Roman architecture as practised by Palladio, Scamozzi and Jones' (Colvin).

To further his aim, Burlington set up what was virtually an architectural training school and among the 'students' was Henry Flitcroft, who, originally a joiner, developed into an accomplished draughtsman and a competent architect in his own right, as shown, for example, by the church of St Giles-in-the-Fields. He re-drew many of Burlington's designs, although in fact the noble architect was quite able to 'draw and design as well as pay the bills'. This Chiswick elevation shows the Villa as built except, that is, for the obelisk chimneys, and it is accurately and elegantly drawn. The naturalistic drawing of the rusticated masonry has precedents in Palladio's own villa drawings but not, though, the softly-cast shadow of the portico. Palladio seems to have used such shadowing only for sculptured monuments and its use is associated with Baroque draughtsmanship. Flitcroft's purpose was, no doubt, to achieve greater legibility for his elevational drawing and make the presence of a portico quite apparent.

C6. **Attributed to Bartholomew Dandridge** (1691-1755)
Portrait of Henry Flitcroft (1697-1769), *c.* 1740
Oil on canvas (1130 x 930)
Provenance: unknown
Like Isaac Ware, (no. C7) Henry Flitcroft was drawn into the circle of Lord Burlington. In 1726, he procured Flitcroft the post of Clerk of Works at Whitehall, Westminster and St James's and as a result he became known as 'Burlington Harry'. However, Flitcroft is famous for his private houses, for example, Wentworth Woodhouse and Woburn and in this field he remained faithful to the Palladian canon throughout his life. His portraitist, Dandridge ran a prosperous business and in 1731 took over Kneller's old studio where he became a pioneer of the rococo conversation piece; Vertue considered him the ablest and most original exponent of such pictures of his time.
Lit: P. & L. Murray, *A Dictionary of Art and Artists*, 1977; *Rococo, Art and Design in Hogarth's England*, exhibition catalogue, Victoria & Albert Museum, 1984, p. 162.

28. **William Kent** (1685-1748)
Design for the State Barge for H.R.H. Frederick, Prince of Wales, 1732
Pen & brown wash (330 x 520)
Provenance: J. D. Crace (Hon. ARIBA) by whom presented, 1911.
Like Inigo Jones, Balthazar Gerbier, and to a certain extent James Gibbs, Kent began as a painter and this shows in the fluency of this freehand drawing for a State Barge. Though it has to be said that as a history painter his work has been characterised as pedestrian and uninspired and his book illustration for *The Faerie Queene* was described by Horace Walpole as revealing 'Wretchedness of drawing ... [and] total ignorance of perspective', Kent's genius lay in design, in which a sense of scale, composition and, often, witty detail had its place.

The State Barge for Prince Frederick has a wealth of watery detail: mermaids, dolphins, scallop shells, seaweed festoons, fish-scale ornament and, on the gunwale, Vitruvian scroll (or wave) moulding. The waterman's uniform includes a cap of fish-scales, and seaweed-like lace decoration. As executed, the 57-foot hull was extended by 6 feet and the beam widened by 8 inches. Later another 8 feet was added on, so that 21 oarsmen, instead of the 12 provided for here, could more easily row the tidal waters of the Thames. The barge was in use until 1849 and is now at the National Maritime Museum, Greenwich.
Lit: G. Beard, 'William Kent and the Royal Barge', *Burlington Magazine*, CXII, 1970, pp. 488-93; *Drawings by William Kent*, catalogue of an exhibition at the Victoria & Albert Museum, 1984, pp. 2-3.

C7. **Andrea Soldi** *c.*1703-1771
Portrait of Isaac Ware (*c.*1707-1766) and his daughter, *c.*1754
Oil on canvas (1350 x 1120)
Provenance: Unknown
Isaac Ware directs our attention to a drawing of Wrotham Park, one of his principal works which Summerson has described as 'perhaps the most significant house of the decade'. In the background one of its corner pavilions can be seen under construction which dates the portrait to about 1754.
Lit: *RIBA Journal* 1947, p. 350; *Rococo*, LIV, *– Art and Design in Hogarth's England*, exhibition catalogue, Victoria & Albert Museum, 1984 p. 296; J. Ingamells, *Andrea Soldi – A checklist of his work*, Walpole Society XLVII, pp. 1-20.

29. **Robert Adam** (1728-1792)
Sketchbook, 1749-50
43 pp; pen & pencil, no covers (160 x 100)
Provenance: presented by the Wellcome Historical Museum, 1944.
In the winter of 1749-50 Robert Adam went to London and from there made an architectural tour in England which is recorded in this sketchbook. It was during this tour, according to John Clerk of Eldin, that 'he first began to curb the exuberance of his fancy and polish his taste'. Intricate Gothic designs still seem to dominate the book, although he appears to have gone to Wilton, as a design for some Jonesian pavilions there is dated *May 1750* (f13). But the sketchbook does contain a fascinating list of items *To carry to Arderseer*, the point on the Moray Firth where Fort George was being built. It is particularly interesting in describing his drawing instruments: *Cambdens Brittannia & Gibson/ Builders Jewels/ Estimator/ Book of Memorandums/ Case of Paralel Rulers/ A Book or two of Architecture/ My Book of sketches/ Colours in the Ivory Case/ Viz. Sap Green/ Carmine Gumd/ Gall Stone/ Wood Sutt/ Lead pencils. Hair pencils. Crowquills/ Sketch of Johnies house.*
Lit: J. Fleming, *Robert Adam and his Circle*, 1962, pp. 85-6.

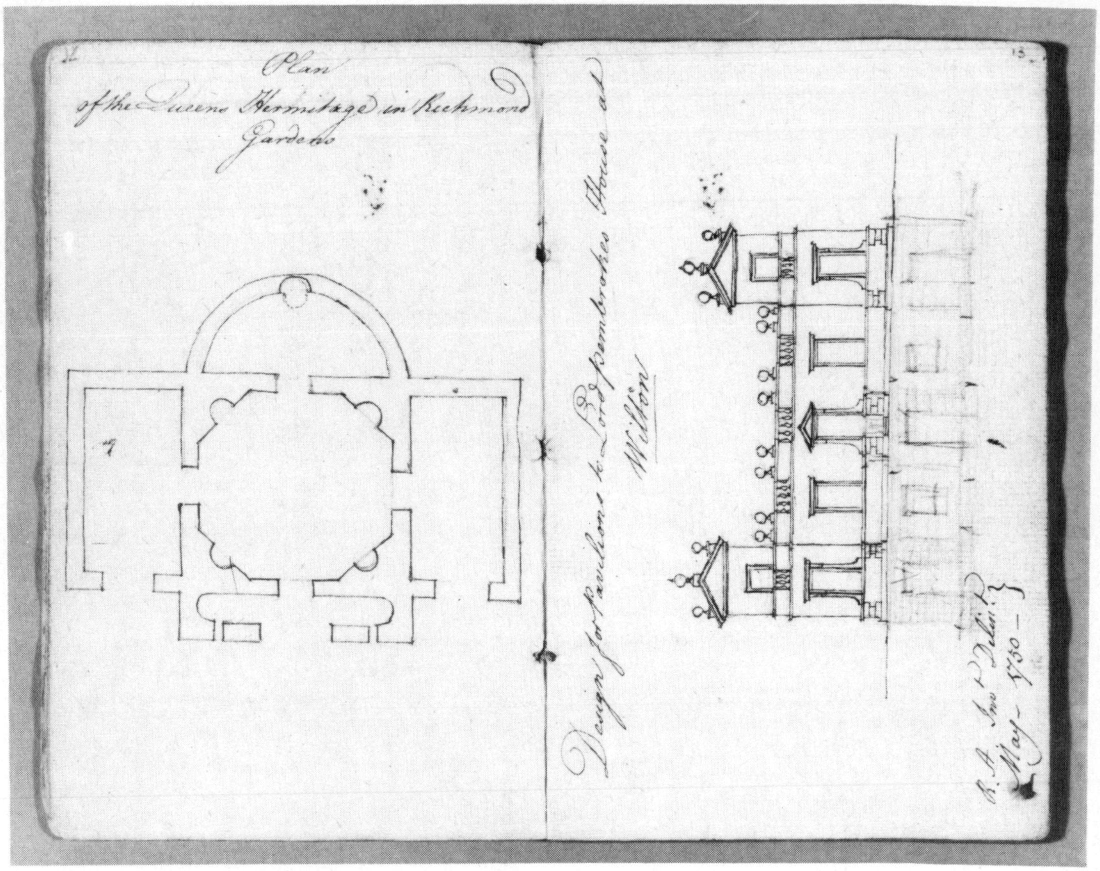

D5. **Giovanni Battista Piranesi,** (1720-1778)
Vedute di Roma. Rome [1748-78].
Issued accumulatively throughout his publishing career in Rome, Piranesi's *Vedute* reflect not only the full range of his extraordinary development as an artist but are important touchstones for understanding that complex revolution in European taste called 'Neo-classicism', a revolution that owed its momentum in no small part to Piranesi's highly successful evocation of the 'magnificenza' of ancient Rome. As the most widely disseminated of all his works probably no other purely topographical book before or since can claim to have altered so radically how contemporary artists and lay public alike looked at architecture in general and the monuments of ancient Rome in particular. The Institute's copy is part of the superb Tubbs collection which, when it was presented to the Library by Grahame Tubbs in 1947, transformed an already 'good collection' (Hind) into one of the best in the world.
Provenance: Tubbs donation, 1947.

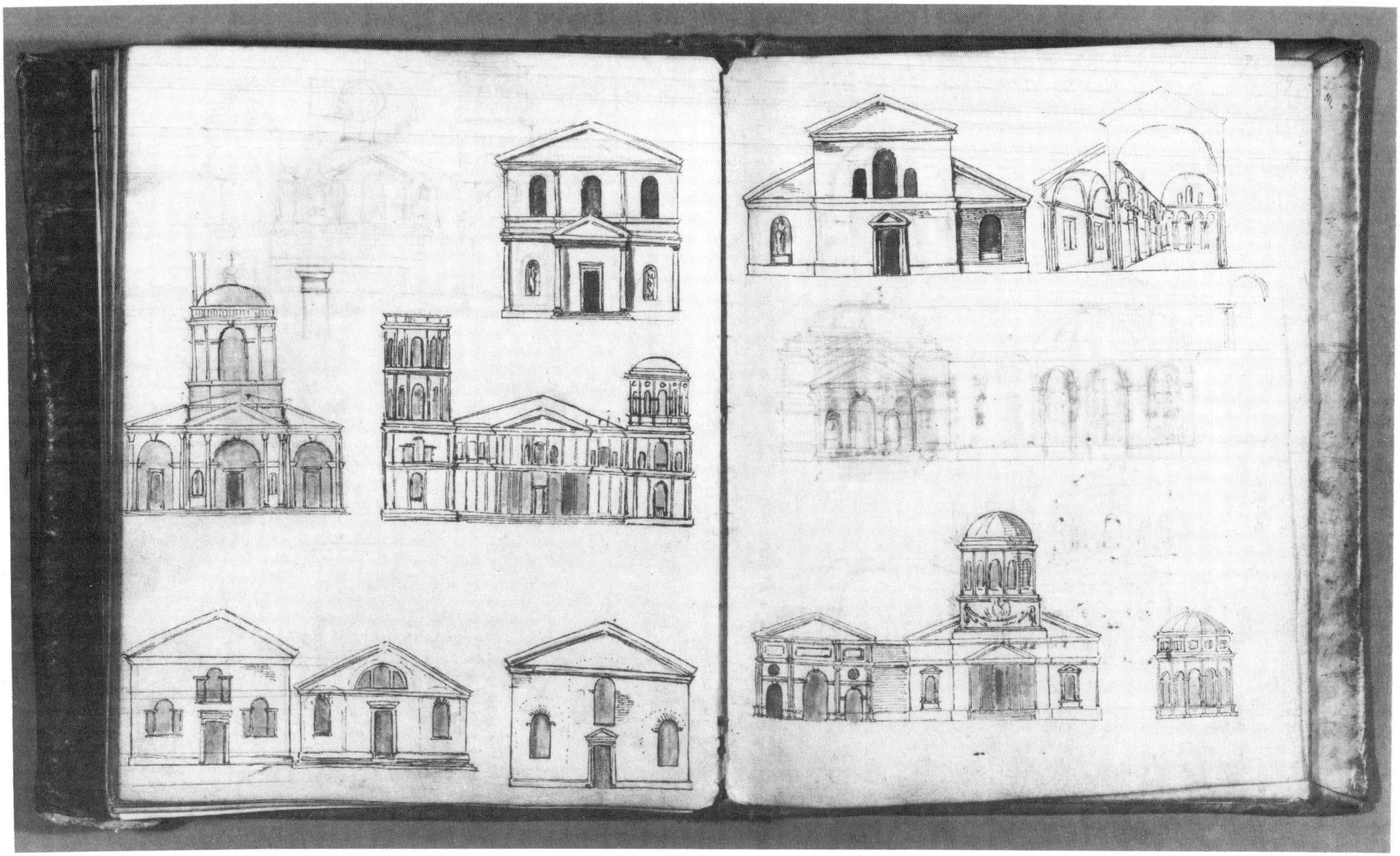

30. **Matthew Brettingham** (1725-1803)
Sketchbook, compiled in Rome and its environs, *c.* 1750
93 leaves, bound in vellum; pencil, pen, brown wash & red chalk (265 x 205)
Provenance: an inscription on the flyleaf reads: *Presented by A. Newton Associate/per A.J. Style, Student/ Dec. 1869.*

Matthew Brettingham was the son of the architect Matthew Brettingham (1699-1769), whose influence with the Earl of Leicester at Holkham Hall enabled him to spend the years between 1747 and 1754 in Italy, not only as a student of architecture but as a dealer buying antique sculpture and paintings for Lord Leicester and other 'milordi'. The income derived from his dealing seems largely to have relieved Brettingham from the need to develop an extensive architectural practice, and the only important independent commission with which he can be credited was Charlton House, Wiltshire, 1772-76, which shows him as a very competent, novel architect.

Very few eighteenth century design sketchbooks survive: Brettingham's was made in Italy in *c.* 1750, and although it has several topographical sketches of scenes in and around Rome, is largely packed with his own sketch designs for various projects which include public buildings and country houses. They show that he was much influenced by Palladio. His free brown pen drawings, both in their manner of execution and composition (for example, ff78v & 79), are particularly close to Palladio's – so much so that it seems very likely that he had seen Lord Burlington's collection of Palladio drawings and based his own drawing style upon them. This is very probable as Lord Burlington was a close friend of the Earl of Leicester at Holkham where Brettingham's father was employed from 1734 onwards.

C8. **John Theodore (Dirck) Heins** (1697-1756)
Portrait of Matthew Brettingham the Elder (1699-1769), 1749
Oil on canvas (1040 x 900)
Provenance: bequeathed by Rupert Gunnis, 1965.
Matthew Brettingham proudly presents us with a design that is not his: the Triumphal Arch at Holkham Hall was designed for the Earl of Leicester by William Kent. Although Brettingham supervised the erection of Holkham, the ideas behind its design came from the 'Earls of Burlington and Leicester assisted by Mr. William Kent'. In 1761 when Brettingham published the 'Plans and Elevations of the late Earl of Leicester's House at Holkham', he forbore to mention Kent and inscribed his own name on the plates. Clearly his professional conduct was in complete contrast to his behaviour in society where 'being a man of mild manners' he earned the name of 'Rectitude' at White's Club. A Norfolk man, he engaged a Norfolk artist to paint his portrait – Heins was a portrait painter and mezzotint engraver of German origin, who had settled in Norwich in 1720.

31. **James 'Athenian' Stuart** (1713-1788)
View of the Tower of the Winds, Athens, Greece, *c.* 1751-53
Gouache (315 x 430)
Provenance: Elizabeth Ann Stuart, daughter of the artist, by whom 20 views where sold to Jermiah Harman, sale 12-21 May 1823; by 1861 they were in the possession of Thomas Howard of Blackheath, by whose executors they were presented to the RIBA, 1873.
This gouache watercolour of the Tower of the Winds is one of twenty similar views of Greek antiquities by Stuart in the RIBA Drawings Collection. They were engraved, with measured drawings by Nicolas Revett, for the *Antiquities of Athens*, the first accurate survey of Greek classical remains and the principal source book of the Greek Revival in Britain. Stuart and Revett arrived in Athens on 18th March 1751, where they stayed with some intervals until March 1753. Stuart painted these general topographical views in a lively gouache technique – consisting of opaque watercolour paint mixed with gum and honey, a method he had learnt from Louis Goupy, the well-known French fan painter, for whom he had worked as a boy. The 'indefatigable' Revett did most of the measuring and produced the precise and detailed drawings, which when published simplified the whole process of design and made the buildings of antiquity particularly easy to grasp and copy by the later architects of the Greek Revival. The Tower of the Winds was published in the first volume of the *Antiquities* (1762, I, Ch. III, pl. 1) and was especially widely copied, for example by Stuart himself in the Tower of the Winds at Shugborough, Staffordshire, 1794 and by William and Henry Inwood as part of the spire on the St Pancras New Church in London, 1819.
Lit: J. Mordaunt Crook, *The Greek Revival*, 1972, *passim*; D. Watkin, *Athenian Stuart, Pioneer of the Greek Revival*, 1982, *passim*.

32. **Sir William Chambers** (1723-1796)
Design for a Mausoleum in the form of a 'ruined' domed temple with peristyle, *c.* 1751-2
Brown pen & brown, grey & pink washes within a double ruled & wash border (430 x 335)
Provenance: unknown.
Robert Adam reported hearing from Wilton, when in Florence in 1755, that Chambers owed all his 'hints and notions' to C L Clérisseau, who had tutored Chambers in drawing in Rome in the early 1750s. John Harris has suggested that Chambers probably took from Clérisseau the 'novel idea of representing an architectural design in a pictorial manner'. The first known example of a standard design in a landscape setting is Chambers's 'ruined' section of 1751-2 of a mausoleum for Frederick, Prince of Wales; this drawing can be tentatively related to it and was probably drawn in Rome *c.* 1751-2. Here, a sense of timelessness and antiquity is implied by presenting a *new* design as a decaying ruin, a method often used by Clérisseau and taken over by Chambers and Adam in several of their designs later on in the 1750s.
Lit: J. Harris, *Sir William Chambers*, 1970, *passim.*

33. **Charles Louis Clérisseau** (1722-1820)
View of the Porta Aurea at the Palace of Diocletian, Spalatro, now Split, Yugoslavia, 1757
Pen, brown pen & washes (465 x 385)
Provenance: presented by Sidney Kitson in 1929.
On 11th July 1757 Robert Adam set sail from Venice to visit Spalatro, taking with him his drawing master, Charles Louis Clérisseau, and two draughtsmen. He was determined to publish an imposing folio of antiquities which would establish his reputation in English society on his return, and wrote that 'this jaunt to Dalmatia makes a great puff even in Italy and cannot fail doing much more in England'. The original set of drawings for the engraved plates was largely, perhaps entirely, drawn by Clérisseau although when published, Adam omitted all the names of the draughtsmen and Clérisseau's share in the work was relegated to a brief mention in the Preface as 'a companion on the voyage'.

Clérisseau had studied at the Académie in Paris under J.F. Blondel and from 1749 in Rome under G.P. Pannini, but had advanced to a more avant-garde interest in the antique. In the early 1750s he was patronized by English students in the Neo-Classical circle around Gavin Hamilton, and in 1755 was adopted by Adam as a drawing master. In little more than a week Adam could feel his taste improving every day: 'he draws in architecture delightfully, in the free manner I wanted ...'.

This drawing is a good example of Clérisseau's fluent wash technique which was to have such a great influence on both Adam and Chambers: the details are picked out in sepia pen and the shadows indicated in darker tones of grey – a technique which well conveyed the stained patina of ancient ruins.
Lit: R. Adam, *The Ruins of the Palace of the Emperor Diocletian at Spalatro*, 1764 (plate XII, engraved by Santini); J. Fleming, 'The Journey to Spalatro', *Architectural Review*, CXXIII, 1958, pp. 103-107.

34. **Edward Stevens** (1744-1775)
Design for a 'London house fit for a person of distinction', 1763
See colour plate page 11.

35. **John Vardy** (?-1756)
Design for a double chaise-longue, drawn to a scale of 1 inch to 1 foot, *c.* 1755-61
Brown pen with pink, yellow & brown washes (430 x 490)
Provenance: ?; with other drawings from the Milton Abbey Collection purchased in Dublin, 1931
Vardy's design for a double chaise-longue with its unusually long 14-foot rectangular frame was probably made for Joseph Damers, 1st Lord Milton. If it was executed it seems, alas, not to have survived. Besides his job at the Office of Works, Vardy also received private commissions, and one of his specialities was the design of carved pieces of furniture, architectural fittings and ornament, some of which were probably carried out by his brother Thomas, a carver.

A faithful colleague and disciple of William Kent, Vardy's style in architecture and design often reflects the older man's work. Here the carved ornament of the chaise-longue is derived from Kent but used in a lighter and more fluid manner that reveals the influence of Rococo. On the other hand the linearity and chaste decoration of the seat rail and legs are Neo-Classical. The jaunty domed canopy, with its (fictive) coat-of-arms, frieze, tasselled pelmet and ostrich feathers, that gives the day bed such importance, was borrowed from the kind of arrangement more often seen over state beds. The draughtsmanship also shows a matching eclecticism. Thus the finely-ruled pen lines of the seat rail, the fluting carefully shaded, contrast with the free drawing of the hangings that are shaded in a brown wash, reinforced by broad pen hatching.
Lit: J. Lever, *Architects' Designs for Furniture*, 1982, p. 42, pl. 1.

36. **Sir William Chambers** (1723-1796)
View of the Place Louis XV (de la Concorde), Paris, from the 'Paris Sketchbook', 1774
Pen with grey & blue washes within black & blue ruled borders (215 x 365)
Provenance: Thomas Hardwick to P.C. Hardwick, by whom it was presented to the RIBA, 1885.
The unexpected decision to build public offices at Somerset House could have become known to Chambers in late April or early May 1774. He did not have the commission at that date and immediately left England for Paris – writing to Thomas Worsley on 20th May 1774: 'Many great things have been done since I last saw Paris which I must examine with care and make proper remarks upon'. The results of his 'examination' are in this sketchbook of wash drawings of the latest Parisian *hôtels* and public buildings, many of which became models for his own Somerset House.

This view of the Place Louis XV shows it in its completed state with Bouchardon's equestrian statue of the king; Nicholas Marie Potain directed the works begun in *c.* 1754 to Ange-Jacques Gabriel's designs. It is fluently drawn in pen with blue and grey washes which give the effect of watercolour. The technique has much in common with Clérisseau's monochrome sketches and is also similar to the architectural *capricci* by Charles Michel-Ange Challe which Chambers would have known in Paris.
Lit: J. Harris, 'Sir William Chambers and his Parisian Album', *Architectural History*, VI, 1963, pp. 54-90 (fig 13); J. Harris, *Sir William Chambers*, 1970, pp. 14, 97.

37. **Charles Joachim Benard** (1750-?)
Design for a triumphal arch
See colour plate page 12.

38. **Robert Adam** (1728-1792)
An imaginary landscape showing a castle and domed city set on the banks of a river winding through a rocky mountain landscape, *c.* 1777-87
Brown pen & coloured washes (350 x 465)
Provenance: unknown.

In the last fifteen years of his life, as his office procedure became increasingly standardized, Robert Adam produced a series of picturesque landscape fantasies which he never exhibited but which were the recreation of his leisure hours. His favourite subject is a castle, most often based on the fourteenth and fifteenth century Scottish castles that his brother-in-law, John Clerk of Eldin, had taught him to draw in his youth. Often it is perched on a high rock, approached by a winding road over a bridge and encircled by a river. Nearly always a beam of light falls on the central object and casts a strongly marked angular shadow. Adam uses the predominant tones of mid-blues and soft browns, applied with heavy washes over dark paper and subscribed to the landscape formulae of Alexander Cozens and William Gilpin that the foreground should be dark, the middle distance light and the horizon misty.

It is to these drawings, and not to his office

productions, that his obituary in the *Gentleman's Magazine* referred: 'His talents extended beyond the line of his own profession: he displayed in his numerous drawings in landscape a luxuriance of composition, and an effect of light and shadow, which have scarcely ever been equalled'.
Lit: P. Oppé 'Robert Adam's Picturesque Compositions', *Burlington Magazine*, LXXX, 1942, pp. 56-57; A.A. Tait, *Robert Adam and Scotland. The Picturesque Drawings*, exhibition catalogue, Scottish Arts Council, 1972, no. 31, plate 12.

39. **Antonio Pietro Zucchi** (1726-1795)
An Architectural Allegory, *c.* 1778
Oil on canvas, (620 x 445) en grisaille
Provenance: Robert Adam (Sale, Christie's, 1818, 20 May, no 5); Richard Cosway, *c.* 1818-1820; Sir Jeffry Wyatville, by whom it was presented to the Institute in 1838-39. It is recorded in a Report of the RIBA Council 1839: 'List of Contributors, 7 May 1838-8 May 1839'.
Zucchi's Architectural Allegory was engraved by Bartolozzi as the frontispiece for Volume 1 of Robert and James Adam's *The Works of Architecture*, 1778. It sets out allegorically the Neo-Classical basis of the Adam style: 'A student conducted to Minerva, who points to Greece, and Italy, as the countries from whence he must derive the most perfect knowledge and Taste in elegant Architecture'. Minerva points to a map which is arranged with Italy to the North of Greece, as if to emphasize the fact that Roman architecture was itself rooted in the previous achievements of the Greeks. Zucchi became associated with Clérisseau and Robert Adam when they were in Venice preparing the drawings made at Spalatro for publication. In 1776 he came to London where he was occupied chiefly in supplying pictures for Adam's designs for decoration. He married the painter, Angelica Kauffman, in 1781, to whom this painting was attributed for many years.
Lit: H. Hawley, *Neo-Classicism, Style and Motif*, exhibition catalogue, Cleveland Museum of Art, 1964, no. 87.

40. **Robert Mylne** (1734-1811)
Elevation of the Principal Front of Wormleybury, Wormley, Hertfordshire, for Abraham Hume, *c.* 1767
Pen with grey & ochre washes, within a triple-ruled border (480 x 640, three sheets joined)
Provenance: presented by Mrs Green, late owner of Wormleybury, 1962
Mylne is perhaps best known for designing the old Blackfriars Bridge (demolished in 1868), and was as much civil engineer as an architect. He designed relatively few country houses and in this

field had to compete with Robert Adam and James Wyatt. He did, however, obtain a number of commissions in Shropshire, and outside that county one of his principal country houses was Wormleybury, for Abraham Hume, created a baronet in 1769. The exteriors of Mylne's houses are, in Colvin's words, 'characterised by a fastidious restraint that is prophetic of neo-classical simplicity of the 1790s', and this is reflected in Mylne's style of drawing, of which this is a good example – a formal mode of presentation, yet not so severe as to exclude, for example, glazing bars in the windows (a common feature of drawings for neo-classical houses), and enlivened by the judicious use of coloured washes and shadow. This is one of a set of eleven plans, elevations and sections which prove that Wormleybury was a completely new house, built in 1767-70, and not, as was once thought, simply a remodelling of the existing building. In 1777-79 the principal rooms were decorated by Robert Adam, and at about the same time Mylne did work at 17 Hill Street, London, for Sir Abraham Hume, the second baronet.

Lit: A.T. Bolton, 'Wormley Bury, Hertfordshire' *Country Life*, XXXVI, 1915, pp. 144-149

41. **James Wyatt** (1746-1813)
Design for the North front of Badger Hall, Shropshire, for Isaac Hawkins Browne, drawn to a scale of ⅛ inch to 1 foot, *c.* 1779
Brown pen & wash with grey & green washes within a double-ruled & wash border (355 x 520)
Provenance: acquired before 1871.
Wyatt rebuilt Badger between 1779 and 1783, but this early design for a new North front was not actually executed; Badger itself was demolished in 1952. C.R. Cockerell called Wyatt's Dodington Park 'chaste & highly considered in the Exterior' – an estimation that could be applied just as easily to this severe and elegant design with its typically Wyatt feature of semi-circular bowed porch and tripartite window surmounted by a Diocletian lunette.

There is an element of uncertainty in putting forward any drawing as undoubtedly Wyatt's own hand. He had worked for Antonio Visentini, the architect and architectural painter, in Venice in the early 1760's and technically was much influenced by him. This elevation has many of the characteristics of Visentini's drawings – the same manner of shading, spartan presentation and ruled border and even shares Visentini's preoccupation with the Cinquecento palazzo elevation. Farington noted in 1796 'the light manner in which Wyatt had spoken of execution in Architectural drawings, adding that some of the greatest architects could not draw at all'. It is true that the majority of the large collection of Wyatt's drawings at the RIBA are comparatively crude design or working details drawn in pen and pencil on coarse-grained cartridge paper. Only a very few are presentation designs, like this elevation, and coloured with washes, intended to persuade a client or exhibit a scheme at the RA. These could be in his hand or could be by one of his several pupils, particularly the indispensable John Dixon who stayed with him for many years. Cockerell also recorded that Wyatt 'would stay 6 weeks with Sir R C contriving his drawgs, his letters remaining unopened. When recommended to do so, would say, no they can wait. Would make any no. of drawgs & destroy them for others with pleasure. Always doubtful & uncertain of himself – would sit whole evenings wrapt in consideration of his plans'.
Lit: J. Harris *Georgian Country Houses*, 1968, pl. 22; J. Harris, 'C.R. Cockerell's Ichnographica Domestica', *Architectural History*, 1971, XIV, p. 14; D. Linstrum, *The Wyatt Family, Catalogue of the Drawings Collection of the Royal Institute of British Architects*, 1974; J.M. Robinson, *The Wyatts: An Architectural Dynasty*, 1979, p. 70.

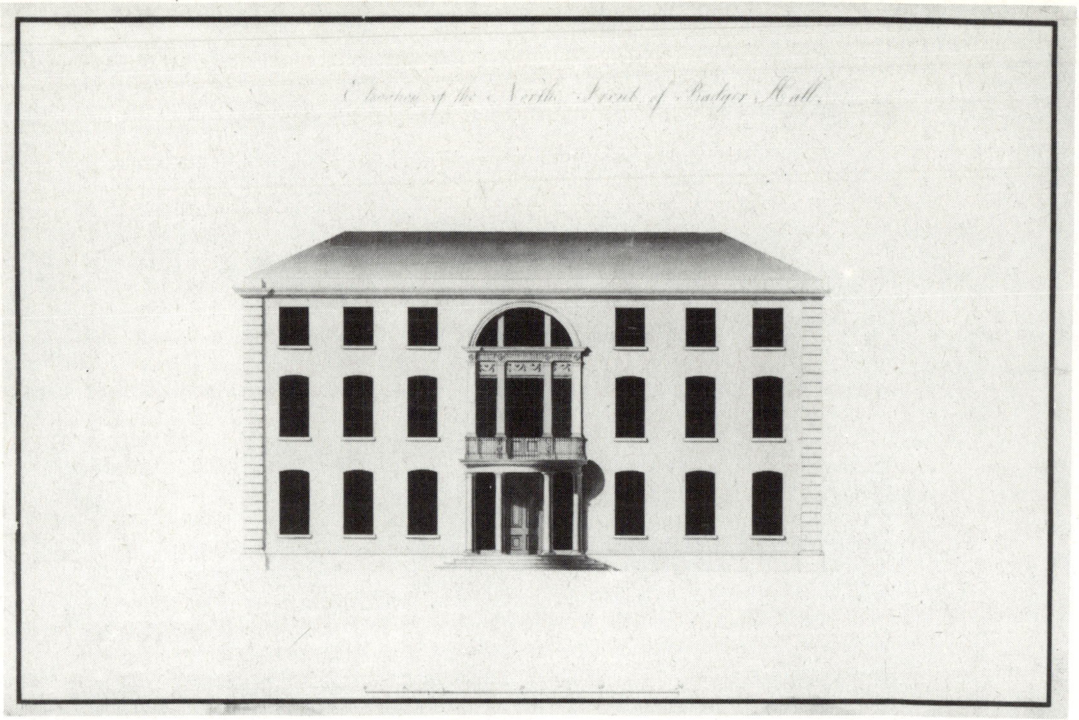

42. **Joseph Bonomi** (1739-1808)
Design for the Great Drawing Room, for Mrs Montagu, in Portman Square, London, 1782
Pen & wash within ruled & wash border (455 x 595)
Provenance: by descent to Anthony de Cosson, by whom presented on permanent loan, 1972.
The architect for Montagu House, 22 Portman Square (destroyed by bombing in 1941) was James Stuart. His dilatoriness and general irresponsibility (he drank too much) explains why Bonomi took over the completion of the interior. The perspective shown here is dated 1782 and was presumably the 'Design for a drawing-room' exhibited at the Royal Academy in the following year. The richly ornamented, elliptically vaulted ceiling, massive Corinthian columns and life-size sculpted figures create a sombre air of Graeco-Roman monumentality. Watkin has written that 'most of the decorative and architectural features of Bonomi's drawings for interiors at Montagu House' (in the RIBA) are 'realisations of Stuart's original intentions'. It follows then, that the essentials of these unexecuted schemes are owed to James Stuart.

Bonomi came to London from Rome in 1767 to work for the brothers Adam and he remained in their office for several years. In a paper given by Wyatt Papworth, the view was expressed that 'many of the beautiful drawings of internal decoration ... and many of the drawings for their book ... were special objects of Bonomi's employment'. A comparison of some of the engraved interior perspectives of *The Works in Architecture of Robert and James Adam* (published in 1773 and 1779) and Bonomi's drawing for Mrs Montagu's drawing room shows the same use of dark tones relieved by shafts of daylight, and mannerisms such as the use of reflections or the representation of marble floors, tend to confirm Papworth's view.
Lit: W. Papworth, 'Memoir of Joseph Bonomi, architect and A.R.A. ...', *RIBA Transactions*, XIX, 1868-9, pp. 123-134; D. Watkin, *Athenian Stuart, Pioneer of the Greek Revival*, 1982, pp. 46-51.

Design of the Great Drawing Room, for Mr. Montagu, in Portman Square, London.

43. Giacomo Antonio Domenico Quarenghi
(1744-1817)
Preliminary design for a palace for Prince Bezbarotko, Moscow, *c.* 1785
Pen & wash (465 x 635, 2 sheets joined)
Provenance: found in a copy of Quarenghi's *Edifices Construits à St Petersburg d'après les Plans du Chevalier de Quarenghi et Sous sa Direction*, 1810, presented to RIBA Library by G.R. Burnell, 1869.
A prolific designer and draughtsman, Quarenghi studied as a painter, first at Bergamo (where he was born) and then in Rome. Here he turned to architecture, studying and drawing the monuments of that city and later, of the Veneto. In 1779 he was invited by Catherine the Great to go to Russia were he stayed for the rest of his life. Among Quarenghi's works was a palace for Prince Bezbarotko, first minister to the Empress Catherine. The design shown here is an alternative design, for it differs both from the published design in Quarenghi's *Edifices* ... and from other drawings in the Biblioteca Civica, Bergamo.

Quarenghi's painterly beginings probably explain the delectable quality of his architectural drawings. Many of them, including his colour-washed sections, have figures that do more than just suggest scale; they also add drama to the design. In the perspective shown here the figures of a peasant and child standing near their rustic cottage make a deliberate contrast with the grandeur and size of the palace. Quarenghi also drew many *veduta ideata* (imaginary views) and he has used a *vedutisto* manner for this design, where the figures, trees, plants, fences and so on are arranged so as to direct the eye into the centre picture space.
Lit: V. Zanella and others, *Disegni di Giacomo Quarenghi*, 1967, *passim*.

44. **George Steuart** (*c.* 1730-1806)
Design for the library at Stoke Park, Wiltshire, for Joshua Smith, *c.* 1786.
Pen & watercolour within ruled & wash border (355 x 490)
Provenance: one of eight drawings for Stoke Park bound in a volume with the label 'Miss Smith 1820' and with a bookplate engraved with the coat of arms and motto of Charles Scrase Dickens; purchased, 1963.
Steuart's country house architecture has been characterised, by Colvin, as having an elegant restraint verging on bleakness. A Highland Scot, said to have been a house-painter, the details of Steuart's architectural training are not known. Stoke Park (most of it was demolished in 1950) had the thinly modelled elevations, chaste neo-classical motifs and compact planning associated with Steuart. It was not a large country house: sufficient for polite society but not grand. As well as the library, there was also an eating parlour, breakfast room, drawing room, and saloon. So as not to lose too much space for circulation, Steuart did away with any external doors to the main part of the house. Behind the steps and portico *in antis* of the principal front were three tall sash windows, and entry was through an inconspicuous door in the west wing. However, if Steuart virtually banished all external doors, he had plenty inside the house and a rather obsessive concern with symmetry led to many of them being false; two out of the six doors of the library are blind.

The interior perspective of the library uses a subtle technique of finely-drawn pen lines, a varied density of shading and telling use of pale washes combined with paper left white. The puzzle is whether it was Steuart who drew it or not, for the preliminary designs for Stoke Park are clearly by another hand. It seems that Steuart employed a perspectivist, perhaps a member of his artistic family.

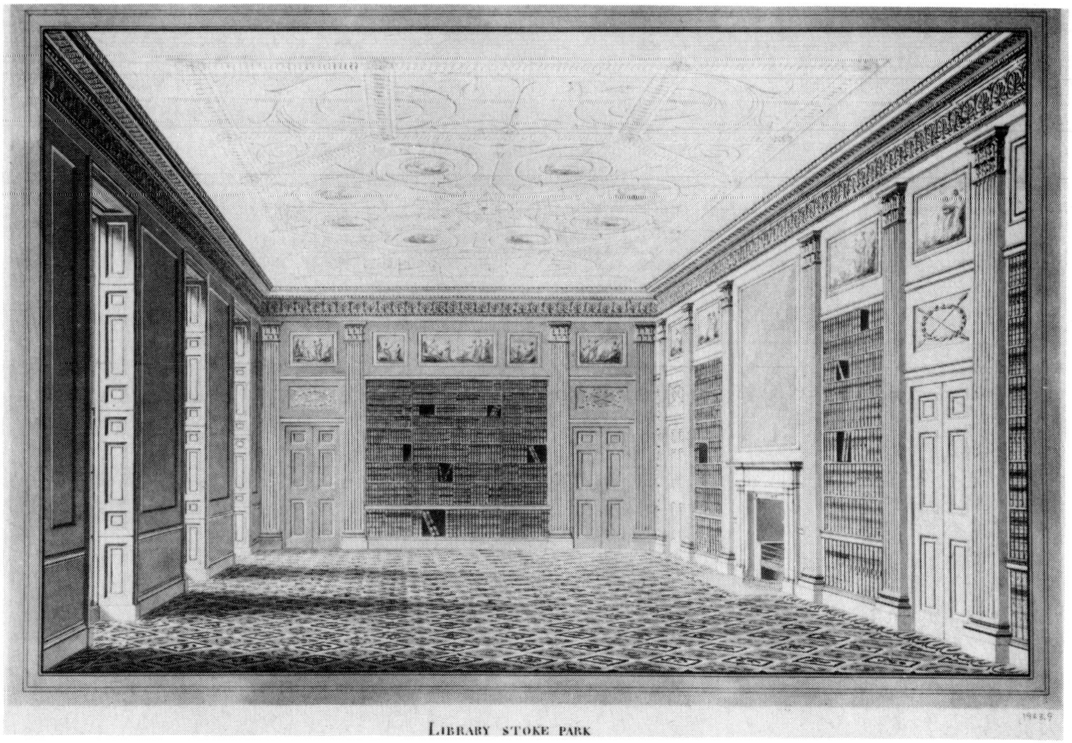

45. **Joseph Bonomi** (1739-1808)
Design for Roseneath, Dumbartonshire
See colour plate page 13.

46. Sir Robert Smirke (1780-1867)
View of the Tower of the Winds, Athens, 1803
Pencil, pen & watercolour (290 x 260)
Provenance: purchased, 1967.
This is presumably the sketch that Smirke records in his journal entry for July 18, 1803 (no. B2). It makes no pretence to be anything more than a sketch, and the notes on it suggest that he used pencil on the spot and filled in with brown pen and watercolour later on. It does not provide a precise record of the architectural details of the building; but it is, on the other hand, an interesting record of its actual state, which Smirke could compare with the view by James Stuart published in *Antiquities of Athens* (no. 31).

B2. **Sir Robert Smirke** (1780-1867)
Journal of a tour: Athens to Messina, 1803
Entry for July 18
Speia pen (190 x 250 open)
Provenance: purchased 1967
Robert Smirke travelled extensively in Europe between 1801 and 1805, visiting France, Italy, Sicily, Greece, Austria and Germany. Two volumes of his journal cover his journey, in the company of the landscape painter William Walker, a pupil of Smirke's father, from Rome to Athens and back to Messina, between April and September 1803. In these journals Smirke describes his personal fortunes and misfortunes, his general impressions of the country and its inhabitants (at a time when Greece was occupied by the Turks) and, of course, the archaeological and architectural sites that he visited and which provided so much valuable material for a young man who was to become one of the leading Greek Revival architects of his day. Sketches made on the spot were a vital part of the process, and the Tower of the Winds, built by Andronicus of Cyrrhus in the middle of the first century B.C., was one of the key monuments that had to be seen by all grand-tourists; it was the only surviving "horologion", or clock tower, and originally had sundials attached to the outside and a water clock inside. The octagonal shape of the building, and individual elements of it, were often borrowed by Greek Revival architects, one of the best-known versions being James Wyatt's Radcliffe Observatory at Oxford.
Lit: J.M. Crock, *The Greek Revival*, 1972; A.W. Lawrence, *Greek Architecture*, 1957

B3. **Sir Robert Smirke** (1780-1867)
Journal of a tour: Rome to Athens, 1803
Entry for July 4
Pen (190 x 125)

Provenance: purchased, 1967.
Smirke was often afflicted with fever on his travels, which he attributed to the climate, and this bout at the beginning of July 1803, just after their arrival in Athens, also struck down his companion William Walker; so it was that he went alone to see W.R. Hamilton, Lord Elgin's private secretary, whose acquaintance they had made the week before. Hamilton was at this time superintending the removal of the marble frieze from the Parthenon (then commonly referred to as the Temple of Minerva) to England; the fragments (better known as the Elgin Marbles) were purchased by the British Museum in 1816 for £35,000, somewhat less than half the probable cost incurred by Elgin in rescuing them (with the full authorisation of the lawful government and owner of the property, the Turkish Empire) from what seemed at the time to be certain destruction; the Parthenon had deteriorated rapidly since 1687, when the use of the cella as a gunpowder store came to a sudden and explosive end. The rest of Smirke's afternoon was spent walking round the south side of the Acropolis.
Lit: J.M. Crook, *The Greek Revival*, 1972; A.W. Lawrence, *Greek Architecture*, 1957.

47. **Thomas Harrison** (1744-1829)
Design for a military and naval monument, 1814
Pen & wash (275 x 635)
Provenance: purchased, 1966.
Thomas Harrison of Chester is one of the most interesting English Neo-Classical architects and his Chester Castle complex of 1788-1822 forms the finest group of Greek Revival buildings in Britain. In his own day his taste and judgement were highly appreciated – particularly by Lord Elgin, who owed to Harrison the original idea of acquiring the Marbles and wrote to him in 1802: 'You and you alone gave me the idea, and the notion of its importance' – but he never really received the recognition he deserved and several of his schemes came to nothing. This design, which is almost certainly the drawing he exhibited at the Royal Academy in 1814, was also never executed. It was for 'A National Building to record by painting and sculpture the Victories of the Marquis of Wellington and the other commanders by sea and land during the present war' (before the Battle of Waterloo). It has the austerity of the best French Grand Prix designs and the device of framing the project in the arch of a bridge probably derives from Piranesi's Triumphal Bridge, engraved for *Opere Varie* in 1750. Harrison's lack of success in London was no doubt due to his unworldly temperament. Joseph Farington described him in 1795 as 'a plain man in person and manners, with an embarrassed delivery in conversation; but very clear and ready in explaining with his pencil'. His drawings, certainly, are some of the most accomplished and 'European' of all the English Neo-Classicists and owe much to his early training in Rome from 1769-76, where he was championed by Pope Clement XIV. They are fastidiously executed in pencil and pen and washed in cool greys and ochres, the medium emphasising the austere Grecian qualities of the design.
Lit: J.M. Crook, *The Greek Revival*, 1968, pl. 16; J.M. Crook, 'The Architecture of Thomas Harrison', *Country Life*, CXLIX, 1971, pp. 876-879, 944-947, 1088-1091.

Dijon

48. **George Maddox** (1760-1843)
Sketchbook, *c.* 1819-20:
21 leaves bound in red leather; pen (135 x 210)
Provenance: presented by Decimus Burton, 1869.
George Maddox was an architect who never really established himself in regular architectural practice; for most of his life he earned his living making designs and drawings for other architects and, above all, by teaching draughtsmanship. His pupils included Sir George Gilbert Scott (who praised his 'wonderful power of drawing') and Decimus Burton for whom Maddox made these drawings (according to the letter accompanying his gift to the RIBA) in about 1819-20. Burton would then have been 19 or 20, his master 59 or 60, but the drawings give no indication of the age of the artist; they are extraordinarily precise and delicate. These exqusite classical compositions must have been made to demonstrate technique to the young man; there is no suggestion that they were intended for publication, or any other practical purpose, although at the time of his death Maddox was said to have been engaged upon a series of etchings of 'architectural groups and fragments'. Nor can they have been intended to teach Burton much about ancient Greek architecture; although reminiscent of the Acropolis, the views in this and the other landscapes in the sketchbook are probably as fanciful as the 'butterfly' on the opposite page (f.lv).
Lit: *RIBA Journal*, X, 1903, p. 202.

49. **Thomas Hope** (1769-1813)
Travel sketchbook, Italy and France, *c.* 1812.
86pp bound in green paper-covered boards, pen, some pencil (105 x 160).
Provenance: purchased, 1978.
Thomas Hope, connoisseur, author and amateur architect, travelled to Italy in about 1812 and this sketchbook is a record of his journey. His route took Hope from Rome through Siena, Florence, Parma, Piacenza and Rivoli and then through France to Paris. Hope's interests were wide and this is reflected in his drawings of buildings, gardens, furniture and ornament. As in many architectural sketchbooks, there are also studies for designs.

While sketchbooks are invaluable as a visual aide-memoire to the architect, to the scholar they offer an insight into the mind of the compiler. Unexpectedly (for a neo-classicist) Hope concentrates in this sketchbook mostly on Italian Romanesque and Gothic architecture, though there are many details of designs in, for example, the French Empire style. Twelve of the drawings were later used for some of the engravings in Hope's *Historical Essay on Architecture ...* (1835) while others became the sources for Hope's designs. The pages seen here (pp. 78,79) show a screen in the Empire style, funerary monuments, a draped pelmet in the manner of Fontaine and Percier, and an entrance façade labelled *Dijon* (probably of the Hospital built there in 1690 by M. de Noinville). All drawings are in a plain pen line. There are no plans or sections in the sketchbook and not many perspectives, for Hope preferred the simple and informative, direct elevation drawn economically and often with some elegance.
Lit: D. Watkin and J. Lever, 'A Sketchbook by Thomas Hope', *Architectural History*, XXIII, 1980, pp. 52-9, pls., 37-43.

A2. **Design model for a Regency country house or suburban villa,** c. 1820s
Wood, painted cream & grey (119 x 280 x 160)
Provenance: purchased, 1980.
The architect and location of this Greek Revival house are unknown. It is reminiscent of the designs of J.B. Papworth, but equally may be the work of a speculative builder.
Lit: *Architectural Review*, CXLII, 1967, pp. 26-32.

50. **Francis Goodwin** (1784-1835)
Design for a National Cemetery on Primrose Hill, London, 1830
Pen & watercolour (115 x 210)
Provenance: purchased at Sotheby's, 12 June, lot 138, 1980
In 1830 Goodwin made designs for a 'National Cemetery' on Primrose Hill, consisting of an outer area 'disposed somewhat after the manner of Père Chaise' at Paris, and an inner enclosure containing temples and mausolea which were to be 'facsimiles of some of the most celebrated remains of Greek and Roman architecture'. These designs he exhibited gratuitously in an office taken in Parliament Street, but his proposals were not taken up by the General Cemetery Company which eventually laid out Kensal Green Cemetery under the direction of another architect.

Goodwin was a skilful purveyor of styles: he produced a showy late Gothic for a series of Commissioners churches, Grecian for public buildings and Italianate and Old English for domestic houses. His office drawings, and those of his chief pupil, Thomas Allom, are of a high standard and he spared no expense in preparing them and in promoting himself.

C10. **Unidentified Artist**
Portrait of W.H. Playfair (1790-1857), *c.* 1818
Pencil & watercolour (700 x 350)
Provenance: purchased, 1940

51. Thomas Sandby (1721-1798)
Design for an idealized bridge, called 'A Bridge of Magnificence', intended to span the Thames between Somerset House and Lambeth, *c.* 1770
Pen with blue & ochre washes (650 x 5230)
Provenance: presented by John Britton in 1835.
Sandby was appointed Professor of Architecture at the Royal Academy in 1768; in 1770 he began a series of six lectures which he repeated annually until his death, and which all the architectural students had to attend. The original text of these lectures is in the RIBA Library, where one can see that the sixth was accompanied by about 40 designs including this large-scale elevation of a 'Bridge of Magnificence'.

Sandby taught that the 'beauty and perfection of Architecture' consisted principally in the 'great and magnificent joined with symmetry and proportion', and that it was necessary for the student to study the sublime and the beautiful as seen in the stupendous works of nature. His use of the words 'sublime' and 'magnificent' were derived from Edmund Burke's *Philosophical Enquiry into the Origins of Our Ideas of the Sublime and Beautiful*, and his concept of 'magnificence' meant primarily greatness of size: only in viewing buildings of great dimensions could the 'imagination soar to the idea of infinity'. (Sixth lecture.) To illustrate this point he unfolded a drawing which in itself extended more than half the width of the lecture room at Old Somerset House. Soane himself could recollect from his student days the 'powerful impression the sight of that beautiful work produced on myself and on many of the young artists of those days'. Sandby's bridge was always intended as an ideal project – but the site was real. It was to extend for 1153 feet from the Strand, just near Somerset House across the river to Lambeth and in so doing 'to open another communication between the great commercial city and its suburbs'. It is an imposing structure of seven arches with colonnades running its full length, joining an arched central feature of two storeys to domed terminal blocks – all three to contain private dwellings and shops. His sources of inspiration were almost certainly Piranesi's triumphal bridge in his *Opere Varie* of 1750 and Palladio's reconstruction of the Roman Ponte Elio.

Sandby, like his brother Paul, was an accomplished topographical artist. His architectural drawings have a subtlety of technique which is possibly not best suited to a dramatic presentation such as this one. He first drew in the bridge in lead pencil, shaded and coloured it with blue and ochre washes and outlined it in sepia pen. He did not normally

recommend the use of a 'penned outline' – especially in a perspective – where a 'soft & agreeable appearance' was required to give a 'nearer approach to that of Nature'.
Lit: D. Stroud, 'Soane's design for a triumphal bridge', *Architectural Review*, CXXXI, 1957, pp. 260-262; *The Age of Neo-Classicism*, exhibition catalogue, Council of Europe London, 1972, p. 622; P. de la Ruffinière du Prey, *John Soane. The Making of an Architect*, 1982, pp. 63-4.

52. **Alexander Carse** (*fl. c.* 1794-1838)
View of the 'Willow Cathedral' built under the direction of Sir James Hall, drawn by Alexander Carse, 1792.
Watercolour with a touch of gouache (205 x 255).
Provenance: presented by Sydney D. Kitson, 1937.
Sir James Hall (1761-1832), a Scottish country gentleman, MP, geologist and chemist, developed a theory on 'The Origin and Principles of Gothic Architecture' which was published first as an essay in 1797 and later, in 1813, as a book. Briefly his argument was that Gothic architecture derived from simple wattle buildings reproduced in stone. Sir James put the idea to the test when 'with the help of a very ingenious country workman' he constructed a 'Willow Cathedral'. Ash posts were placed at four-foot intervals and willow rods, ten feet long, were bound to the posts and at their tops so as to form a frame for a thatch roof. The door was copied from that of Beverley and the windows from 'various Gothic edifices'. In addition 'soon after the work was finished, a very accurate drawing of it was made by an ingenious young artist, Mr A. Carse, which it is proposed to engrave for the illustration of this Essay when published at full length'. In fact, the published frontispiece was quite different to the one shown here and was drawn by W.H. Lizars.

Alexander Carse came from Edinburgh and is best known for his genre paintings, examples of which (for example *The Penny Wedding*, 1819) are in the National Gallery of Scotland. His view of the 'Willow Cathedral', painted on Whatman paper watermarked 1794 seems to be his earliest known work. It quaintly conveys, perhaps with unconscious irony, Hall's rather eccentric idea as to the roots of Gothic architecture.
Lit: J. Hall, *Essay on the Origin and Principles of Gothic Architecture*, 1797, *passim*; *Catalogue of the Drawings Collection of the Royal Institute of British Architects* (entries under Blore, Carse, Hall).

See colour plate page 14.

53. **Humphry Repton** (1752-1818)
'Red Book' for *Langley Park, In the County of Kent. One of the Seats of Sir Peter Burrell, Bart.*, 1790.
26 leaves bound in brown calf; watercolour (215 x 295)
Provenance: Sir Peter Burrell Bt; presented by J.M. Lockyer, 4th March 1850.
At the age of 36, with a growing family and having lost his capital in a business venture, Repton decided on a career as a landscape gardener. He designed a trade card (there is one stuck into this Red Book) and in August 1788 sent off 'circular letters addressed to former friends' asking for commissions. These soon came and with them the idea of presenting 'Red Books' (as often bound in brown calf as red morocco) to his clients. They were wonderfully successful as advertisements and are now invaluable records of Repton's design philosophy. Most of them are of the size of this one, though about a dozen, including the Sheringham Red Book (no. 54) are larger, folio volumes. Each is a combination of watercolour designs and text (written in copperplate) explaining proposals and recalling conversations with the client.

Landscape design is a difficult subject to draw and Repton had only such precedents as Capability Brown's maps (some of which he owned). He also had a knowledge of surveying and there is a plan with a plant list in the Langley Park Red Book. But mostly he relied on description and on watercolour sketches. To some of these were added a device of Repton's own invention, the slide (or flier or overlay) which helped to demonstrate 'before and after': 'before' on the slide, and underneath, the 'improvement' as shown in this *View from the house, towards the North of the Avenue*.

Repton's bill for his work at Langley Park has been preserved. The total was *£53:11:0*, of which the *digest of Plan Sketches & c in proportion to time employ'd at home* came to *£15:15:0*. Since he charged ten guineas a day for work done at home, this Red Book must have taken about a week to make. For work done away from home Repton charged Sir Peter Burrell, £5:5:0 a single day, £8:8:0 for two days which included expenses.
Lit: *Humphry Repton, landscape gardener, 1752-1818*, exhibition catalogue, Sainsbury Centre for Visual Arts, UEA, Norwich, 1982, *passim*.

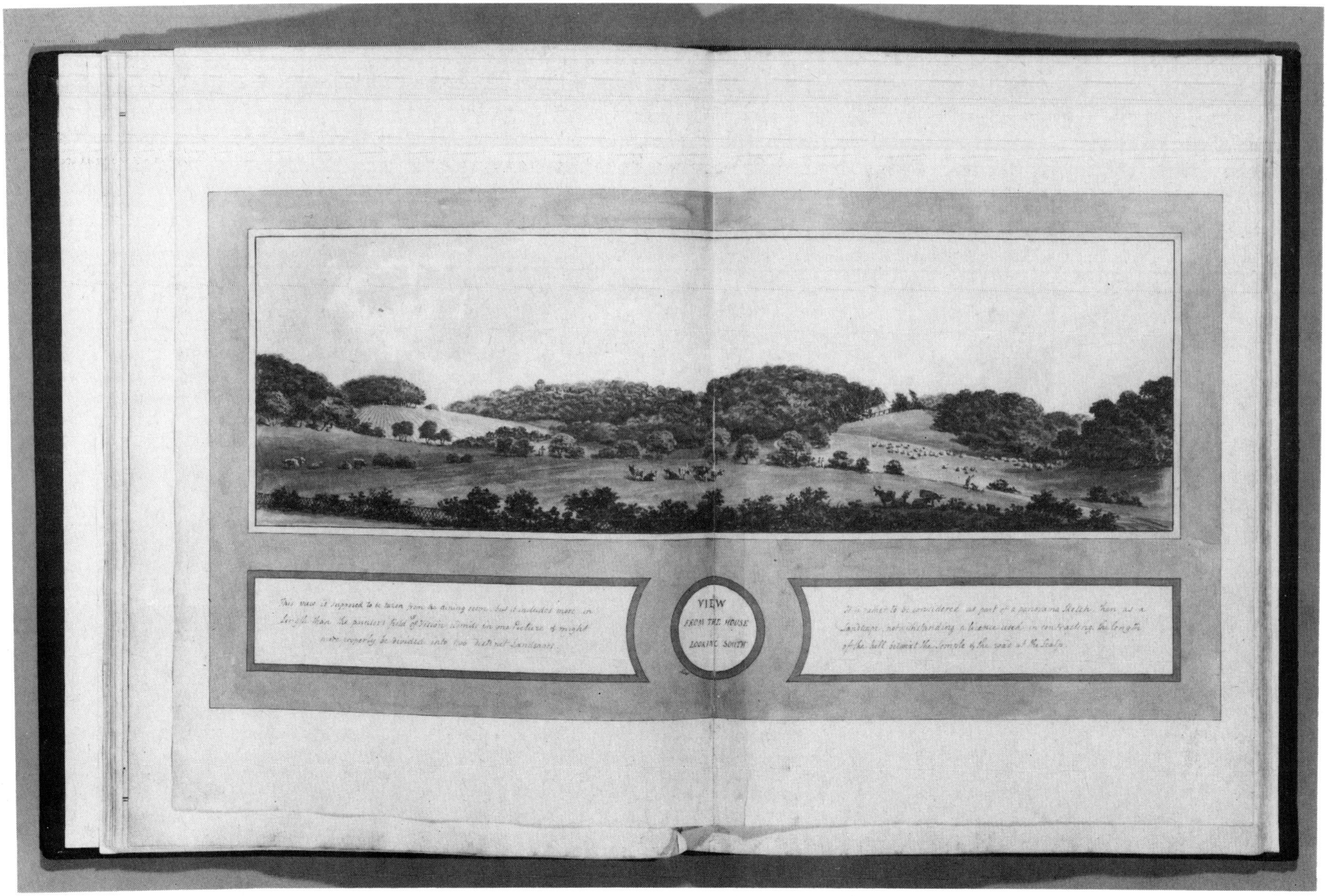

54. **Humphry Repton** (1752-1818)
'Red Book' for *Sheringham in Norfolk, the Property of Abbot Upcher Esq by H. Repton assisted in the Architecture by his son J.A. Repton, MDCCCXII*.
36 leaves bound in red morocco; watercolour (450 x 340)
Provenance: Abbott Upcher; by descent to the H.T.S. Upcher Settlement, presented on indefinite loan to the RIBA, 1979.
Sheringham was Repton's masterpiece and in his preface to the Red Book he wrote *this may be considered as my most favourite work*. It was the combination of a location that possessed *more natural beauty and local advantages, than any place ... ever seen*, young and sympathetic clients, and the chance to design (with his son John Adey Repton) both house and landscape that so delighted Repton. His enthusiasm spilled over into verse (mostly his own), used as well as drawings to emphasise his arguments in what was as much a prescription for a conduct of life for Mr and Mrs Upcher as an explanation of the designs. The architectural drawings in the Red Book were done by J.A. Repton with Repton Snr 'humanising' them, adding figures, furniture, curtains, and so on. As a watercolourist, Repton was self-taught and his technique, after some initial experiments, was to use brush and watercolour and little or no pen and ink. Generally, he used warm brown for the foregrounds and 'for my distances a cold grey, or neutral tint, and afterwards I glaze over the whole with colour'. The later watercolours such as this *View from the House looking south*, (f12v, f13r) are both more detailed and more romantic than the ones made earlier in his career.
Lit: as for no 53.

55. George Stanley Repton (1786-1858)
Sketchbook compiled while a pupil in the office of John Nash *c.* 1802-*c.* 1804.
94 leaves bound in brown calf with a brass clip; brown pen & wash, pen. (100 x 160)
Provenance; presented by George S. Repton (?descendant), 1935.
George Stanley Repton was the fourth and youngest son of Humphry Repton. When he was about sixteen, he became a pupil of his father's friend, John Nash. His sketchbook covers the first two years or so in Nash's office and offers a fascinating insight into architectural education at that time. From the 1770s an increasing number of architects had one or more pupils in their offices, articled for a period of five or six years. As part of their training they were required to copy working drawings, and many of the plans, details and elevations for houses and cottages in G.S. Repton's sketchbook are reduced copies of Nash's designs. The details for two fireplace surrounds for *Mr Legh* (G.J. Legh of High Legh Hall, Cheshire, a house that Nash altered and added to from 1797 to 1818) are characteristic examples of Repton's impeccable draughtsmanship. Other drawings in the sketchbook include topographical views of buildings that caught his eye. One of these was Norris Castle on the Isle of Wight, designed by James Wyatt in 1799. Here Repton has experimented with brown pen and washes while other sketches show him using pen alone. Eventually his drawing style became virtually indistinguishable from that of his eldest brother, John Adey Repton. Both of them at times, assisted their father 'in the architectural department' of his practice.

56. Attributed to **John Nash** (1752-1835)
Design for a road bridge in a neo-Norman style, over the Long Walk, Windsor Great Park, drawn by G.S. Repton.
Brown pen & watercolour (355 x 565)
Provenance: purchased, 1973.
Unsigned, undated, uninscribed and undocumented, this unexecuted design for a road bridge in a Norman castle style has to rely on attribution. Dr Tim Mowl suggests that, on stylistic grounds, John Nash is the most likely author of the design. This is because the capitals and mouldings on the arches match Nash's documented neo-Norman work on the library façade of Kentchurch Court, Herefordshire (*c.* 1795) and also correspond to Nash's work at Killymoon Castle, Co. Tyrone (1801-3). Nash was joint architect (with Soane and Smirke) to the

Office of Works, and was responsible for Windsor Great Park.

The perspective shows the Long Walk with Windsor Castle in the background and was, almost certainly, drawn by G.S. Repton. He (and his brother J. A. Repton) used pen and monochrome wash (grey or brown) for many of their perspectives. They also used pen and local blue watercolour, a technique suggested by the work of watercolour artists like J.R. Cozens and, by now, rather old fashioned.

57. **John Buckler** (1770-1851)
View of Ashridge Park in Hertfordshire, 1822
Watercolour (355 x 500)
Provenance: presented by Basil Ionides, 1938.
John Buckler was an architect but is best known as the prolific topographical artist of cathedrals, country houses and other buildings, many of which were published as aquatints. At the end of his life he calculated he had made over 13,000 sketches, mainly of topographical subjects, and his careful drawing of ancient buildings form an invaluable record of much that has since been altered or destroyed. Forty-two volumes of original sketches by himself and his sons are preserved in the British Museum, which include a record of most of the parish churches and other ancient buildings in Buckinghamshire, Hertfordshire, Oxfordshire, Somerset, Staffordshire, Wiltshire and Yorkshire. He was also often commissioned to produce sets of finished drawings for private patrons, and this view of Ashridge forms part of such a set – one of ten drawings made of the house in 1813, the year of James Wyatt's death, and in 1822, after Jeffry Wyatt, his nephew, had completed the house.

Ashridge was James Wyatt's last great Gothic house. This view shows the symmetrical nature of Wyatt's Gothic: the square mass of the house builds up to a central 'keep', with the Chapel in the background. Jeffrey Wyatt (later Sir Jeffry Wyatville) added the lower buildings which join the house on the right.

Buckler's style has been characterized by Iolo Williams as 'smooth' and 'painstaking' with a 'narrowly restricted range of colours in which browns, brownish-greens and grey-blues dominate'. This is a topographical drawing, but the accuracy and precision with which the intricate Gothic details have been indicated in brown pen make it hard to distinguish it from a design perspective produced in the Wyatville office.
Lit: I. Williams, *Early English Watercolours*, 1970, p. 62.

58. **John Nash** (1752-1835)
Design for a dairy at Blaise Castle, near Bristol, for John Scandrett Harford, drawn by John Adey Repton or George Stanley Repton *c.* 1804
Brown pen & washes, some chinese white
(215 x 335)
Provenance: by descent to Guy Repton, by whom bequeathed, 1935.
The dairy at Blaise Castle was built in about 1804 and G.S. Repton's sketchbook (no. 55) compiled while in Nash's office has the elevation, section and plans. Though these are drawn with elegant precision, it seems unlikely that at the age of, say seventeen, he could have produced as sophisticated a perspective as the one shown here. It is more probable that it was drawn by George's eldest brother, John Adey Repton. But he had left Nash's office in 1800 after working there as an assistant for four years, leaving because Nash would not publicly acknowledge his design contribution.

A building such as this dairy was as much an ornament and a place of rest, refreshment and amusement, as a work place. J.A. or G S. Repton's perspective is one of their finest for, unusually, it is invested with a mysterious and magical quality. The thatched, six-sided dairy is shown framed by dark, vaguely menacing trees that contrast with the rustic building, its sheltering roof and welcoming seats lit by the afternoon sun.

59. **William Henry Bartlett** (1809-1854)
View of the Deepdene, the house of Thomas Hope, 1825.
Pencil & watercolour (235 x 175)
Provenance: from a bound MS volume entitled *Historical and Descriptive Account of The Deepdene ...* presented by Mrs Irene Law, a descendant of Thomas Hope, 1965.
As an amateur architect Hope designed (strictly speaking, enlarged and embellished) two houses – both for himself. Besides the London house in Duchess Street, Hope also had a country seat, the Deepdene, near Dorking in Surrey. Bought in 1807, the work of transformation seems to have been finished by 1823. To mark this, Hope commissioned from the antiquarian and topographer John Britton an *Historical and Descriptive Account of the Deepdene ... To accompany a Series of Drawings*. Dedicated to Mrs Hope and not intended for publication, the incomplete text and the drawings are in two volumes (the other is at the Minet Library, London.)

Many of the drawings were done by William Henry Bartlett who began his seven-year apprenticeship to John Britton when he was fourteen and was sixteen years old when he worked on the drawings for the Deepdene. His preparatory study of the entrance court, looking towards the loggia-topped tower, subtly conveys the Italianate Picturesqueness of Hope's designs for the Deepdene. Cream and buff washes and a low viewpoint emphasise the irregular, picturesque composition, and the glowing greens of the luxuriant trees and shrubs and the cerulean blue sky turn Surrey into Italy. Bartlett went on to become a most prolific topographical water-colourist, book illustrator and travel writer.
Lit: D. Watkin, *Thomas Hope and the Neo-Classical Idea*, 1968, ch. VI; P. Ferriday, 'A Victorian Journeyman artist', *Country Life*, CXLIII, 1968, pp. 348-9.

60. **Joseph Michael Gandy** (1771-1843)
The Tomb of Merlin, 1815
Watercolour (760 x 1320)
Provenance: from the collection of Gandy's friend, Richard Westmacott; sold at Christie's, 25 March 1899, lot 96; acquired from Mr R.A. Robson, 1941.
It has been said that Gandy was born at an unpropitious time for an architect, reaching maturity just before the lean years of the Napoleonic Wars; also that he was 'odd and impracticable in disposition'. The result of this is that little more than a dozen buildings can confidently be attributed to him. He published, in 1805, two series of bizarre designs for cottages and other rural buildings; and he spent much of his working life employed by Sir John Soane as a perspectivist. Whatever Gandy's psychological shortcomings, he undeniably had great energy, and much of this was put into painting the architectural fantasies which he exhibited at the Royal Academy, almost without a break, between 1789 and 1838. *The Tomb of Merlin* was exhibited in 1815, accompanied by the sort of spurious scholarship which characterised so many of Gandy's catalogue entries: quotations from the inspiration for the scene, Harrington's translation of *Orlando Furioso*, and the statement that this was a 'composition from the school of Constantinople, where the adoption of early Christian emblems began, giving rise to a new style of architecture ...' In fact, the style is closer to Anglo-Norman, and a more direct source of inspiration was probably the Rosslyn Chapel, which Gandy had measured and drawn. As a fantasy, it combines the themes of 'sepulchral chamber', 'subterranean temple' and 'a tomb as a beacon' – all titles of earlier works by Gandy exhibited at the Academy.
Lit: J. Summerson, 'The Vision of J.M. Gandy', *Heavenly Mansions*, 1949; B. Lukacher, 'Gandy's dream revisited', exhibition catalogue, Architectural Association, London, 1982.

61. **Joseph Michael Gandy** (1771-1843)
An Imperial Palace for Sovereigns of the British Empire, 1825
Watercolour (760 x 1500)
Provenance: unknown.
From 1825 to 1830, John Nash was engaged upon the conversion of Buckingham House into a palace for King George IV. Between 1824 and 1828, Gandy exhibited at the Royal Academy a series of five watercolours, forming a design for 'an Imperial Palace for the Sovereigns of the British Empire, estimated to be built in ten years at £300,000, per annum'. Just how serious Gandy's proposal was, is a matter of opinion,and part of the whole problem of how to approach Gandy's work; although he designed a few buildings he cannot really be called an architect, and although he worked in Soane's office he was more than just an architectural draughtsman, because he treated his subjects – including his perspectives of Soane's designs – with so much imaginative artistic licence. To find people with whom to compare Gandy one must either look back to Piranesi, or forward to the visionary painter John Martin, eighteen years his junior. In this work he gave some details of the construction of the new building, and was at pains as the years went on to point out that each new view of the palace conformed with those previously exhibited so that he must have had some idea of the overall conception of the scheme. But this is precisely what the views never give us; we see only portions of the whole, with vague suggestions of vast domes shrouded in mist, while one view purports to show the palace in the year 2500. The view shown here was exhibited in 1825, and depicts 'one of the interior courts ... viewed from the audience chamber'. Some of Gandy's contemporaries gave him the benefit of the doubt, and criticised the scheme as a serious proposal; the terms 'Imperial Palace' and 'British Empire', and the lavish use of caryatids, implying captivity and slavery, were all considered most unsuitable for the residence of the constitutional monarch at the head of the free British nation.
Lit: as for no 60

62. **Decimus Burton** (1800-1881)
Design for Adelaide Crescent, Hove, Brighton, Sussex, *c.* 1831
Pen & watercolour (585 x 960)
Provenance: purchased, 1966.
Burton exhibited his design for 'Queen Adelaide's Crescent at Brighton' at the Royal Academy in 1831. The site was part of the 200 acres of farmland, bought by Isaac Lyon Goldsmid, that lay between Brighton and the small village of Hove. Burton (as he did for other of his town planning schemes) used a bird's eye view to show his design for the Crescent. A fine, sometimes broken line, much of it freehand, delineates the architecture. The delicate penmanship was learnt from his drawing master, George Maddox, and is perhaps more successful than the watercolour landscape. In the background are the South Downs with grazing sheep and in the foreground, the seashore with pebble beach and fishing boats on a choppy sea. The scene is animated by horses and carriages, and residents taking the sea air. It was a charming picture of life at the seaside in the reign of William IV and, when lithographed, made an excellent advertisement.

Adelaide Crescent, however, was not completed to Burton's design. Ten houses at the south-eastern end were built and then work stopped. In about 1840, David Mocatta (architect of the London, Brighton and South Coast Railway Company) proposed a Royal Marine Palace for the north side of the Crescent but this was not built. Instead, from 1850 Adelaide Crescent was completed to a modified design that included the addition of Palmeira Square.
Lit: A. Dale, *Fashionable Brighton, 1820-1860*, 1969, ch. XI.

63. **Charles Fowler** (1792-1867)
Design for Hungerford Market, Charing Cross, London, *c.* 1832
Brown pen & watercolour with some pencil
(380 x 545)
Provenance: presented (with other drawings for Hungerford Market) by the architect, 1835-6 and 1862.
Fowler's best known works are the conservatory at Syon House, Middlesex (1827-30), and Covent Garden Market, London (1828-30). Hungerford Market, the greatest of his market buildings, was demolished in about 1862 to make way for Charing Cross Railway Station. As Colvin wrote: 'it is these buildings which give Fowler the distinction of being one of the few nineteenth-century architects who, like the engineers Telford and Rennie, were able to handle structure and form with equal assurance'.

Structurally, Hungerford Market exemplified Fowler's principle of 'enough for security and not more than enough'; walls were one-and-a-half bricks thick and the roof was of laminated tiles. A freestanding, double-butterfly roof made from prefabricated, cast iron components was designed for the fishmarket. The planning of the market complex that stretched from the Strand to the Thames included a huge central hall and shopping galleries on two levels. The *South View of Hungerford Market*, seen here, shows the wholesale fish market that lay behind a Tuscan colonnade (with an open terrace above) linking two taverns. A wharf and stairs allowed for the loading and unloading of fish.

As a draughtsman, Fowler was very competent but seems to have felt the need for some help with his perspectives. For while he drew the architecture and the background, another hand (probably that of an artist rather than an architectural draughtsman) did the watercolour foreground with its reflecting water, boats and people. As architectural perspectives became more pictorial the practice of two hands contributing to a single drawing became less unusual.
Lit: C. Fowler, 'Some Remarks on Hungerford Market', *RIBA Transactions*, 1st. series XIII, 1862-3, pp. 54-7.

B4. **Charles Robert Cockerell** (1788-1863)
Personal diary, 1823
Provenance: purchased from Mrs Anne Crichton in 1984
C.R. Cockerell, who was one of the leading architects of his time, a Royal Academician, first recipient of the Royal Gold Medal for architecture and first professional president of the RIBA, kept a personal diary from 1821 to 1832. It consists of 11 volumes of Richards's Universal Daily Remembrancer with additional pages of notes interleaved.
The diaries are full of information about his clients, fellow architects and others. They also provide detailed information about many of his projects and notes, sketches of ground plans and architectural details of the many country houses and other buildings which he visited or saw by chance on his extensive travels in Britain and Ireland to monitor the progress of his projects. Cockerell also made notes on his daily reading and on the Sunday sermons he listened to so attentively. His most private thoughts he wrote in French, perhaps to protect them from the prying eyes of servants. After his marriage to Anna Maria Rennie in 1928 the diaries become increasingly perfunctory.

The volume shown here is the one for 1823, a year in which he was exceptionally busy. In the three days covered by these particular pages, December 9th-21st, Cockerell travelled by coach and boat from London to Carmarthen via the Grange, Amesbury Abbey, Longleat and Bristol. The left-hand page shows Amesbury Abbey, Wilts, built by John Webb in 1661 and pulled down in 1830, where Cockerell was particularly intrigued by the design of the staircase. The right-hand page includes details of progress on the construction of a new conservatory designed by Cockerell at the Grange, near Alresford, Hants.

In addition to these diaries the British Architectural Library has some of Cockerell's lecture notes and correspondence and a manuscript scrapbook by John Eastly Goodchild, Cockerell's devoted assistant, called 'Reminiscences of my twenty-six years association with Professor C.R. Cockerell Esqr.'
Lit: Watking, David *The life and work of C.R. Cockerell*, London, A. Zwemmer Ltd, 1974. Chapter 2 'The man and the diaries, 1821-1828'.

64. **Charles Robert Cockerell** (1788-1863)
Design for the Westminster Life and British Fire Office, Strand, London, 1832
Pen, pencil & watercolour (540 x 395)
Provenance: presented by the daughters of F.P. Cockerell, 1930-32.
Cockerell's premises in the Strand were an important early instance of the employment of an architect of distinction and scholarship by a private commercial company. He served his client well in providing an image of dignity and security in the form of a Doric temple standing on a rusticated podium; his allusions both to Greek Doric and to Palladio are immensely learned and formed the stylistic theme for his well-known branch Banks of England.

Cockerell's perspectives have great quality. He himself always wanted to be a painter, much to his father's dismay, and wrote from Greece in 1815, 'Art is certainly my forte and I was born a *Painter* not certainly an architect.' His drawing combines an accurate sense of line and perspective with a particularly subtle rendering of planes by colour. He differentiates the stone of the Strand Office from the brick façade next door, and in a most sensitive way shows the varying gradations of stone on the main façade. The building is also beautifully lit with an almost Mediterranean sunlight.

It is also one of the first architectural perspectives in which the figures in the foreground – the excited pedestrians and the fire-engine rushing off to a fire somewhere further up the Strand – are engaged in an activity that relates to the character of the building represented. The building was demolished in 1907 to make way for Charles Holden's British Medical Association (now Zimbabwe House).
Lit: J.H. Worthington, 'Drawings by Charles Robert Cockerell, *RIBA Journal*, 1932, XXXIX, pp. 268-71; D. Watkin, *The Life and Work of C.R. Cockerell*, 1974, *passim*; G. Stamp, *The Great Perspectivists*, 1982, no. 26.

65. **Edward Walters** (1808-1872)
Design for a palace for Sultan Mahmut II, on the shores of the Bosphorous, Turkey, *c.* 1835
Pencil & watercolour (290 x 705)
Provenance: by office descent to A.W. Jones, by whom presented, 1976.
In March 1832, Edward Walters left England for Constantinople. He had been sent by the civil engineer John Rennie to superintend the building of a small arms factory for the Turkish government. At some time during his five year stay, Walters made an 'elaborate design for a palace for the Sultan' that was not, though, carried

out. The sultan was Mahmut II who began the process of reformation and modernisation of the Ottoman state.

Pevsner has described Walters's style as 'founded on Italian Renaissance treated in the fullest, freest and most intelligent manner' and this is what we see in his palace design. Using an assymetrical plan with a raised portico and a domed tower crowned by a golden crescent (the emblem of the Turkish Sultanate), Walters uses the same tall, arched openings for portico and tower and this and other unifying details integrate what seems at first, a rather wild scheme.

The perspective, shown here, is intensely romantic: the rising sun casts a golden glow on the palace, warming away the mauve shadows of night. Only the predatory bird standing on a purple-shadowed cliff, is a reminder of the darker side of Turkish history. It seems that Walters may have been helped in the making of the drawing for the watercolour technique of the foreground is quite different from the rest. Walters's architect cousin Edward I'Anson, on an occasion when Walters's drawings were exhibited at the RIBA, commented that the drawings 'were all his own work, but he was assisted in them by his friend Mr William Wild (sic) ... particularly in the backgrounds', that is, the non-architectural details. But though William Wyld (1806-1889), a well-known watercolourist, is known to have travelled in Algiers and Egypt during the 1830s it is not certain that he was in Turkey.

Lit: E. I'Anson, 'A Short biographical notice of the late Edward Walters, architect of Manchester', *RIBA Proceedings*, 1871-2, pp. 113-4; *Builder*, XXX, 1872, pp. 199-201.

66. **William Grellier** (1807-1852)
Competition design for the Royal Exchange, London, 1839
Pen & grey wash, in a contemporary ebony frame (735 x 1310)
Provenance: presented by Cecil Grellier, the architect's grandson, in 1965.

The old Royal Exchange burnt down on 10th January 1838; by early 1839 the Gresham Trustees announced a competition for a new Exchange which should be in the 'Grecian, Roman or Italian style' with a price limit of £150,000. In October the assessors presented their report: of the designs capable of being erected for £150,000 they felt unable to recommend any to the Committee, but made a selection of eight designs which were to be judged as 'works of art' rather than as 'designs which we can certify in their present state to be practicable and capable of being made durable edifices'. Grellier's design was judged the best of these and he was awarded the First Premium of

£300; his drawing certainly presents the Victorian business world in an ideal light, where London financiers mingle with baggy-trousered merchants from the Orient. This was only the start of a competition which turned out to be one of the most notoriously mismanaged in history. Sir William Tite's design was eventually chosen and still stands today.

Grellier's elegant design is executed in Indian ink and grey wash – in accordance with the Institute of British Architects new recommendations for competition procedure that drawings 'should always be to one scale, and limited to one style of finishing, as in Indian ink, with no colour, unless for such a purpose as that of distinguishing different materials in sections'.

Lit: J.A. Gotch, *The Growth and Work of the Royal Institute of British Architects*, 1934, pp. 104-105;
N. Taylor, *Monuments of Commerce*, 1968, pl. 3;
D. Watkin, *The Life and Work of C.R. Cockerell*, 1974, *passim*.

67. **Thomas Allom** (1804-1872)
An imaginative view of Rome, *c.* 1830s-40s
Watercolour & pen, in contemporary carved & gilded frame (765 x 1345)
Provenance: purchased, 1940s.

This imaginative view of Rome is both an architectural fantasy and an archaeological reconstruction. It tells a story, having much in common with Professor C.R. Cockerell's large and learned subjects of the 1820s – 'Athens at the time of the Antonines' or 'The Theatre at Pompeii as it might have appeared in the Interval between the Earthquake of AD 68 and the final catastrophe of AD 79' – both of which are in the RIBA Drawings Collection.

Allom's drawing is untitled but shows a papal procession proceeding up a wide flight of steps on the right and passing past a triumphal arch and the Castel Sant'Angelo, which has been recased with two storeys of colonnades surmounted by a dome. The embankment, arch and many buildings in the background have also been inserted or redesigned.

Allom was a founder member of the Institute of British Architects and became an Associate in 1835, being number 9 in the register of membership. He had worked for the Greek Revival architect, Francis Goodwin, for seven years and many of the reconstructed buildings in this fantasy are close to Goodwin's designs. He was as much an artist as architect and acted as perspective artist to many leading architects (see no. 73) as well as being employed by Messrs Virtue & Co and Messrs Heath & Co to produce a series of topographical books.

Lit: *Builder*, XXX, 1872, p. 840, (obituary);
S. Rowland Pierce, 'Some Early RIBA Travellers', *RIBA Journal*, 1962, LXIX, pp. 410-11.

68. **Thomas Rickman** (1776 - 1841) and **Richard Charles Hussey** (1806-1887)
Competition design in a Decorated Gothic style for the Fitzwilliam Museum, Cambridge, 1834-5
Pencil & watercolour (745 x 520)
Provenance: Thomas Miller Rickman; Miss Mary A. Lynan (TMR's niece), by whom presented, 1912.

The competition for the Fitzwilliam Museum was announced in July 1834 and Rickman's office time-sheets (British Museum Add.MSS 37802) show that he began work on the design on the 2nd of August. After a discussion with the Vice-Chancellor on 'Grecian or Gothic', 'tower or none' and other points, work went on steadily with Rickman recording the time spent on the competition on fifty occasions until, on 9 April, 1835, he noted: 'Examining designs and signing Report and packing up Box, 2 hours'. In the box were three alternative designs: design A in a Roman Corinthian style, design B in a Decorated Gothic style and design C in a Ledoux-inspired Greek Doric style.

The Gothic design, shown here, with its soaring, functionless tower has something of the dreamlike, fabulous quality of James Wyatt's Fonthill Abbey (1796-1807). None of the competition perspectives are by Rickman, or by Hussey who became Rickman's partner early in 1835. The most likely candidate is Jonathan Anderson Bell (*c.* 1809-1865). Bell studied art in Rome (1829-1830) before becoming Rickman's

'favourite pupil' and, later, assistant. His watercolour drawings were 'of a high order of excellence and ... finished with the greatest delicacy' (DNB). In the event none of the entries were successful and the Fitzwilliam was built to the Graeco-Roman design of George Basevi.
Lit: D. Watkin, *The Triumph of the Classical: Cambridge Architecture 1804-1843*, exhibition catalogue, Cambridge, 1977, pp. 46-9.

B5. **Institute of British Architects**, founded 1834
Original royal charter of incorporation, 1837

Thomas Philip Earl de Grey (1781-1859), a member of the Privy Council and first President of the Institute of British Architects, was instrumental in obtaining this first royal charter which was granted by William IV by writ of privy seal on 11th January 1837, only two and a half years after the foundation of the Institute in 1834. De Grey, who after a successful military career served as First Lord of the Admiralty, 1834-1835, and Lord Lieutenant of Ireland, 1841-1844, was a Fellow of the Royal Society and of the Society of Antiquaries and remained President of the Institute until he died in 1859. The charter conferred on the Institute the legal status and rights of a person. It states the main principles or enabling powers while the first official by-laws, ordained on 1 May 1837, set out the methods of application of those principles. General meetings of the Institute's corporate members could adopt, alter, add to or revoke these by-laws, subject only to the laws of the realm. The charter states the purpose of the Institute to be 'the general advancement of civil architecture, and for promoting and facilitating the acquirement of the knowledge of the various arts and sciences connected therewith –'. It stipulates three classes of members, Fellows, Associate and Honorary Fellows, of whom only the Fellows could exercise a vote, and a Council composed exclusively of Fellows to direct and manage the affairs of the Institute.

In August 1837 Queen Victoria consented to become the Patroness of the Institute; in 1848 the first annual Royal Gold Medal for architecture was awarded and in May 1866 the queen commanded that the Institute be styled the 'Royal Institute of British Architects' (the Institute had in practice been calling itself 'Royal' ever since the grant of the charter in 1837). Supplementary royal charters were granted in 1887, 1909, 1925 and 1971 and since 1887 all amendments, suspensions and additions to the by-laws have had to be approved by the Privy Council. The current charter of 1971 revoked the previous supplementary charters and parts of this original charter.

In the address by the Council of the Institute to the members upon laying the charter before them this sentiment was expressed 'The charter . . . should serve as a stimulus to our continued progress onwards and to a gradual increase of attainments and knowledge until the science which directs us shall be as well defined and as accurately laid down as astronomy now is . . . until the regions of taste, 'the music of the eye' as it has been aptly termed by Aristotle, shall have been thoroughly investigated; its effects resolved to their first principles and its laws as well understood and as universally recognised as the exquisite beauties which in literature distinguish the productions of a Homer, Dante and a Shakespeare.'
Lit: RIBA, *Charter byelaws and annual reports 1836-1849*: *RIBA Kalendar*, 1926/27, pp. 39-61: RIBA, *The charter, supplemental charter 1971 and byelaws*: J. Parris, 'For crown, charter and corporation', *Building Design* no. 520, 1980 Nov 7, p. 16.

C11. **John Wood** (1801-1870) after William Robinson (1799-1839), ?1859
Portrait of Thomas Phillip, Earl de Grey (1781-1859)
Oil on canvas (1590 x 1280)
Provenance: presented by the members of the RIBA, 1889-60. A list of subscribers was published in *RIBA Proceedings*, 1889-60, p. 36.
As the first President (1835-59) of the small new Institute of British Architects, Earl de Grey was an ideal choice. He was a man with a strong sense of public duty, who deeply respected the Duke of Wellington. George Godwin said in his obituary that Earl de Grey 'brought together in support of the Institute the most distinguished persons of all classes, whether belonging to the aristocracy of rank or talent'. He persuaded Queen Victoria to found the Royal Gold Medal in 1848 which was to 'advance the interests of the Institute abroad, and to increase the importance of its position at home'. A distinguished amateur architect himself, he completely redesigned his home, Wrest Park in Louis XV style (1834-1839) as well as designing the capacious staircase at the United Services Club where he was Chairman of the Building Committee.

William Robinson exhibited portraits of Earl de Grey at the Royal Academy in 1827 and 1833 but John Wood's portrait is probably derived from the earlier one since it shows the sitter in Baron's robes; de Grey was Baron from 1786 to 1833. Robinson had worked in the studio of Thomas Lawrence and the pose of the Earl is exactly that of George IV painted by Lawrence in 1822; clearly de Grey favoured this pose for he chose it for his portrait by H.W. Pickersgill (1836) in the United Services Club.
Lit: J.A. Gotch (ed.), *The Growth and Work of the RIBA, 1834-1934*, 1934, S. Houffe, 'Wrest Park I', *Country Life*, CXLVII, 1970, p. 1251; J.C. White, *Earl de Grey of Wrest, 1781-1859*, Bedfordshire County Council County Record Office exhibition catalogue, 1982.

69. Sir Charles Barry (1795-1860)
Design for the West Front, Houses of Parliament, Westminster, London, 1836
Brown & blue pen (215 x 585)
Provenance: presented in 1938 by Caryl Arthur Ransome Barry, son of E.M. Barry.
One of a collection of drawings kept by the family, probably to prove Barry's authorship of the design in a dispute with the heirs of A.W.N. Pugin.
The drawing shows Barry's revisions to his winning competition entry of 1835, and the officially adopted design. The most important features are the Gothic refronting of Soane's Law Courts and the arcade running around Old Palace Yard and New Palace Yard. The design is substantially different from that executed, hardly surprising as construction started on the river front and it was 1850 before this elevation was reached. Although Barry was predominantly a pencil draughtsman, the assured hand seen here suggests his authorship. He is also known to have drawn on this scale. The atmospheric use of blue for the more distant parts of the palace was probably a device to clarify the design and indicate what stood where. The care taken suggests that the drawing was intended for presentation to a Committee.

70. Sir Charles Barry (1795-1860)
Design for the Clock Tower (Big Ben) Houses of Parliament, Westminster, London, *c.* 1851
Pen & wash (870 x 230)
Provenance: as no. 69.
The clock tower presented several design problems: how to make the clock-face prominent (it was corbelled out in the final design), from what sort of super-structure to suspend the bells, and how to keep walls and clock-face steady under the swing of the pendulum. Barry worked closely with the Astronomer Royal, who supplied him with drawings for the layout of the clock mechanism. They did not always agree: the Astronomer opposed Barry's proposal to illuminate the dial from within, as it would require substantial alterations to the chosen hand and dialwork. The design eventually adopted (not shown here) was based on Pugin's clock tower at Scarisbrick Hall.

This is an office drawing and represents the second stage in Barry's procedure for selecting a design, when an assistant would carefully draw up his preliminary sketches. He would judge from these more finished drawings the success of his original concept.
Lit: Correspondence between Astronomer Royal and Barry, RIBA MSS Collection, Ba Fam/1/3/4.

C12. **John Henry Foley** (1818-1874)
Marble bust of Sir Charles Barry, 1871 (1795-1860)
Provenance: presented by John L. Wolfe, 1873.
Sir Charles Barry, awarded the Royal Gold Medal in 1850, enjoyed an almost unrivalled reputation in his lifetime as one of the leading members of the architectural profession; and his fame was kept alive after his death largely by the efforts of his biographer, Alfred Barry, and of his life-long friend, John L. Wolfe. It was Wolfe who was the leading spirit behind the erection of a memorial statue to Barry in the Houses of Parliament (by public subscription, to which Wolfe's contribution was by far the greatest), completed in 1864. The sculptor for this memorial – which showed Barry seated, in modern dress, holding plans of the building in which it was housed – was John Henry Foley, whose most famous work is the seated figure of the Prince Consort and the 'Asia' group for the Albert Memorial. Foley had, in 1844, submitted a figure in the competition for the decoration of the Houses of Parliament – his first real success – and this led to commissions for statues of Hampden and John Selden, both in St Stephen's Hall. Foley was, therefore, acquainted with Barry, and for the statue, carved posthumously, had to rely on personal memory, photographs, and an existing bust by William Behnes of 1849. According to Wolfe, he commissioned the RIBA's bust immediately after the completion of the statue, but he was not told of its completion until 1873, when it was presented, with great ceremony, to the RIBA. The pose is quite unlike that of the statue; it is more

classically stylised and heroic, and in a style often used by Foley, with the sitter looking to one side, his shoulders covered with drapery. The bust is signed and dated on the back, *J.H. Foley, R.A. Sc./ London 1871.*
Lit: R. Gunnis, *Dictionary of British sculptors 1660-1851*, 1953; A. Barry, *Life and Works of Sir Charles Barry*, 1867, p. 351; *RIBA Transactions*, XXIV, 1873-4, pp. 51-53.

71. **Augustus Welby Northmore Pugin**
(1812-1852)
Designs for floor tiles for the Central Hall or Lobby, Houses of Parliament, Westminster, London, 1851
Pencil & watercolour on tracing paper, mounted on linen-backed cartridge (560 x 635)
Provenance: presented by Charles J. Marshall, 1941. Marshall had been apprenticed to E.M. Barry, and when he died was among those assistants allowed to take a selection of drawings. Pugin had many 'ancient specimens' of encaustic tiles in his antiquarian collection. From 1843-44 he collaborated with Mr Minton of Stoke-on-Trent, first in an effort to re-establish the method of making these tiles, then in providing designs for the firm to manufacture.

Although the tiles were evolved principally for church decoration, Pugin incorporated them with great success into his decorative scheme for the Houses of Parliament, where the most elaborate design is to be found in the Central Lobby. We know from his accounts that he was working on the tiles in 1851; they were actually laid in 1852.

This sheet – as executed and with very accurate colours – gives a good idea of Pugin's linear design, but is not in his hand. It would have been drawn in Minton's studio, following the rough sketch he had provided.
Lit: B. Ferrey, *Recollections of A.N.Welby Pugin*, 1861, pp. 250-256.

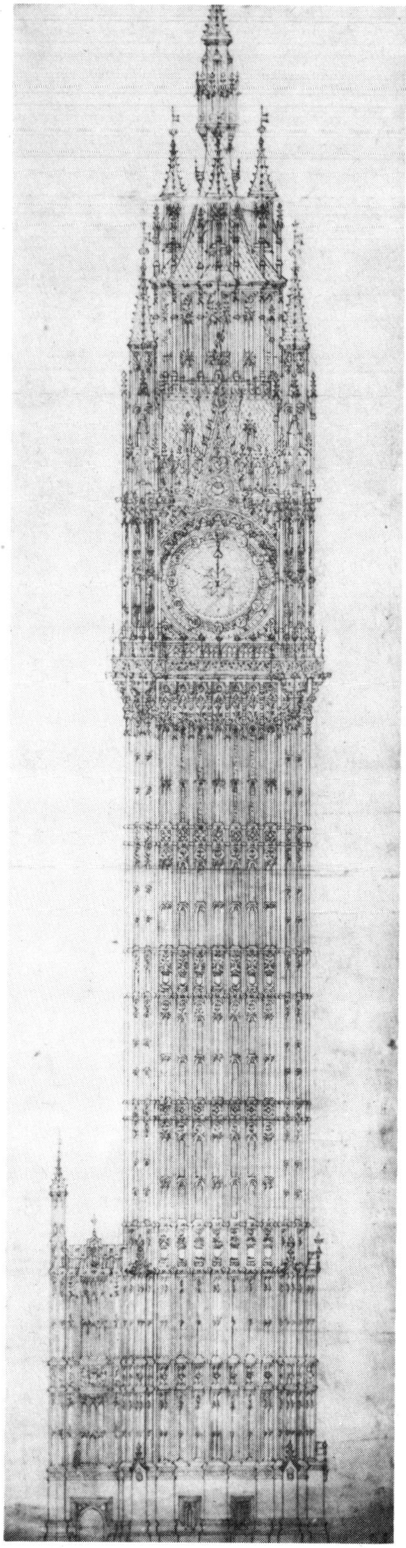

72. **Augustus Welby Northmore Pugin** (1812-1852)
Design for the Roman Catholic Cathedral of St George, Southwark, London, 1838
Pen, brown pen & brown wash (310 x 215)
Provenance: purchased, 1982.
In 1838, a group of prelates and influential laymen formed a committee with the aim of providing a cathedral, convent and schools for London's growing Roman Catholic community. Pugin was invited to prepare drawings, and this dramatic perspective was probably among those he presented. He wanted to impress those gathered with the grandeur of his design and used tiny figures to emphasize the vast size of the building. But the committee, frightened by the cost and time needed for such a scheme, rejected these initial proposals. A competition was held in 1839 which Pugin won with a less ambitious design. Later he complained of sacrificing height and proportion to accomodate 3000 people 'at a limited price'.

This drawing was subsequently engraved, and became one of his most famous ecclesiastical designs. Its format suggests that it could have been drawn with publication in mind; engravings of proposed churches were frequently sold to raise funds.

Lit: B. Ferrey, *Recollections of A.N.Welby Pugin*, 1861, pp. 162-171.

73. **Sir Charles Barry** (1795-1860)
Design for Highclere, Hampshire, 1840
Watercolour (495 x 940)
Provenance: as for no. 69
In 1840 Barry exhibited this perspective at the Royal Academy: it shows the second of his three schemes for refronting the 3rd Earl of Carnarvon's eighteenth-century house, in the ornate style he termed 'Anglo-italian', based on the architecture of the Elizabethan and Jacobean periods.

The draughtsmanship is that of Thomas Allom, who also made a set of drawings of Barry's design for the Houses of Parliament in 1844. It was probably as a result of his involvement at this stage that Allom was employed by the 4th Earl to design the interiors of Highclere in about 1862. Although Allom trained in the office of Francis Goodwin and was a founder of the RIBA he achieved greater critical success as a topographical artist. His landscape here is of a higher quality than many found in

perspectives of the day, and the horses and carriage are particularly characteristic of his free use of wash.
Lit: M. Girouard *The Victorian Country House*, 1971, pp. 68-70; *Marble Halls*, exhibition catalogue, Victoria & Albert Museum, London, 1973, pp. 16, 91; *Builder*, vol XXX, 1872, p. 840.

74. **Anthony Salvin** (1799-1881)
Design for Scotney Castle, Kent, 1838
Watercolour (555 x 755)
Provenance: unknown. It is likely that the drawing came direct to the Collection from the Salvin Office.
The new house at Scotney Castle was sited to take full advantage of the picturesque qualities of the surrounding landscape and old castle ruins, and it was designed in the Tudor style to the same effect. The owner, Edward Hussey, probably employed Salvin on the basis of work at Parham, built in a similar stone to that found in Hussey's quarries.

The perspective was exhibited at the Royal Academy in 1838 and served as a publicity exercise. To ensure the production of a watercolour of quality, the talents of two men were combined: James Deason (*fl.* 1831-59) drew the proposed house, and George Arthur Fripp (1813-1896) added colour, landscape and figures. Fripp had just moved to London from Bristol and had yet to establish his reputation (he later became the Secretary of the Old Watercolour Society, where he exhibited over 500 works). Deason remains a somewhat enigmatic figure; he was one of Salvin's assistants and accompanied him on sketching expeditions, usually to churches in the vicinity of a building project. He appears never to have exhibited a scheme in his own right.
Lit: J. Allibone, Antony Salvin, PhD thesis, London University, 1974, ch. VII; Victoria & Albert Museum, *Catalogue of Watercolour Paintings*, 1927, p. 216.

75. **Robert Lewis Roumieu** (1814-1877)
Design for a *campanile* for the Church of All Saints, Ennismore Gardens, London, *c.* 1850-5
Pen & watercolour over pencil with gouache & chinese white & green pen & ink added
(1110 x 745)
Provenance: presented by J. Fox Jones, 1956.
Trained in the office of Benjamin Dean Wyatt, an exceptionally skilful draughtsman, Roumieu went on to develop his own colourful and pictorial drawing style. Generously invested with anecdotal figures, his perspectives must have greatly appealed to the newly prosperous middle classes whose houses, offices and shops he designed. His commission here was for a campanile, an addition to the church built by Lewis Vulliamy (1848-9) and later re-fronted by C. Harrison Townsend (1892). The campanile was built in the 1870s but not to this design and probably not by Roumieu. His design is in a muscular Romanesque style and fairly restrained, though his fondness for emphatic and complex detailing shows itself, particularly in the flattened beakhead ornament of the central arch that seems unpleasantly like teeth.

When Roumien made his perspective he seems first to have drawn the architecture, figures and other details of *milieu* in pencil. The pencil lines of the building were then gone over in pen with black and brown inks and the pencil erased. Watercolour was added, used 'pure' (that is, without pencil outlines) for trees and skies. Touches of gouache and chinese white were then added and pen and coloured ink (as here, for the green railings). Neither a purist as a designer nor as draughtsman, Roumieu went for effect and, in his own terms, succeeded brilliantly.

76. **Robert Louis Roumieu** (1814-1877)
Design for a house in an Italianate style
See colour plate page 15.

77. **Cuthbert Brodrick** (1822-1905)
Competition design for the Corn Exchange in Mark Lane, London, 1870
Brown pen & watercolour (470 x 400)
Provenance: presented by H. Trevor Field, 1940.
Brodrick was an assiduous competition entrant and originally made his reputation by winning the competition for Leeds Town Hall in 1852. In 1860 he was also successful with the Leeds Corn Exchange, but failed with many others – including the National Gallery and Government Offices in London and the Royal Exchange in Manchester – and in 1869 retired to Paris.

It was presumably because of his success with the Leeds Corn Exchange that he was invited to send in designs for the competition to rebuild the Corn Exchange in Mark Lane. In this presentation design, Broderick envisaged a Crystal Palace shed above and behind a showy and highly ornamental – and very Continental – façade, which was to be fully glazed between 'bronze' mullions. His design was unplaced and the winner was H. Stock, who never carried out his design. The Corn Exchange committee must have been very conservative; they peremptorily refused admittance to any member of the press, even the establishment representative from the *Builder*, and waited until 1878 before they commissioned Edward I'Anson to build. His façade to Mark Lane took the form of a dignified stone *palazzo*, which was no doubt more to their taste.
Lit: *Builder*, XXVIII, 1870, pp. 91, 210, 569;
N. Taylor, *Monuments of Commerce*, 1968, pl. 23;
D. Linstrum, 'Cuthbert Brodrick: an Interpretation of a Victorian Architect', *Journal of the Royal Society of Arts*, CXIX, 1971, pp. 80-1.

78. **Cuthbert Brodrick** (1822-1905)
Design for the Oriental Baths in Cookridge Street, Leeds, Yorkshire, 1866
Pen & watercolour (480 x 770)
Provenance: as for no. 77.
The Turkish association, naturally, suggested the style adopted for these baths – but Brodrick has characteristically responded with a full-blown design of exotic domes, fretwork details and crowning minaret. He was, as Michael Darby has shown, interested in structural polychromy, and the *Builder* in 1862 had noted his use of red, blue and black brick, moulded brick string courses, encaustic tiles and terracotta at the Leeds Corn Exchange – all materials used again here. Brodrick's drawing style and the symmetrical monumentality of his designs were influenced by French architecture and French architectural drawings, owing much to his visit to France in 1844-45 and to his continuing love for that country. This particular drawing, for example, has much in common with J.I. Hittorff's design for a racing stand at Longchamps, Paris, of 1855. The Oriental Baths were refaced in a dreary Gothic style in 1882 and demolished in 1969.
Lit: D. Linstrum, 'Cuthbert Brodrick' *Country Life*, CXLI, 1967, p. 1379, fig. 2; *Marble Halls*, exhibition catalogue, Victoria & Albert Museum, London 1973, p. 134, no. 86; M. Darby, *The Islamic Perspective*, exhibition catalogue, Leighton House, London 1983, no 110.

79. **Sir Matthew Digby Wyatt** (1820-1877)
Design for Oak Lodge, Addison Road, Kensington, London, 1870s
Pencil & coloured washes (430 x 605)
Provenance: unknown.
Sir Matthew Digby Wyatt, Architect to the East India Company, Honorary Secretary of the RIBA, Royal Gold Medallist and Slade Professor of Fine Art, was an ecclectic who never committed himself to a particular style. The unexecuted design for Oak Lodge was based on the popular French Second Empire Style that he had experienced first hand on his visits to Paris. The open segmental pediments and bull's eye window recall Lefuel's Guichets du Carrousel at the Louvre, which he saw when writing his "Report on the Art of Decoration at the International Exhibition" in 1867.

His published works were better received than his architecture, although his draughtsmanship was much admired. The *Builder* described the 'great freedom of touch and marked and individual style' of some of his drawings, characteristics we can apply to this picturesque rendering of the house and its 'wild' garden.
Lit: N. Pevsner, *Matthew Digby Wyatt* 1950, *passim*; *Builder*, XXXV, 1877, p. 541 ff.

80. **Alfred Waterhouse** (1830-1905)
Revised design for the Manchester Assize Courts, 1861
Brown pen & watercolour, some pencil
(700 x 1140)
Provenance: presented by Michael Waterhouse (architect grandson of A.W.) and Cedric Ripley, 1933.

Winning the Manchester Assize Courts competition brought Waterhouse 'national attention', 'almost universal praise' and launched a highly successful career. The competition success justified his decision to use Gothic for a civic building, proved his mastery of planning and was to allow him scope as a designer of interiors, furniture, crockery and even livery.

The working programme for the Courts building moved fast. The competition results were announced in April 1859, work on demolition of the buildings on site began almost straightaway, detail drawings were promised for the end of January 1860 and some revisions to the original design were agreed. Externally, the most significant change was the re-design of a clock tower some time after 14 June 1860 when the contract drawings were signed. A lofty gable pierced by a rose window replaced it and can be seen in this perspective, made in 1861. Waterhouse may have intended to exhibit the drawing at the Royal Academy but did not, in fact, do so, for he was reticent about self-advertisement and did not exhibit regularly at the RA until 1868. It is interesting to note that from 1884 he exhibited, along with his architectural perspectives, large topographical watercolours. Of one of these a critic commented 'we feel not a little proud of an architect who can ... meet a painter on his own ground and on equal terms'.

The Manchester Assize Courts perspective shows Waterhouse's abilities both as an architect and as artist. Sadly the building, bombed during World War II, was later demolished.

Lit: S. Allen Smith, *Alfred Waterhouse* ... PhD thesis, London University, 1970; S. Maltby and others, *Alfred Waterhouse, 1830-1905*, exhibition catalogue, RIBA Heinz Gallery, London, 1983, *passim*.

81. **Alfred Waterhouse** (1830-1905)
Competition design for the Royal Courts of Justice, Strand, London. 1866
Brown pen with brown & grey watercolour, chinese white, some pencil (845 x 1360)
Provenance: as no. 80.

The competition for the Law Courts was announced in 1866 and of the invited architects, eleven agreed to compete, among them, E.M. Barry, William Burges, J.P. Seddon, G. Gilbert Scott, G.E. Street and Alfred Waterhouse. All offered designs in a Gothic style, Waterhouse giving as his reasons (in a letter signed 'one of the Eleven', to the *Pall Mall Gazette*, March 1867) that 'Gothic work may combine picturesqueness of external form with the most rigid utilitarianism'. He submitted thirty drawings, six of which were extra perspectives that he wished to have returned 'when the competition is decided', giving as his reason that 'for me they possess a certain value in being all of them the work of my own hand'. One of them, the drawing shown here, was described in the *Builder* (XXV, 1867, p. 144) as 'a shadowy, suggestive waterview of ... odd beaconlike towers' (that included a clock tower, a ventilating tower 300 feet high and Will Towers), the critic fancifully adding that it was a 'mystic piece, showing the rising site, the slow waters, the pile darkening in the gloom thrown upon it by the cloudy darkening sky'.

A man of prodigous energy but with a heavy workload, Waterhouse saved time when he could, by judicious shorcuts. Perspectives often had the outlines done by an assistant with Waterhouse doing the rest. Here, the rather coarsely ruled lines of the design are clearly in an office hand, the freehand drawing (of, for instance, Somerset House, the Temple and York Water Gate) and watercolour being done by Waterhouse. Preparing drawings for the competition was a hectic business. The office Day Books show that Waterhouse spent a total of 121 hours on the Law Courts drawings; in December 1866 he spent 17 hours; eleven of his staff (just about all of them) spent 226 hours.

The competition results were, typically, fudged. The lawyers voted Scott first and Waterhouse second, the architectural assessors placed E.M. Barry first and Scott second. Argument followed and eventually, G.E. Street another competitor, was chosen. Lit: Day Book, 1865-78 (private collection); as for no 80.

82. **Alfred Waterhouse** (1830-1905)
Design for the door of the Natural History Museum, London
See colour plate page 25.

C13. **Sir William Quiller Orchardson** (1832-1910)
Portrait of Alfred Waterhouse (1830-1905) *c.*1891
Oil on canvas. (1440 x 1220)
Sir William Quiller Orchardson's portrait of Alfred Waterhouse is one of the finest in the Institute's collection of presidents' portraits. Of Waterhouse, Thomas Cooper said, 'his great distinction was the inexpressible charm of his personality' and the *Times* obituarist wrote 'even those who did not like his architecture loved the man'. These qualities Quiller Orchardson has understood perfectly and the atmosphere of the portrait is one of gentle benevolence. Waterhouse himself was a magnificent watercolourist and was elected to the Royal Academy in 1885. It is said that his Quaker upbringing prevented him from pursuing a career as an artist. It is not surprising therefore, that he chose one of the best portraitists of the day to paint his own portrait. The silver gilt frame blends with Orchardson's deliberately muted colours – yellows and browns – which Chesneau described 'as harmonious as the wrong side of an old tapestry'. His treatment of his sitter's hair and beard is supreme, the pose too is unusual. Waterhouse appears relaxed and at the same time alert, seated in his chair. He is holding a ground plan for his own house, Yattendon Court, Berkshire, and it seems typical of the man that he should be portrayed holding plans of his own house rather than one of his prestige buildings such as the Natural History Museum (1873-1881) or the Prudential Assurance Building in Holborn (1878). He was President of the Institute from 1888 until 1891.
Lit: S. Maltby and others, *Alfred Waterhouse, 1880-1905*, exhibition catalogue, RIBA Heinz Gallery, London, 1983, *passim*.

83. **John Ruskin** (1819-1900)
View of the Tomb of Can Signorio della Scala, Verona, 1869
Watercolour on buff paper (555 x 400)
Provenance: presented on indefinite loan by the Architectural Association, 1963.
Ruskin was always strongly attracted to his 'beloved' Verona; the three tombs, in particular, of Can Grande, Castelbarco and Can Signorio, illustrated his belief that architecture and sculpture were not separate arts and that

ornamentation was an integral part of a building. His attention had first been drawn to the Can Signorio tomb in 1834, when he had seen Prout's engraving of the subject, and he always particularly admired it for its sumptuousness, for the 'picturesqueness of its pinnacles', the 'varied size and design of the crockets' and 'the beauty of its cornices'. His two longest visits to Verona were in 1851-52, when he was working on the *Stones of Venice*, and seventeen years later in 1869 when he spent much of May and June tirelessly drawing the three monuments in both pencil and watercolour. As in his drawings of nature, Ruskin endlessly sought to capture the essential character of a building in his drawings of architecture: his diary entries throughout May and June convey this struggle: 'Got pencil Can Signorio right in early morning' or 'Tired and working in colour against time'. Although critical of inaccuracy in others, Ruskin's own architectural drawings, like this one, are often freely and broadly painted. He himself stated that in drawing architecture 'the most expressive and truthful effects were to be obtained by bold Rembrandtism, that is to say, by the sacrifice of details in the shadowed parts, in order that greater depth of tone might be afforded on the lights'. This drawing has much in common with his wonderful study of flying buttresses at St Wulfran, Abbeville of 1868, which calls to mind Ruskin's verbal evocation of the 'grey, shadowy, many-pinnacled image of the Gothic spirit within us'.

Lit: E.T. Cook & A. Wedderburn, *The Works of John Ruskin*, 1905, *passim* (reprd vol XI, p. 90, plate B); J. Evans and J.Howard Whitehouse, *The Diaries of John Ruskin*, 1956-59; *Ruskin a Verona*, exhibition catalogue, Museo di Castelvecchio, Verona, 1966, no 18, fig 15; J. Unrau, *Looking at Architecture with Ruskin*, 1978.

84. **William Butterfield** (1814-1900)
Working drawing for the chapel of Keble College, Oxford, *c.* 1872. Elevations drawn to a scale of 1 inch to 4 feet and details drawn full size
Pen & coloured washes, some pencil revisions
(665 x 970)
Provenance: presented by R.P. Easton, 1954.

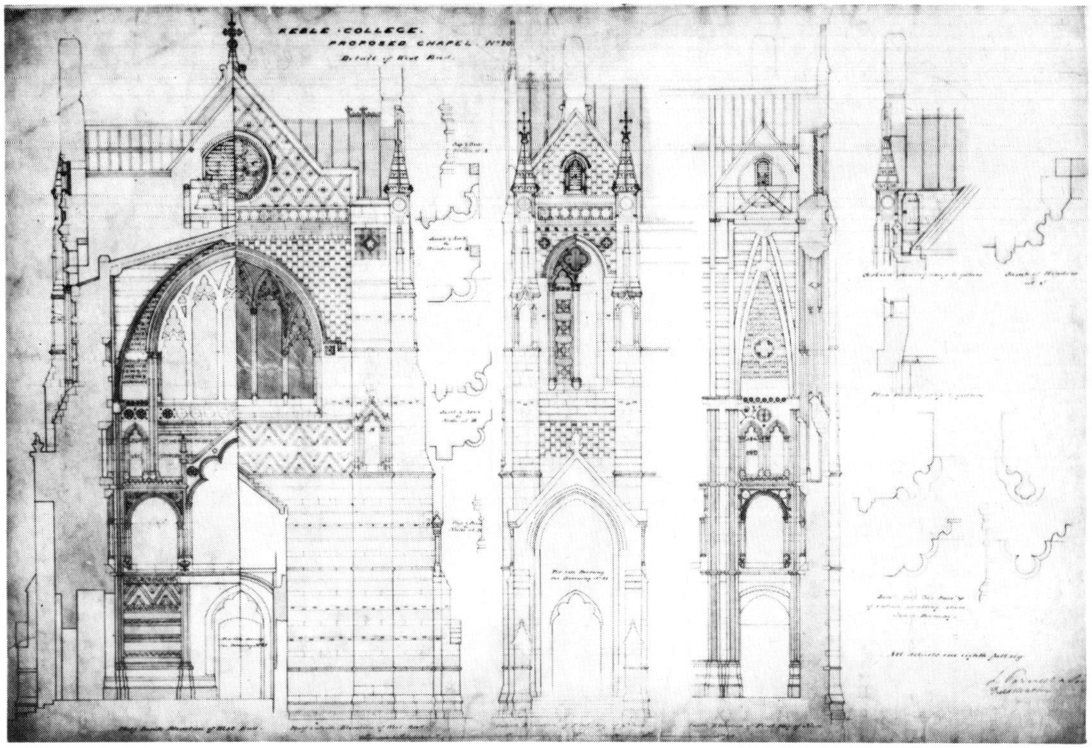

The chapel of Keble College, Oxford is a fine example of Butterfield's highly individual Gothic Revival style: asymetrical, daringly proportioned, emphatically detailed and built in multi-coloured brick and stone with patterns of bands, chevrons, chequers and lozenges.

The working drawing shown here is for the west end of the chapel and includes detailed elevations of the inside and outside with details, to a larger scale, of mouldings. With others, it formed part of a set of drawings that, with the specification, contained all the information that a builder needed to price a building. The same set then became part of the signed contract. The system of coloured washes is much the same as that used in other offices at that time. For example light red for brickwork (sections in a darker tint), cobalt blue for lead and so on. But suprisingly, considering the very strong, even garish, colours of Butterfield's architecture and decoration, the effect here is gentle – even feminine.

Butterfield's drawing office practice was rather unorthodox so that, for instance, he had neither a drawing-board nor a T-square, working with only a pair of folding compasses and a two-foot rule. He considered it a waste of time to make detailed drawings himself and employed assistants to make them from his own 'small and highly unattractive drawings'. The assistants' work was then revised again and again until they got it right. The pencil revisions to a gable crocket, a canopied niche and to the banded decoration, seen here, are in Butterfield's hand, as is the sketchy design for a tower. Having a 'wholesome horror of self-advertisement', Butterfield did not exhibit any drawings and seems never to have published any of them in the architectural journals. And perhaps this reticence explains why (with one known exception) he never signed his drawings or, for that matter, dated them.

Lit: *RIBA Journal*, VII, 1900, pp. 241-8 (obituary); J. Summerson, *Heavenly Mansions*, 1949, pp. 159-76.

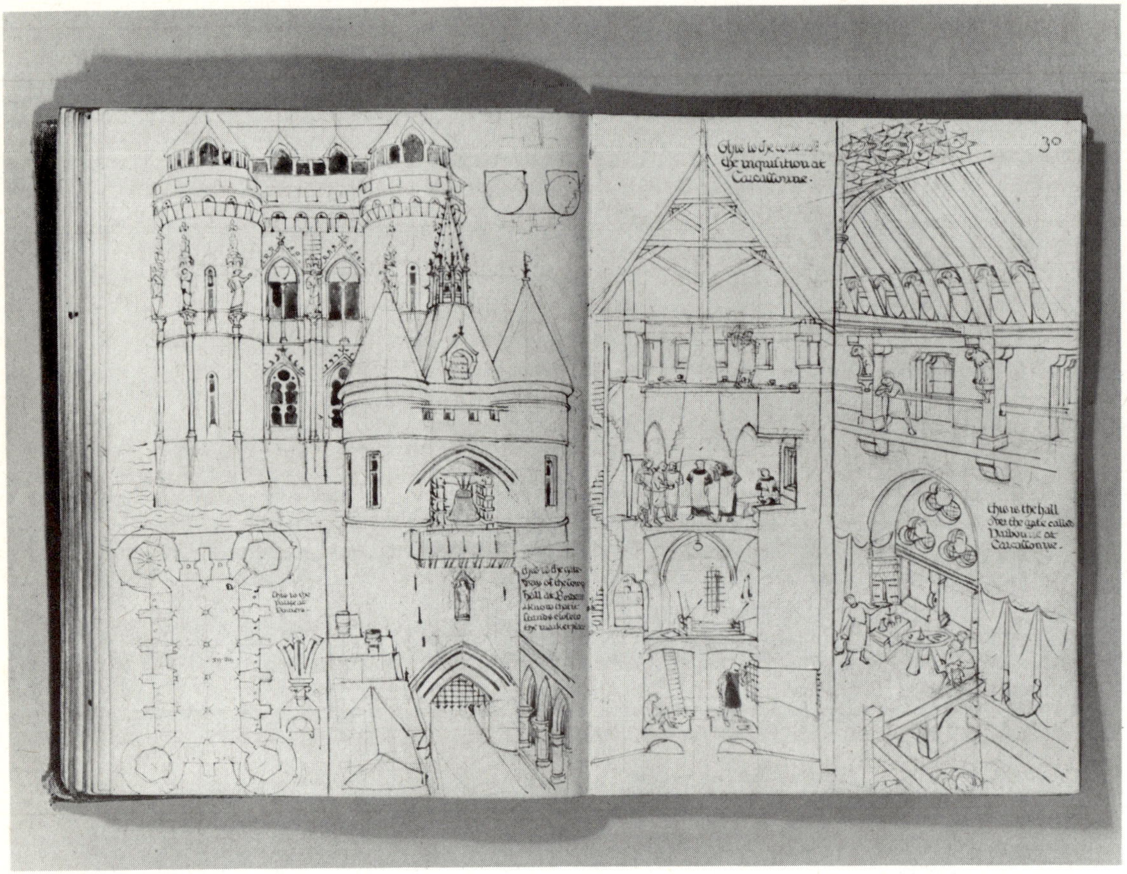

85. **William Burges** (1827-1881)
'Vellum Sketchbook', 1861
36 vellum leaves bound in a dark green, limp pigskin folding cover; brown pen, brown pen & wash, some gouache (235 x 170)
Provenance: Lot 281, sale of Burges's effects, 1882; bought by Sir William Emerson (1843-1925), a former pupil of W.B., and presented to the RIBA, 1910.

The thirteenth century was more than any other period the source for Burges's architecture and design. His 'Vellum Sketchbook' was consciously modelled on the thirteenth century sketchbook of Wilars de Honecourt (Bibliothèque Nationale, Paris) published in facsimile in 1858 but already studied by Burges in the original. Thus, physically, the sketchbook is more or less an exact copy of Wilars's: that is, the vellum pages, the binding and size are pretty much the same. Burges used a pseudo-Gothic script for his inscriptions and the freehand pen drawings made with a crow-quill pen and brown ink over pencil are in a similar manner, except that is, for Burges's naturalistically drawn animal, flower and figure studies. Burges, speaking of Wilars's sketchbook in a talk at the RIBA, said 'another peculiarity of our architect was, that, when he copied any executed work, he copied it not as he saw it but with variations of his own, as he would execute it himself'. This 'peculiarity' is one that is general to most architects (including Burges himself) when sketching other architects' buildings! Burges considered that 'Wilars presents us with a decidedly good style of drawing ... we should join our improved knowledge of perspective and of the figure to the energy, simplicity and firmness of our confrère of the thirteenth century'.

Burges's work includes Cardiff Castle, Castell Coch and his own Tower House in London and the drawings of French castles, shown here, (f29r, f30r) suggest the sources of his castle style architecture. Burges labelled them: *This is the palace at Poitiers; This is the gateway of the timber hall at Bordeaux & know that it stands close to the market place; This is the tower of the inquisition at Carcassonne; This is the hall over the gate called Narbonne at Carcassonne*. Burges's sense of humour emerges in the section of the Carcassonne tower, where a cross-bowman is shown on the top floor, soldiers, priests and a prisoner on the floor below, while a rack is mercifully unoccupied above a dungeon in which two prisoners languish.

Lit: W. Burges, 'Architectural drawing', *RIBA Transactions*, 1860-1, pp. 15-28; J. Mordaunt Crook, *William Burges*, 1981, pp. 63-5; *The Strange genius of William Burges*, exhibition catalogue, National Museum of Wales, Cardiff, 1981, p. 132.

86. **William Burges** (1827-1881)
Design for a house at Park Place, Cardiff for James Mc.Connochie, drawn by Axel Haig, *c.* 1872
Brown pen over pencil, watercolour, gouache & chinese white (455 x 545)
Provenance: unknown.
In 1871 James Mc.Connochie, a Scots engineer, commissioned Burges to design a house in Park Place, Cardiff. The perspective, shown here was exhibited at the Royal Academy in 1872 and the *Builder* (XXX, 1872, p. 358) described the style of the building as 'a plain, simple treatment of Early Gothic of a somewhat French character, a little heavy, but very solid and satisfactory-looking'. More positively, Henry-Russell Hitchcock later wrote of the Mc.Connochie house (now used as local government offices) as 'one of the best medium-sized stone dwellings of the High Victorian Gothic'.

An excellent draughtsman himself and one who urged the use of 'strong thick lines', Burges disapproved of coloured, pictorial perspectives but since these were expected in the Architecture Room at the Royal Academy, he got perspective artists such as E.S. Cole and, in particular, Axel Haig (1835-1921) to do them for him. Haig's first drawings for Burges were the astonishing bird's eye and worm's eye views for the Law Courts competition (1866-7). After this, Haig worked steadily for Burges (as well as for other architects) making many stunning perspectives including, for example, one for Studley Royal church (RIBA). Haig had trained as an architect before he turned architectural draughtsman and then watercolourist and etcher, so that his perspectives are accurate as well as seductive. His sympathy for Burges's medievalism allied to his artistic skills – above all his luminous use of watercolour – made him an ideal collaborator, and one who shared Burges's sense of humour. Is the workman painting the railing (on the right of the drawing) a self-portrait?
Lit: H.-R. Hitchcock, *Architecture: nineteenth and twentieth centuries*, 1963, p. 188; J. Mordaunt Crook, *op. cit.*, pp. 305-6; J. Mordaunt Crook & C.A. Lennox-Boyd, *Axel Haig*, 1984, *passim*.

C14. **Henry Wyndham Phillips** (1820-1868)
Portrait of Owen Jones (1809-1868), 1856
Oil on canvas (1510 x 1110)
Owen Jones – 'the most potent apostle of colour that architectural England has had' – so wrote the obituarist in *The Builder* in 1874. In 1836, Jones had published the first part of his *Plans, Elevations, Sections and details of the Alhambra*, which marked the advent of colour printing as an industry; in 1851 he had been appointed a Director of Decoration at the re-erection of the Crystal Palace at Sydenham, for which he designed the Alhambra Court, and the success of his colour scheme for this, and the publication of his *Grammar of Ornament* in 1856, ensured him international esteem. That same year the RIBA, where Jones had been elected Vice-President in 1843, commissioned this superb portrait by Henry Wyndham Phillips. The design above the dado in the portrait is derived from a room in the Alhambra Court, which is in turn based on the Hall of the Ambassadors at the Alhambra itself. The design below the dado echoes strongly that in the alcove of the Hall of the Two Sisters, also at the Alhambra in Spain. Jones's obituary in *The Architect* described him as 'unassuming in his eminence, gentle, blameless and kind' and this portrait is testimony to these characteristics. This is not a portrait of a self-important man: Jones has a peaceful, almost resigned look on his face, his coat is slung loosely over his right shoulder and the fur lining continues the soft contours of his beard. The year after this portrait was painted, the RIBA further honoured Jones by awarding him the Royal Gold Medal.
Lit: M. Darby, *The Islamic Perspective*, exhibition catalogue, Leighton House Gallery, 1983, *passim*.

87. **John Pollard Seddon** (1827-1906)
Design for the restoration of the chancel, Church of the Holy Trinity, Ingham, Norfolk, drawn by Howard Gaye, 1877
Watercolour on board (710 x 515)
Provenance: presented by J.P. Birch, 1969.
John Pollard Seddon was one of the most original of the Gothic Revival architects. His best known work is the University College of Wales, Aberystwyth, begun originally as an hotel in 1864 – but after that date he increasingly concerned himself with church restoration and the design of furniture, metalwork, tiles and stained glass. He held a passionate belief in the unity of the arts and wrote and lectured on painting, sculpture, polychromy and ornament: the collection of Seddon's working drawings at the RIBA were presented in 1890 to accompany a paper in *RIBA Transactions* on 'Church fittings'.

This perspective was painted by the architect Howard Gaye, who often prepared Seddon's exhibition drawings and later worked in a rather different style for C.F.A. Voysey, who had been Seddon's pupil. It shows a design for restoring the chancel screen at Ingham church. Also shown are a stone pulpit, decorated with painted and gilded carving, an elaborate carved lectern surmounted by a Majolica eagle, a reredos, new glass in the East window, decorative painting on the walls and decorative tiles on the floor. Seddon did build a new South aisle and clerestory in 1876, but, except for the lectern, nothing else in this perspective was executed. The *Builder* reviewed the drawing at the 1877 RA exhibition as being 'rather strong and overdone', but it won the bronze medal at the Paris International Exhibition in the following year. In its jewel-like colouring and lighting it has an almost Pre-Raphaelite intensity and it is interesting to note that Seddon was a close friend of both Rossetti and Ford Madox Brown and employed Rossetti, Morris, Burne-Jones and Thomas Woolner to work on his restoration of Llandaff Cathedral in the 1860's.
Lit: *Builder*, XXXV, 1877, p. 474; J.P. Seddon, 'Church fittings', *RIBA Transactions*, VI, 1890, pp. 165-186; M. Darby, *John Pollard Seddon*, 1983.

88. **John Dobbin** (1815-1888)
View of the Alhambra, Granada, Spain, 1870
Watercolour (695 x 1020)
Provenance: presented through the National Art Collections Fund, 1939.
An important aspect of the Romantic and Picturesque movements was the taste for the exotic. Throughout the eighteenth century a growing number of travellers included the

countries of the Near East in their Grand Tours, and published accounts of their journeys upon their return. By the 1870s interest had extended to Spain and India. Published views and measured drawings of the Alhambra appear from then on, the most influential being Owen Jones and Jules Goury's *La Alhambra Palais* of 1836-45, illustrated with colour lithographs.

John Dobbin, a London based watercolourist, was one of the many artists to exploit the market for exotic landscapes. He appears to have made an initial journey to Spain in 1858/59, and while there made sketches to be worked up into finished paintings once back in England. These must have sold successfully for, of the hundred and fifty odd watercolours he exhibited at the RIBA and RA from 1859 to 1871, only a handful had other than Spanish subjects.

Lit: A. Graves, *RA exhibitors 1769-1904*, 1905-6; J. Johnson *Works Exhibited at the Royal Society of British Artists 1824-1893*, 1975; M. Darby, *The Islamic Perspective*, exhibition catalogue, Leighton House, London, 1983, *passim*.

89. **George Aitchison** (1825-1910)
Design for the decoration of the *Front Drawing Room* at No. 15 Berkeley Square, London.
see colour plate page 25.

C15. **Sir Lawrence Alma-Tadema** (1836-1912)
Portrait of George Aitchison (1825-1910), 1900
Oil on canvas (1500 x 1240)
On 4th December 1899, the RIBA Council 'resolved that the President (Sir William Emerson was President 1899-1902) be requested to see Sir Lawrence Alma-Tadema, R.A., and ask him whether he could see his way to paint a portrait for the Institute of his old friend Professor Aitchison'. Alma-Tadema accepted the President's request and 'generously offered to accept whatever sum was subscribed to the portrait fund'. It is perhaps the warmth of the friendship that existed between the artist and the sitter which makes this such a very attractive portrait – sittings were probably a pleasure rather than a chore. Aitchison's obituarist in *The Builder* stated that the portrait is a 'good likeness and very characteristic of the man', whilst the book he holds is probably his 'beloved Vitruvius'. In 1887 he was elected Professor of Architecture at the Royal Academy and he raises a finger in the portrait as if making a point to his students.

90. **Sir Thomas Graham Jackson** (1835-1924)
Competition design for the new Examination Schools, High Street, Oxford, 1876
Pen (635 x 890)
Provenance: presented by the architect's son, Basil H. Jackson, 1951.
Jackson won the competition for the new Schools in 1876 largely due to the fact that his planning made the best use of an awkward site. His was also the only entry of the five in the limited competition which was not in the Gothic Revival style, and the fact that he won was a victory for the eclectic principles he had expounded three years earlier in his *Modern Gothic Architecture*. The building provided accommodation for holding examinations, lectures and other public functions, and, because of its prominence, established Jackson's reputation in Oxford and beyond. Slight modifications to the design were made in execution, principally to the porch and the layout of the quadrangle; the Schools were inaugurated in 1883, and the buildings to the left in this picture were replaced by a further block by Jackson in 1886-88 – the fact that these were not yet designed is neatly concealed by the scrolled edge of the inset bird's eye view. The drawing also shows, on the right, part of Frank Cooper's shop – the home of Oxford marmalade.

Jackson was an accomplished draughtsman, and drew his own perspectives; but although he was a water-colourist of great skill, he used only pen and ink for drawings such as this because they were intended partly for publication in the journals of the day, a process greatly improved by the introduction of photo-lithography in the late 1860s – which meant that drawings no longer had to be engraved but also precluded the use of half-tones. Figures were not his strong point, but they always added life and a touch of humour to his drawings.
Lit: J. Bettley, 'T.G. Jackson and the Examination Schools', *Oxford Art Journal*, VI, 1983, pp. 57-66.

91. **Sir Horace Jones** (1819-1887)
Design for a "Bascule" Bridge Across the River Thames, 1878
Brown pen & wash (305 x 710)
Provenance: unknown
As Architect and Surveyor to the Corporation of London from 1864 to 1887, Horace Jones designed, among other buildings, the markets at Smithfield, Billingsgate and Leadenhall. His solutions to the structural and mechanical problems of large covered markets proved Jones to be a practical and technically inventive designer well able to contribute to the debate over a new crossing for the Thames. His solution favoured a bridge rather than a tunnel or ferry and in particular a *bascule* or 'see-saw' bridge. It was to have two side spans of 190 feet each and a centre span of 300 feet that would be bridged by two hinged platforms. Jones presented his scheme to a meeting of the Special Bridge or Subway Committee of the Corporation of London on 16 October 1878. The members of the Committee were shown two perspectives of the *bascule* bridge design: one showing the bridge open (seen here), the other with the bridge closed (also in the RIBA Collection). The design was shelved and not revived until 1884, and Jones died before the completion of what is now Tower Bridge in 1894. As built, the design differs in many ways from Jones's original idea but the essentials of the scheme, including the castle style architectural treatment, are owed to him.

It is unlikely that Jones drew the presentation perspectives of his scheme. The draughtmanship does not correspond with drawings known to be in his hand and it is difficult to imagine that the busy City architect could have spared the time. What the perspective artist was required to put over was an explanation to a lay committee of how a *bascule* bridge worked, then to convey the volume and variety of river traffic and the problematic height of masted ships (a survey showed that this ranged from 45 to 90 feet), the easy gradients and access for road traffic that Jones achieved, the economy of the two piers required instead of the three or four needed for, say, a swing bridge and the 'beauty of form' that made Jones's bridge 'the most picturesque ... on the river'.
Lit: C. Welch and others, *History of the Tower Bridge*, 1894, *passim*; J. Freeman, 'Sir Horace Jones 1819-1887', *Victorian Society Annual*, 1981, pp. 45-54.

92. **Sir Ernest George** (1839-1922) and
Harold Ainsworth Peto (1854-1933)
Design for Nos 35 and 37 Harrington Gardens, London, for Walter Richard Cassels, 1882
Brown pen & wash (510 x 655)
Provenance: presented by Alfred B Yeates, 1935.

Lutyens, who was in Sir Ernest George's office, remembered him with amused contempt as 'a distinguished architect who took each year three weeks holiday abroad and returned with overflowing sketchbooks. When called on for a project he would look through these and choose some picturesque turret or gable from Holland, France or Spain, and round it weave his new design.' George, it is true, was an inveterate sketcher and did much to popularize the Dutch and Flemish styles in England; he had one of the busiest practices in the country and was best known for his houses in Harrington and Collingham Gardens. When not sketching he spent all his time in his office at No. 18 Maddox Street in a room panelled in the Dutch style. In designing he would start with a brilliant watercolour perspective, rather than a plan or section, and drew all his own perspectives for exhibition at the Royal Academy.

This perspective is a good example of his fine penmanship, drawn in brown ink and wash, (with ink produced by the laborious method of grinding a chinese stick round and round in a small pool of water), on high quality Whatman paper which had first been stretched on a board in the office. The effect is 'artistic' and spontaneous with many breaks in the ruled lines to give the impression of a freehand sketch.

A pair of town houses are shown, built of red brick with a quiet Dutch feeling. W.R. Cassels, the theological critic, lived in the larger of the two, the house on the right. He was a bachelor, with an income derived from a Bombay trading company, and had a fine collection of paintings which he hung in the immense 40 foot drawing room overlooking the garden on the first floor.

Lit: *Building News*, XLIII, 1882, p. 10; Darcy Braddell, 'Fugaces Anni', *Builder*, CLXVIII, 1945, p. 6; C. Hussey, *The Life of Sir Edwin Lutyens*, 1950 p. 17; G. Stamp, *The Great Perspectivists*, 1982, no 79.

93. **Colonel Sir Robert William Edis** (1839-1927)
Design for the Constitutional Club, Northumberland Avenue, London, drawn by George Nattress, 1886
Pen & watercolour (885 x 1070)
Provenance: puchased, 1982

The Constitutional Club was always one of the most sumptuous of the London clubs. Pevsner called it 'a prodigious effort'; with its five storeys, terracotta dressings and picturesque skyline of Dutch gables, it abandoned the traditional *palazzo* formula so often used by club-houses and presented instead an image that was much closer to a luxurious London hotel.

Colonel Sir Robert Edis had been an early convert to 'Queen Anne' and had a large and interesting practice specializing in hotels and clubs, as well as two Bond Street galleries, the Middle Temple Library, flats and houses. He also wrote a book on the *Decoration and furniture of London Town Houses*, 1881. He never saw active service but in 1883 succeeded Lord Leighton as Colonel of the Artists' Volunteer Rifle Corps, which was founded during the anti-French scare of 1859 and whose somewhat unlikely recruits included Millais, Holman Hunt, Swinburne, Rossetti and Morris. This no doubt brought him closely in contact with a more artistic circle, and it is interesting to note that George Nattress, the perspectivist employed here, was principally a landscape and topographical artist who did not usually specialize in architectural subjects. Certainly the treatment of materials and figures is very painterly and the manner of depicting the glass in the windows and drawn blinds adds light and liveliness to the building. The club stood in Northumberland Avenue until 1963, when it was demolished to make way for Standard House by Ronald Fielding.

Lit: *Builder*, 1886, L, p. 703.

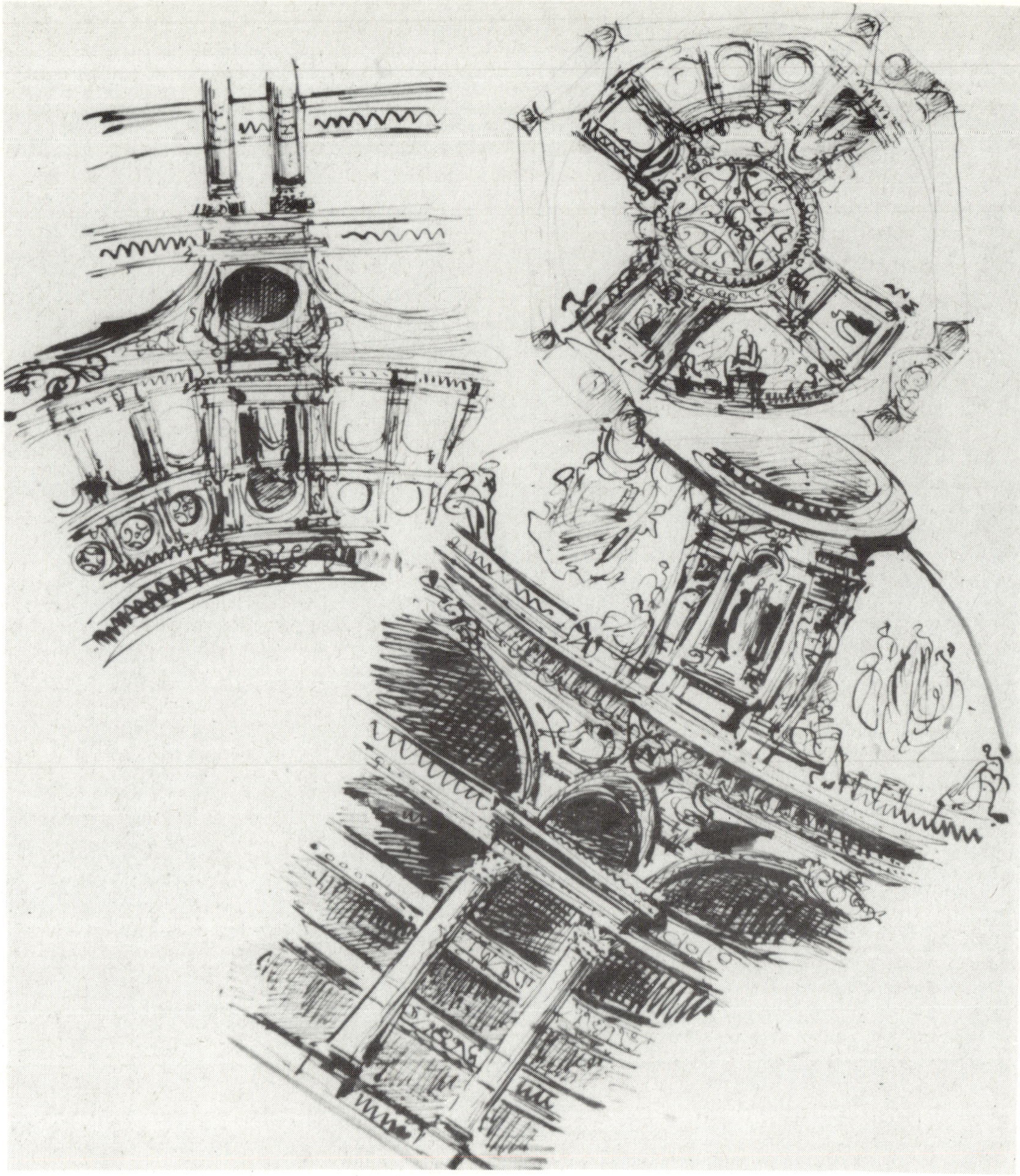

94. **Charles Garnier** (1825-1898)
Designs for the interior of the Opéra, Paris, *c.* 1861
Brown ink, pen & brush (185 x 235, 380 x 325)
Provenance: presented by the French Academy of Architecture, 1958.
Garnier was a founder of the Second Empire style – a re-interpretation of the classical tradition that borrowed from a wide variety of periods and sources. He won the Prix de Rome in 1848 but suffered a decade of anonymity upon his return to Paris. Then in 1860 he came fifth in the first stage of the competition for the new Opéra. This 'competition' of ideas was followed in 1861 by a second stage with a more specific brief. Garnier won, and spent the next fourteen years supervising the construction of his masterpiece.

At the Opéra, gold and polychrome marbles enliven what he considered its dull and sad surroundings. The luxuriousness of his design suited the political role of the building: it was to reflect the prosperity of the age. These preliminary designs are for the ceiling and balconies in the auditorium: their exuberance conveys something of the opulence and drama of the scheme, and the influence of the Baroque.
Lit: J.F. Revel 'Charles Garnier, dernier fils de la Renaissance', *L'Oeil*, no. 99, 1963, pp. 2-11; L. Hautecoeur *Histoire de l'Architecture Classique en France*, VII, pp. 179-193, 1957.

96. **George Devis** (1820-1886)
Design for a model farm in Silesia
See colour plate page 26.

95. **John Belcher** (1841-1913)
Competition design for the interior of the South Kensington Museum, now the Victoria and Albert, London, 1891
Pen & wash (915 x 615)
Provenance: purchased, 1970.
"The just proportions of the rooms, convenience of arrangement for exhibition and the provision of ample light, have been the principles most considered." So wrote Belcher in 1892 of his influential competition entry for additions to the South Kensington Museum. Although not the winning design, his scheme was published, exhibited, and admired, with the result that it encouraged the revival of the Baroque style in the design of public buildings. This impressive perspective recalls the architectural fantasies of the eighteenth century, architecture on a monumental scale made possible by the wealth and technological advances of the nineteenth century.

The perspectivist was William Bingham McGuiness (?-1928), a member of the Royal Hibernian Academy of Arts who specialized in street scenes. His is not a precise projection of the future building, he concentrates instead on the theatre of the large vaulted spaces. Particularly effective is his treatment of light reflected off the marble floors.
Lit: *The Architect*, XLVI, 1891, pp. 96, 107, and pl. preceding p. 234; *Builder*, LXIII, 1892, pp. 378-379; *Builder*, LXVII, 1894, pl. opposite p. 474.

C16. **Sir Frank Dicksee** (1853-1913)
Portrait of John Belcher (1841-1913), *c.*1906
Oil on canvas (1590 x 1360)
It was Sir Aston Webb who said that John Belcher was 'one of the first to introduce real sculpture into architecture'. The building in which he did this was the Institute of Chartered Accountants (1889) where Hamo Thornycroft (1850-1925) designed the exterior frieze consisting of deep panels carved with standing figures. The 'Arts' panel provides the background to Belcher's presidential portrait where three classical figures representing Architecture, Sculpture and Painting may be seen. Belcher stands by a model of the dome of Electra House, Moorgate, of 1902 (now the premises of City of London College.) and he holds a drawing for half of the main elevation. Although Pevsner describes the building as 'Belcher at his most intolerable', when it was designed it was widely illustrated, highly praised and extremely influential. In this carefully constructed portrait, the model of Electra House is balanced by Belcher's T-square. His cravat, Sir Frank Dicksee has painted beautifully, for the rich burgundy colour provides a complete contrast to the other muted tones.

97. **William Eden Nesfield** (1835-1888)
Sketchbook, September 1862-May 1876
180 pages bound in black leather with a metal clasp; pencil with occasional use of coloured washes (225 x 150)
Provenance: purchased out of a fund raised by R. Phené Spiers, 1895.
In September 1862 Shaw and Nesfield went off for a week's sketching in Sussex, intent upon Wealden vernacular subjects. It was a sudden shift of interest for them that was to lead to their 'Old English' houses and vernacular cottages, which later came to have such an influence on the Arts and Crafts Movement. Fortunately both Shaw's and Nesfield's sketchbooks survive at the RIBA Drawings Collection recording this important trip – Shaw's more austerly confined to drawing, Nesfield's accompanied by a concise diary that reflects their humour and enthusiasms. *Tortington Sept 25. Saw 2 sows lying back to back, head and tail for mutual support against the combined efforts of their respective litters of about 13 suckling pigs each. Good dodge'. 'Sept 26th. Left Littlehampton 8.30 saw Rustington Church. Very good plan. Walked on to Angmering which turned out to be an awful sell as it was totally restored by Teulon in his best manner*. He sketched vernacular cottages, details in churches, old oak furniture, carving and ornament. In June 1863 he visited Speldhurst in Kent, and two typical pages, pp. 62 and 63, record his interests: a tile-hung shop with lean-to and hipped roof, a *curious settle at the George and Dragon Inn* and some ancient Egyptian chairs copied from *Der Styl*.
Lit: A. Saint, *Richard Norman Shaw*, 1976, pp. 26-28.

98. **Richard Norman Shaw** (1831-1912)
Design for Grims Dyke, Wealdwood Road, Harrow, Middlesex, for Frederick Goodall, RA, 1872
Pen (465 x 670)
Provenance: presented by Mrs Norman Shaw, 1916.
Grims Dyke is one of Shaw's best examples of the 'Old English' style, that is a free adaptation of Tudor forms with picturesque many-gabled compositions and the warm and rich effects of half-timbering and tile-hanging. The studio (on the right) was placed at an oblique angle to the rest of the building as Goodall wanted a pure north-south light for painting.

One of the paradoxes of Shaw's working method was that he chose not to produce artistic and coloured perspectives to express the picturesqueness of his designs and the textures of the materials he used. He was a cold and literal draughtsman. His RA perspectives are ruled, pen drawings and although he indicated the landscape surroundings, they are not drawn with much subtlety. He never added figures or hansom cabs. It is clear that he felt that any conspicuous display of draughtsmanship was improper: 'our present style of drawing has, I fear, grown up largely from a desire to make architecture more pictorial, and by this means to enlist the sympathies and admiration of those who would not understand it if they did'. Goodhart-Rendel thought there was very little in Shaw's drawings 'to captivate, but a very thorough attempt to explain', and there is no doubt that his designs were widely copied by architects, particularly when the invention of photolithography enabled them to be published in the architectural press.
Lit: H.S. Goodhart-Rendel, 'Architectural Draughtmanship of the Past' *RIBA Journal*, LVIII, 1951, p. 130; A. Saint, *Richard Norman Shaw* 1976, *passim*.

99. **Richard Norman Shaw** (1831-1912)
Full-size design for the weather vane, Pierrepont, Frensham, Surrey, for Richard Henry Croome, 1876
Grey & yellow washes on pink detail paper (2320 x 745)
Provenance: Frank Birch; Harold Falkner, by whom it was presented, 1950
This is one of a large collection of working drawings owned by Frank Birch, one of Shaw's favourite builders. He built many of Shaw's 'Old English' houses in Surrey, Sussex and Hampshire, several of which had interchangeable details. Sometimes the decision on important points was left to Birch: the design for the Pierrepont entrance gable (RIBA, Shaw [44].36) is inscribed *'the bargeboards cornice etc to be all similar to Wispers – or Boldre Grange – or any of our best specimens'* – as though, as Andrew Saint has said – 'architect and builder belonged to one and the same firm.' At other times, as in this example, Shaw would invent and draw out the whole detail to its full size. No expense was spared at Pierrepont. The initial 'C' on the vane flag is that of the client, Richard Croome.

This is one of the earliest 'full-sizes' of this dimension in the Drawings Collection. This is partly because before *c.* 1800 large working drawings would have been made by the builder or craftsman (and therefore tend not to have survived), and partly because from the 1870's onwards architects increasingly felt the need to specify their designs in great detail.
Lit: A. Saint, *Richard Norman Shaw* 1976, p. 164.

100. **John Pollard Seddon** (1827-1906) and **Edward Beckitt Lamb** (1857-?1932)
Design for the Imperial Monumental Halls and Tower, Westminster, a reworking of an 1890 scheme, drawn by John Gaye, 1904
Watercolour on board (650 x 915)
Provenance: presented by J.P. Birch, 1969.
The Monumental Halls were intended to accommodate the monuments in Westminster Abbey, which by the middle of the nineteenth century were causing concern both in their numbers and in their 'taste'. From 1854 onwards Sir Gilbert Scott put forward several suggestions for a new respository but it was only in 1890 that a Royal Commission was appointed to enquire into the lack of space in the Abbey. They inspected plans depicting various proposals submitted by J.L. Pearson, Somers Clarke, E.J. Tarver and Lawrence Harvey and J.P. Seddon, but nothing came of these schemes either.

This drawing represents a later more elaborate version of one of Seddon's 1890 schemes, made in partnership this time with Edward Beckitt Lamb, the son of Edward Buckton Lamb. It shows a great 'valhalla' standing between the Abbey and Houses of Parliament, consisting of an immense tower, the height of which was 550 feet, behind which stretches a Monumental Hall with burial chapels and South transept. The tower, as well as the halls, would be the repository of memorials, and in the interior of the former there would be ascending stages, on each of which monuments would be placed. At the top of the tower there would be a large public viewing platform. The Abbey is also given a central crossing tower for good measure.

The perspective presents a fascinating bird's-eye view of the Houses of Parliament and its adjoining buildings in 1904: Parliament Square has not yet been formally planned and in the lower right-hand corner is Norman Shaw's recently built New Scotland Yard.
Lit: '*Marble Halls*', exhibition catalogue, Victoria & Albert Museum, London 1973, no. 15; M. Darby, *John Pollard Seddon*, 1983, pp. 78-79.

101. **Arthur Beresford Pite** (1861-1934)
Design for mission premises, Old Montague Street, Whitechapel, London, *c.* 1891
Pen (385 x 255)
Provenance: by office descent to G.E.P. Jackson (Pite's last partner), by whom presented, 1959.
Pite learnt to draw at the School of Art, South Kensington where an introduction to the drawings and prints of Albrecht Dürer 'was to become the foundation of a technique absolutely peculiar to

... himself'. He used that technique for the perspective, shown here, of his mission hall in Whitechapel. The design, constrained by costs, is simple, making the best of cheap London stock bricks and red rubbers. The emotional impact of the drawing is strong for Pite evokes the squalid poverty of the East End slums where a mission hall with its light shining over an open door represented some kind of solace. Unusually, in an architectural perspective, the new building with its uneven roofline and ragged brickwork is made to seem almost as dilapidated as its neighbours. Neither the mission hall nor anything else in Old Montague Street survives, all having been since redeveloped.

Pite used his pen and ink technique (employing a Waverly nib that 'could lay a thick and, in reverse, a thin line') all through his working life. But to match a bewildering succession of architectural styles he experimented with other, quite distinctive, drawing techniques. As a student he tried out watercolour rather in the manner of, say, Ernest George and used this afterwards for cottage and garden perspectives. For the plans, elevations and sections of a church in a Free Byzantine style he assumed the Arts and Crafts drawing convention of Halsey Ricardo. The 'Grecian purity' of his Euston Square building was rendered in the cream, buff and grey washes of Neo-Classicist William Wilkins. But for two of his Michaelangelesque buildings in St Marylebone, perhaps because his figure drawing was deficient, he allowed J.J. Joass to make the perspectives.

Lit: H.S. Goodhart-Rendel, 'The Work of Beresford Pite ...', *RIBA Journal*, XLII, 1935, pp. 123-8; notes of a lecture by Robert W. Pite to the RIBA Library Group, January 1960 (RIBA Biography files).

C17. **Frederick W. Pomeroy** (1856-1924)
Bronze low relief roundel of J.D. Sedding (1838-1891) and Rose Sedding (d.1891)
(diameter 160).
Provenance: purchased, 1978.
Surely this commemorative roundel is the most touching item in the Exhibition. It was made in 1891, the year of the deaths of both John and Rose Sedding, by F.W. Pomeroy whom Sedding had met at the Art Workers' Guild in 1887. Pomeroy worked with Sedding on many important commissions, the most prestigious being Holy Trinity, Sloane Street, begun in 1888 where Pomeroy carved the chancel stalls and the screen. In this enchanting roundel, he has captured the essence of the exceptional relationship between husband and wife with enormous sympathy and has revealed the deep intimacy within their marriage. E.F. Russell, at one time the Seddings' vicar in Holborn, wrote that Sedding 'leaned on his wife; indeed I cannot think of him without her' and two days before his death he said 'I have to thank God for the happiest of homes and the sweetest of wives'. She was 'gentle and refined, sensitive and sympathetic to an unusual degree, yet there was no lack in her of the sterner stuff of character – force, courage, and endurance', whilst he was 'loved and admired by the most diverse natures'. Within a week of her husband's death, Rose Sedding was also dead, it was therefore both ironic and pathetic that the following lines of a seventeenth century poet should be found amongst her papers in her own handwriting:

" 'Tis fit one flesh one house should have,
One tomb, one epitaph, one grave;
And they that lived and loved either
Should dye, and lye, and sleep together".

Lit: J.D. Sedding, *Garden Craft, Old and New*, 1891.

C18. **J.H. Lorimer** (1864-1929)
Portrait of Sir Robert Lorimer (1856-1936), 1886
Oil on canvas (410 x 510)
Provenance: unknown.
John Lorimer, the second eldest brother of Robert, painted this charming portrait when the sitter was 22 years old. Lorimer is working on a gateway design with single-minded attention and appears totally unaware of the artist.
Lit: P. Savage, *Lorimer and the Edinburgh Designers* 1980.

C19. **Sir William Orpen** (1878-1931)
Portrait of Leonard Stokes (1858-1925), 1912
Oil on canvas (1440 x 1160)
This portrait caused a sensation at the Institute. Sir William Orpen wished to paint Stokes in something brown but to the horror of his wife the only brown garment that he possessed was his much-patched dressing gown. At the unveiling, the Institute reacted with outrage; all previous presidents had been portrayed in formal dress and the audience themselves were suitably attired in white tie and tails. Consequently on 8th July, 1912, the Council decided that some modification was required to bring the portrait 'into harmony' with the other presidential portraits and 'the President was requested to write to Mr. Orpen and suggest to him the desirability of making the necessary alterations'. However, two weeks later the President stated that 'Mr. Orpen was unwilling to make any alteration in the portrait and it was accordingly resolved that the President and Vice-President be authorised to find some suitable place for hanging the portrait but that it should not be hung in the West Gallery'. A 'suitable place' was found: the basement of 9, Conduit Street, the premises of the Institute, where the portrait was relegated for many years. Today we can see how brilliantly Orpen reveals Stokes's forthright character in his straightforward picture. As President, (1910-12) he made the first major attempt to unify the profession after internal disagreements over the question of Registration. He was an honest man who hated shams of any kind and for this reason perhaps chose Orpen to paint him, for Orpen depicted people exactly as he saw them. Despite the uproar caused by his first presidential portrait, Orpen was commissioned to paint those of Paul Waterhouse, Guy Dawber and William Tapper, by which time he was a highly successful society portrait painter.
Lit: Council Minutes, (RIBA archives), 1912.

102. **Charles Francis Annesley Voysey** (1857-1941)
Design for a textile showing water-lilies growing in a stream, *c.* 1888
Yellow, green, blue & grey washes (780 x 560)
Provenance: presented by Charles Cowles Voysey, 1943.
Throughout his career Voysey was a prolific designer of patterns for textiles, carpets and wallpapers, and in the early 1880s particularly, and right into the 1930s his pattern designs supported him when building commissions were scarce. In later life Voysey said that it was not from Morris but from the work of G.F. Bodley, William Burges, E.W. Godwin and A.H. Mackmurdo, all pattern designers as well as architects, that he learned that nothing inside or outside a home was too small to deserve the consideration of the architect. He was much respected as a specialist in this field and one of his pupil's indentures (in the RIBA MSS Collection) shows that his assistants were articled 'to learn the art, profession and business of an architect *and* the art of pattern designing'.

This particular textile design bears the watermark 1888 and belongs to an early group of designs of the 1880s that were based on the most original use of carefully observed botanical forms, many of them with the flowing curves which so much influenced the later Art Nouveau movement on the Continent. All these patterns are in light, clear, flat colours in deliberate contrast to the dull greens and sepias in vogue in Voysey's youth.
Lit: E. Aslin in *C.F.A. Voysey: Architect and Designer 1857-1941*, exhibition catalogue, Brighton, 1978, pp. 96-100, fig D46.

103. **Edwin Lutyens** (1869-1944)
The 'Munstead Wood' sketchbook, *c.* 1892-93
36 leaves bound in buff cloth covers; pencil, pen & watercolour (125 x 180)
Provenance: recovered by R.A. Wood, of the builders J.W. Falkner & Sons Ltd, from rubbish removed from the Lutyens office at 5 Eaton Gate in 1939; presented by R.A. Wood to Viscountess Ridley (Lutyens's daughter Ursula) in 1956; presented to the RIBA in 1983 on indefinite loan by the Misses Jane, Susannah and Jessica Ridley.
Munstead Wood, near Godalming, built in 1896-7 for Gertrude Jekyll, made Lutyens's name, when not yet thirty, by its seemingly simple composition out of local forms and materials. This sketchbook contains thirty six sheets, of which the first twenty bear thirty-four pen and watercolour drawings with a few pencil sketches interspersed. The remainder are blank,

except for a few scribbles and, on the last sheet, a coloured view looking outward through a vaulted porch. He evidently added this to please; for it is inscribed *To the Egress* and *Au Re (se) voir*. Most of the sketches are for an early project for Munstead Wood itself and depict a much larger house than was eventually built, but two are for the Gardener's Cottage and for 'The Hut', which was the first little 'cottage in a wood' built for Gertrude Jekyll in 1894. This sketch is inscribed in pencil *abandoned Oct 9th 1892*, and, in ink, *Restored to favour July 16th 1893*.

Lutyens did not usually go to such lengths to charm a client and hardly ever added watercolour to his sketch designs. Hussey notes that the sketchbook was probably compiled when 'the weekend at Munstead became a habit' and they began 'the witty and exciting sport of working out the design together'.

Things did not always go smoothly between them as *Au Re (se) voir* indicates. Miss Jekyll remembers when 'the fur flew, when I wound up my objections by saying with some warmth: "my house is to be built for me to live in and to love; not as an exposition of architectonic inutility".'
Lit: C. Hussey in *The Country Seat* (ed. by H. Colvin & J. Harris), 1970, pp. 267-271; *Lutyens*, an Arts Council exhibition catalogue, London 1981, pp. 73-74; M. Richardson, *Architects of the Arts and Crafts Movement*, 1983, pl. V.

104. **Charles Francis Annesley Voysey (1857-1941)**
Design for a Clock Case
See colour plate page 27.

105. **Henry Wilson** (1864-1934)
Design for the staircase for the Chapel-Library wing, Welbeck Abbey
See colour plate page 29.

106. **Frank Lloyd Wright** (1867 or 1869-1959)
The Francis Apartment Building Built for the Terra Haute Trust Co in 1895
Brown pen & cream wash on tracing paper (300 x 430)
Provenance: given by F.L.W. to Henry-Russell Hitchcock, by whom it was presented, 1965.
The Francis Apartment Building in Chicago, belongs to the very early years of Frank Lloyd Wright's long career when the influence of Louis Sullivan (with whom he broke in 1893) was still apparent. It is evident, for example, in the Sullivanesque design of the iron entrance gates and in the Sullivan office characteristic of drawing figures and vehicles that give scale to the building.

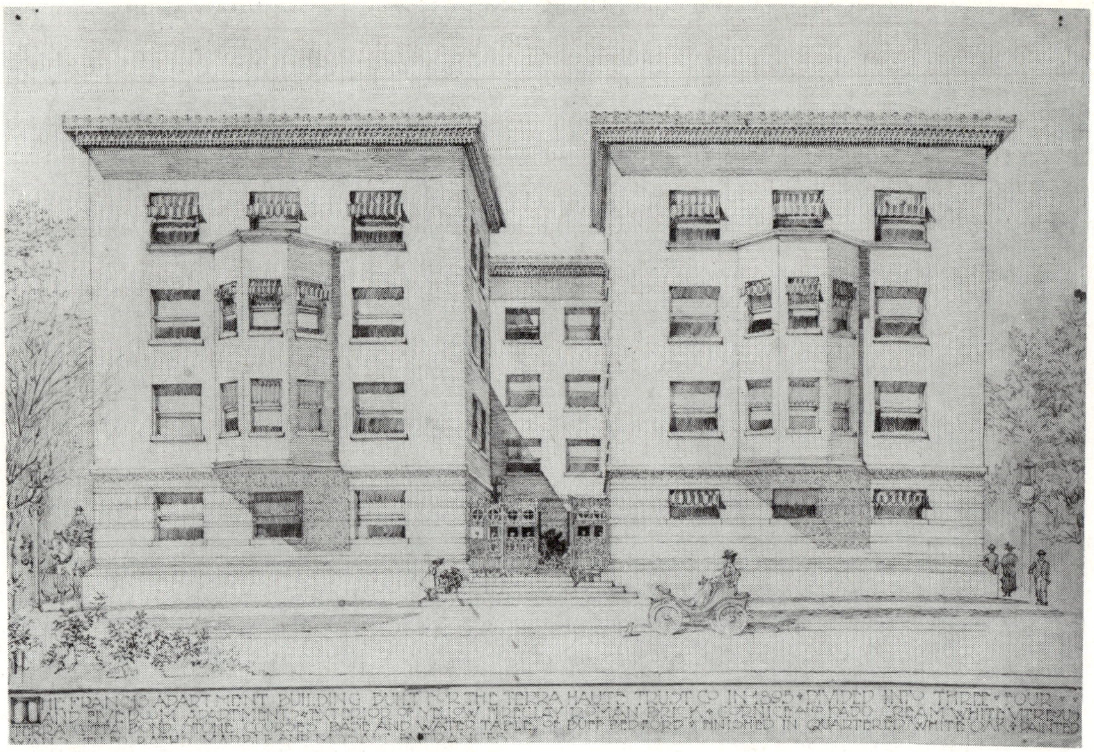

Though Wright used others to help prepare his presentation drawings, it seems certain that the perspective, shown here, is in Wright's own hand. H. Allen Brooks attributes a re-drawing of it (slightly simplified with, for instance, the motor car and window blinds omitted) published as plate 5 in the Wasmuth portfolio as drawn by Wright. And the RIBA's perspective has many of Wright's mannerisms of the 1890s including, for instance, dotted lines, wavy-lined shadows, vertically hatched shading in the window openings and the manner of drawing the foliage (in the foreground). Brook has written, of the Wasmuth drawings, that many of the eye-level perspectives were 'simply *copied* from photographs'. While a cropped photograph published with this perspective (*The Architectural Review* (Boston), June 1900, p. 70) does not correspond with the drawing, other photographs must have been available to Wright and it is possible that one of them was used as the basis of this perspective. On the other hand, many of Wright's perspectives were developed (according to Arthur Drexler) by means of mechanical projection from the plan and that could be the case here.

Another possibility, suggested partly by the use of tracing paper, is that a drawing of the elevation was used, with adjustments, as the basis for the perspective.

The inscription in Wright's inventive lettering reads: *The Francis Apartment Building Built for the Terra Haute Trust Co in 1895 * Divided into Three * Four * and Five Room Apartments * Exterior of Yellow Fireclay Roman Brick * Cornice and Dado Cream White Vitreous Terra Cotta Bond Stone Course Base and Water Table of Buff Bedford * Finished in Quartered White Oak * Painted Walls Tiled Baths Marble and Mosaic Entrances*.
Lit: A. Drexler, *The Drawings of Frank Lloyd Wright*, 1962, pp. 7-16; H. Allen Brooks, 'Frank Lloyd Wright and the Wasmuth Drawings', *Art Bulletin*, XLVIII, 1966, pp. 193-202 (refers to *Ausgeführte Bauten und Entwürfe von Frank Lloyd Wright*, published by Ernst Wasmuth, Berlin, 1910).

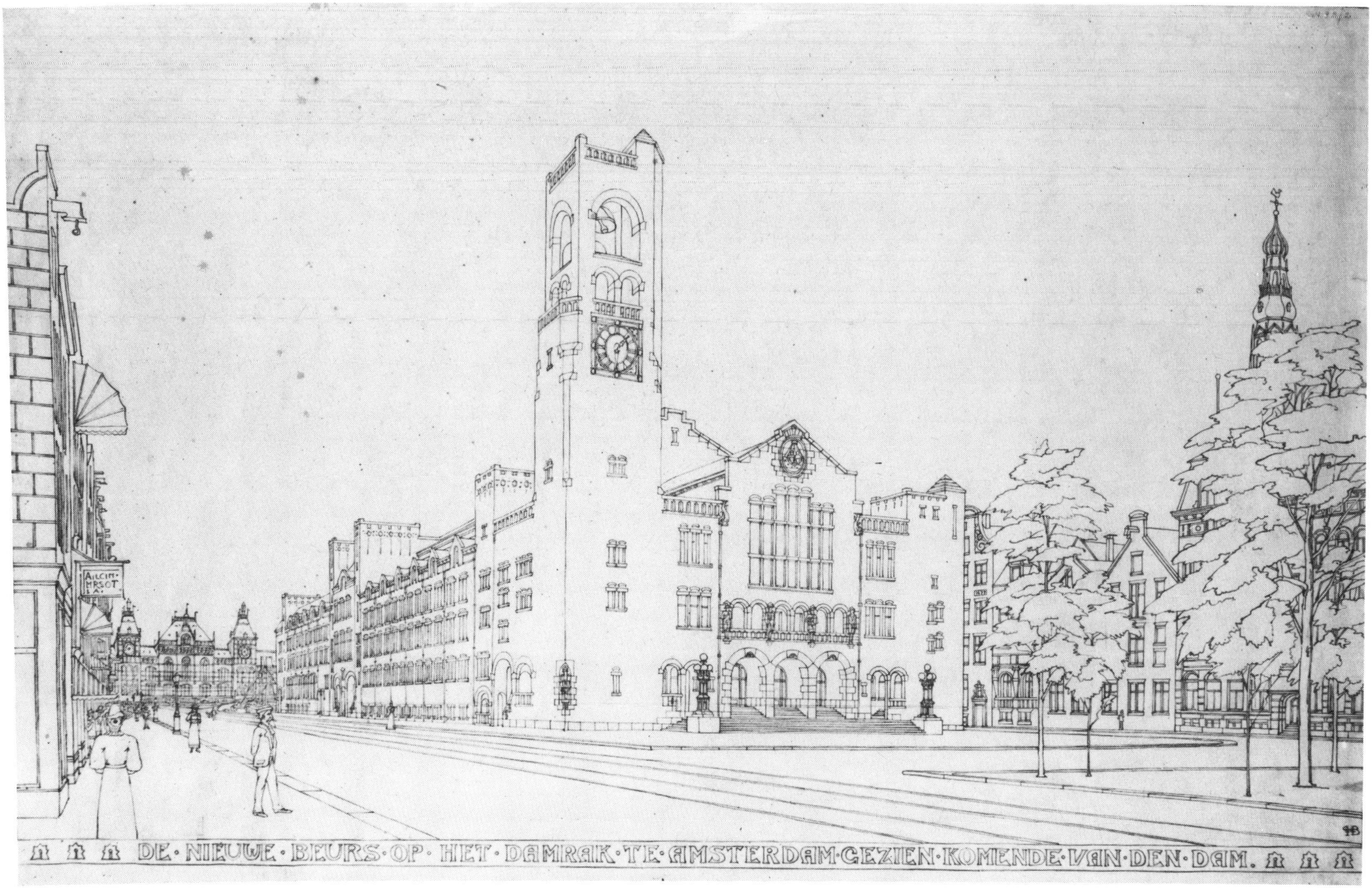

107. **Henrik Petrus Berlage** (1856-1934)
Design for the Stock Exchange, Amsterdam, 1897-98
Brown pen on cream paper (650 x 980)
Provenance: Berlage Archive, B.N.A. Amsterdam (Royal Society for the Advancement of Architecture, Association of Dutch Architects, Amsterdam). Dr H.P. Berlage, Berlage's son presented this drawing, one of his father's finest perspectives in the Berlage Archive, to the Royal Institute of British Architects in 1963 in memory of Berlage receiving the Royal Gold Medal in 1932.

Berlage was a reformer rather than an innovator and a comparable figure in Holland to Voysey in England; the Stock Exchange in Amsterdam was his most notable building. This perspective shows his third design, evolved in late 1897-98, and was made for the purpose of presenting the scheme to the public in early 1898. It was built, with small modifications from 1898-1903.

It is a plain, round-arched building, with a stone trim crudely notched and chamfered, and marked a return to the materials of traditional Dutch building. Berlage's line drawing is equally plain and honest with none of the elaborate colour washes or shading methods of classical nineteenth century architectural perspectives. It makes no attempt to convey the colour or texture of the materials used but instead concentrates on showing the rational and rectangular quality of the building in relation to its site on Dam Square and along the Damrak. In the distance is the Central Station by P.J.H. Cuypers. The integrated artistic lettering has much in common with many European drawings of the period and is uniform with all the lettering produced in the Berlage office from late 1897 onwards.

Lit: H.-R. Hitchcock, *Architecture, Nineteenth and Twentieth Centuries*, 1958, pp. 355-357;
P. Singelenberg, *H.P. Berlage: Idea and Style*, 1972, *passim*.

108. **Edwin Lutyens** (1869-1944)
Preliminary design for Castle Drogo, Drewsteignton, Devon, *c.* 1910-11
Pencil, pen & crayon on squared paper (405 x 530)
Provenance: presented by Robert Lutyens (Lutyens's son), 1951.
Drogo was built for Julius Drewe, founder of the Home and Colonial Stores, who had first approached Lutyens in late 1909 to build him the kind of castle that might have belonged to his thirteenth century ancestor, Drogo de Teynton. Lutyens began working up the first rough sketches on a voyage to South Africa in November 1910 and finalised them in the following April. At that stage he had planned the vast design, shown in this sketch, the main buildings of which were to lie around three sides of a courtyard open to the north. The perspective sketch in this design represents the immense open-roofed Hall on the south side, with three Gothic traceried windows between buttresses (which were, incidentally, a direct quotation from Charles Holden's Bristol Library of 1905). The elevation at the top of the sheet is of the east side, the only range to be built. By 1911 Drewe had doubled the cost by insisting on increasing the thickness of the walls – so the building of the west side was postponed, and after the War the Great Hall was also abandoned. Drogo was not finished until 1932, but its long period of change and reduction enabled Lutyens to perfect the sculptural virtuosity of the elevations – making it one of the greatest 'modern' castles.

This sketch is typical of hundreds Lutyens made throughout his career on a graph pad which he used in the office and which travelled with him on his many voyages to India and South Africa. It is the kind of drawing he would have handed to his assistants for them to work up and draw to scale, but it is also one of the many that he would have shown to Mr Drewe. The added pen and crayon are his only attempts to 'charm' the client.
Lit: C. Hussey, *The Life of Sir Edwin Lutyens*, 1950, pp. 217-25 *et passim*; P. Inskip, 'The Compromise of Castle Drogo', *Architectural Review*, CLXV, 1979, pp. 220-226.

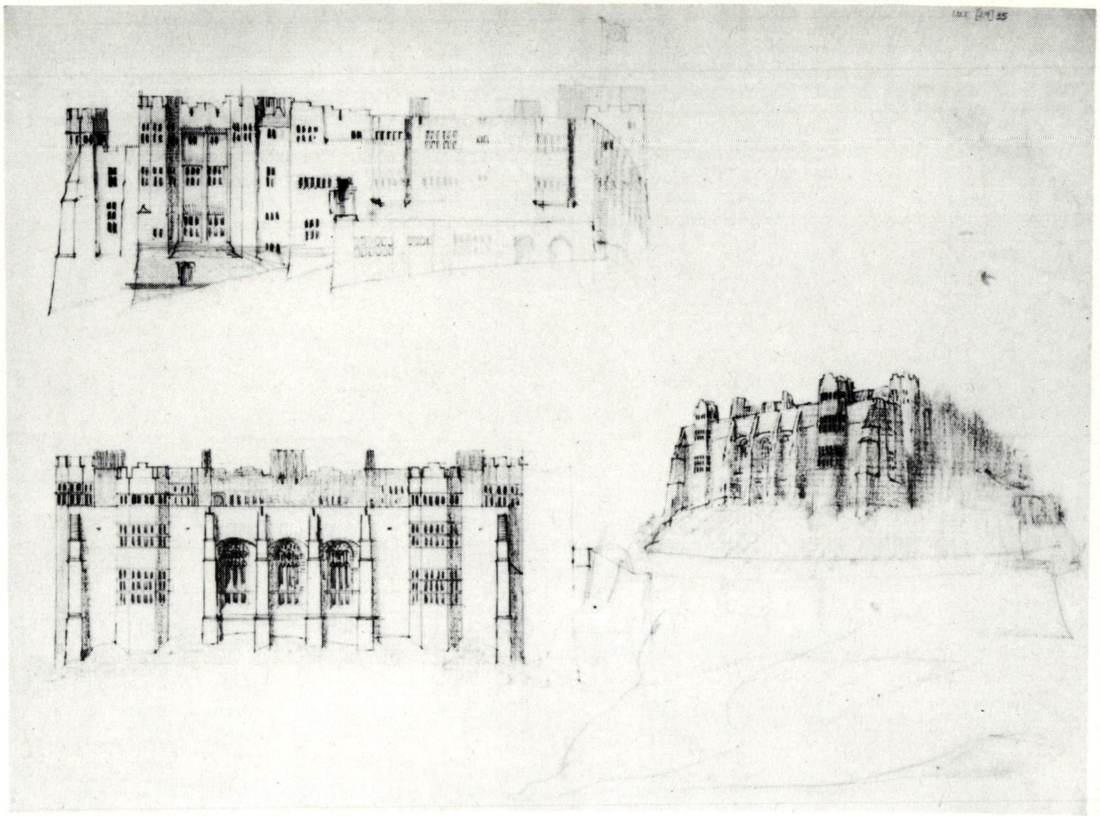

109. **Charles Frederic Mewes** (1860-1914)
Design for a small swimming-pool
See colour plate page 31.

110. **Edwin Alfred Rickards** (1872-1920)
Competition design for County Hall, London, 1907
Pen (835 x 585)
Provenance: presented by J.F. Malyan, 1960.

As a designer and draughtsman, E.A. Rickards was a 'natural'. Without any architectural training except for what he picked up as an assistant in several London offices, he was, from the age of twenty one, a freelance perspectivist and architectural ghost, prepared to design and draw other architects' competition entries as, for instance, G.T. Hine's entry for the Surveyors Institution, 1895-6. In 1897 Rickards collaborated with H.V. Lanchester and James Stewart (died 1902) for the Cardiff town hall competition and when they won, a partnership was set up. It was a practice based almost exclusively on competitions, but one where they were unsuccessful was the competition for London's County Hall (won by Ralph Knott). Rickards's perspective shows his building, with a Thames sailing barge in the foreground, as it would have been seen from Westminster bridge. The design is characteristic: 'big-scale, full blown baroque' with plenty of 'sculptured sweetness'.

The vigour and excitement of Rickards's drawing was widely admired by other architects. Beresford Pite wrote that 'the gift of attractiveness belonged to Rickards' pencil, harnessed to great powers of design ... [a] coveted gift not given to many'. At the same time he voiced a disquiet, felt by others before and since, on the 'moral' problem of superlatively drawn perspectives in architectural competitions. And their influence through publication in the architectural press on architects with a 'thirst for freshness and a zeal for new excitements ... the ready victims to the charms of fancy expressed in talented sketches'.

Lit: A.B. Pite, *Builder*, CXIX, 1920, pp.233-4. (obituary)

111. **Philip Armstrong Tilden** (1887-1956)
Design for a tower for Selfridge's department store, Oxford Street, London, 1918
Pen (920 x 685)
Provenance: presented by Mrs P. Tilden, 1958.
H.G. Selfridge employed Tilden on two monumental schemes: a vast castle at Hengistbury Head and this extraordinary neo-Wren tower for the top of his department store. 'It is, perhaps, fortunate', commented the obituary writer in the *Times*, 'that Tilden's grandiose projects for the late Mr Selfridge ... were never carried out'. The architect was paid a retaining fee to make drawings, and these were viewed and discussed at regular meetings. However, it is difficult to judge how seriously the tower-project was ever considered.

Tilden had been encouraged to draw and design from an early age, and was acknowledged as a gifted draughtsman. He trained in the office of Collcutt & Hamp, where he was employed to make perspectives. This was a job he always enjoyed – 'giving rein to my fancy', as he put it. Clients too, enjoyed his perspectives; Mr Selfridge actually 'revelled' in them, according to Tilden's reminiscences.
Lit: P. Tilden, 'Architectural Reminiscences', *Builder*, CLXVIII, 1945, pp. 147-50; P. Tilden, *True Remembrances* ... 1954 *passim*.

112. **Oliver Hill** (1867-1968)
Design for *The Kitchen Court* at Cour, Kintyre, Argyllshire, 1921
Pencil, black crayon & varnish on detail paper (405 x 535)
Provenance: presented by Mrs Titania Molyneux (widow of O.H.), 1969.
Oliver Hill was an architectural polygamist – a designer in many styles. As a draughtsman he was, in the early years of his career, an experimentalist in a variety of media (often mixed) and techniques. His first designs (dated 1908-11) made while a student at the Architectural Association evening classes, show him using charcoal, and watercolour in an heroically sublime style of great intensity but there are also watercolour essays in a softly romantic, fairy-tale manner.

Hill's practice, set up in 1910, was interrupted by war service but in 1920 he received his first large commission. This was for the mansion house at Cour, Argyllshire and some of the cottages and other buildings on the estate. His design for Cour was influenced by the modern Tudor of Lutyens's Castle Drogo but made more plastic with rounded corners, conical roofs and arched window heads. Hill's perspective for *The Kitchen Court* at Cour, shown here, was made on detail paper, the outlines drawn in and shaded with pencil and some black crayon. Then all of the sheet, except for the sky, was brushed with varnish that when dry was scraped to give highlights. Hill seems to have rejected this drawing in favour of another 'neater' but similar perspective that was exhibited at the Royal Academy in 1921 (and reproduced in *Academy Architecture*, LIV, 1922, pp. 50-1).

From 1921, Hill began to employ perspective artists, trying out H.F. Waring, Walter Keesey, William Walcot and others, but from 1929 to 1962, J.D.M. Harvey (1895-1978) was his preferred perspectivist.

113. **Raymond McGrath** (1903-1977)
Design for the Dance and Chamber Music Studio, BBC
See colour plate page 30.

114. **William Walcot** (1874-1943)
Egyptian temple: 'Antony in Egypt', 1928
Pencil & gouache, in a blue & gold painted contemporary frame (800 x 1040)
Provenance: purchased, 1944.
Walcot was undoubtedly the greatest architectural perspectivist of the early twentieth century and is noted for his bold impressionistic technique. From the time he settled in London in about 1907 he produced perspectives for all the leading architectural practices – notably Sir Edwin Lutyens, Sir Herbert Baker, Sir Aston Webb and E. Vincent Harris. Lutyens, particularly, chose to present the Viceroy's House, New Delhi, through Walcot's eyes, as he liked the heat he gave his buildings, and Walcot's great Delhi perspectives were exhibited at the Royal Academy in 1914 before being shipped out to India.

Walcot also practised as an architect but was better known as an etcher and painter of architectural fantasies. From just before the Great War he embarked on a series of etchings and paintings which were dramatic reconstructions of Ancient Rome and Greece, Egypt, Babylon and Baal. Considerable scholarship went into these – and as in this example – they often had biblical or classical subjects. They were regularly

exhibited and reproduced in the architectural press, especially in the *Architectural Review*. This gouache was one of ten large subjects, the Great Temple series, which were exhibited at the RIBA in 1944, and illustrates very well Walcot's fondness for a loose form of tempera, in which the main lines were applied in thick body colour by the use of a palette knife or the point of a pencil. Philip Frere, Eustace Frere's son, remembered that Walcot could work with both hands at the same time ... 'with his right hand he was doing some intricate detail of fenestration when suddenly he would seize a tube of brown water-colour paint and, with the tube held vertically in his left hand, would smear the nozzle sinously up and down the left hand side of the drawing. The result of this singular operation would turn out to be the trunk of a large tree to be embellished and tidied up a moment or two later when the right hand was once more available' (quoted, Fine Art Society exhibition catalogue)

Lit: *RIBA Journal*, LI, 1944, reprd p. 77; *William Walcot 1874-1943*, Fine Art Society exhibition catalogue, 1974; G. Stamp, *The Great Perspectivists*, 1982, no. 176.

115. **Corbett, Harrison & MacMurray, Hood & Fouilhoux, and C. Howard Crane**
(Harvey Wiley Corbett, 1873-1954, Wallace Kirkman Harrison, born 1895 and William MacMurray, 1868-1941; Raymond Hood, 1881-1934 and Jacques Andre Fouilhoux, 1879-1945; and C. Howard Crane *c.* 1885-1952).

Design for the *Grand Foyer*, International Music Hall and Opera House, Hyde Park Corner, London, *c.* 1933.
Poster paint, gold paint, pencil & chinese white on Strathmore thistle board (725 x 565)
Provenance: purchased, 1972.
A scheme for a music hall and opera house, not carried out, was proposed for the redevelopment of the site of St George's Hospital, London by much the same team of architects that had designed Radio City, New York. In London, C. Howard Crane replaced Reinhard and Hofmeister, and as architect to the Earls Court Exhibition building (opened in 1937) built by Hegeman-Harris Co., the builders intended for the St George's Hospital project, it seems likely that Crane initiated that project; possibly in conjunction with Samuel L. Rothafel (known as Roxy) manager of Radio City, Ns.Yo., 1930-3, whose obituary (*New York Times*, 1.1.4.1936) noted that he visited London and 'dickered with a proposal for the erection of a mammoth motion picture theatre with elaborate stage presentations. His plans did not materialize however'.

The album put together for, presumably, the Court of Governors of St George's Hospital (and from which the perspective shown here comes) is a very grand affair. Cream 'suede' covers, and silvered end papers, enclose plans, photographs and thrilling perspectives drawn by two unidentified hands. The design for the Grand Foyer is virtually identical to that at Radio City, New York and may have been based on a photograph. The slickly drawn perspective uses thickly applied poster paints and gold paint in broad areas. Pencil outlines were added of some of the details and figures and these were then filled in with more poster paint and with chinese white. The final result was 'speckled', in parts, with an atomizer-spray. An interesting example of a commercial techique used for an 'architectural' perspective.
Lit: C.H. Krinsky, *Rockefeller Center*, 1978, pp. 164-87 *et passim*.; A. Balfour, *Rockefeller Center, architecture as theater*, 1978, *passim*.
See colour plate page 31.

D8. **Le Corbusier, Charles Édouard Jeanneret**
(1887-1965)
Design for the terrace on the 'living' floor of the Villa Savoye, Poissy-sur-Seine, France *c.* 1928.
Contemporary print (490 x 860)
Provenance: lent by Alan Irvine
At the Villa Savoye, Le Corbusier applied the principles he had expounded in *Vers Une Architecture* (1923), taking into account the particularities of the site. The layout of the living floor allowed the occupant to take advantage of the view to one side of the house and the sun on the other.

Although he believed there was a need for 'the perspective' in architectural drawing, he avoided using perspective in his painting – it gave only the accidental appearance of objects. In fact his approach was almost architectural, based on the elevation and plan of selected object types. Jeanneret the artist cannot be divorced from Le Corbusier the architect; elements of Purism appear in his designs, and the 'packing-case' lettering featured in his architectural drawings has its origins in Cubism. His choice of medium and manner of execution reflects his general ideology; the pen and ink sketch on which this print is based would have been economical in time and labour.
Lit: R. Banham, *Theory and Design in the First Machine Age*, 1960; M. Jardot, *Le Corbusier desseins*, 1955.

116. **Eric Mendelsohn** (1887-1953)
Preliminary designs for the De La Warr Pavilion, Bexhill, Sussex, 1933-34
Pencil & crayon on tracing paper
3 sketches: (265 x 225), (55 x 150), (125 x 170)
Provenance: presented by Mrs Mendelsohn in 1955.

Eric Mendelsohn was a leading architect in Germany until the Nazis came to power. He came to England in the summer of 1933 and early in 1934 won the competition, with Serge Chermayeff, for a municipal social centre in Bexhill comprising a pavilion and swimming pool. It was one of the earliest examples of the Modern Movement in Britain and a revolution for the English seaside.

Mendelsohn's tiny sketches have a special significance as he is known to have begun by making them, rather than by letting the elevation grow from the plan. The original first sketch in any project became the criterion against which he would check all future development, and he often cautioned his assistants 'Look at my sketch, there is everything in it'. He also had models prepared from his rough preliminaries and worked constantly back and forth between the two mediums. In some senses his sketches were visionary fantasies expressive both of the 'feel' of the machine and of the effects of 'dynamism', which he defined as the 'expression of internal forces'. He drew with a 6B pencil, writing to his wife in 1917 'You must fix all the pencil drawings. I cannot confine myself to ink. Sometimes even fluid is too unyielding. The pencil line appeals more to the imagination because it leaves gaps and room for variation'. The sketches were not just preliminaries – they were often all he did for the client. He told Rabbi Cohen of the Cleveland Synagogue, 'Please do not mind if the lines are not straight for I have one glass eye and cannot draw a straight line, but my draughtsman will be accurate.' They were also, not only a means to an end, but came to have great influence in themselves; an early exhibition at the Paul Cassirer gallery in Berlin in 1919 led to a collection being published in *Wendingen* in 1920.

Lit: A. Whittick, *Eric Mendelsohn*, 1964, *passim*.
E. Mendelsohn, *Letters of an Architect*, 1967, *passim*.

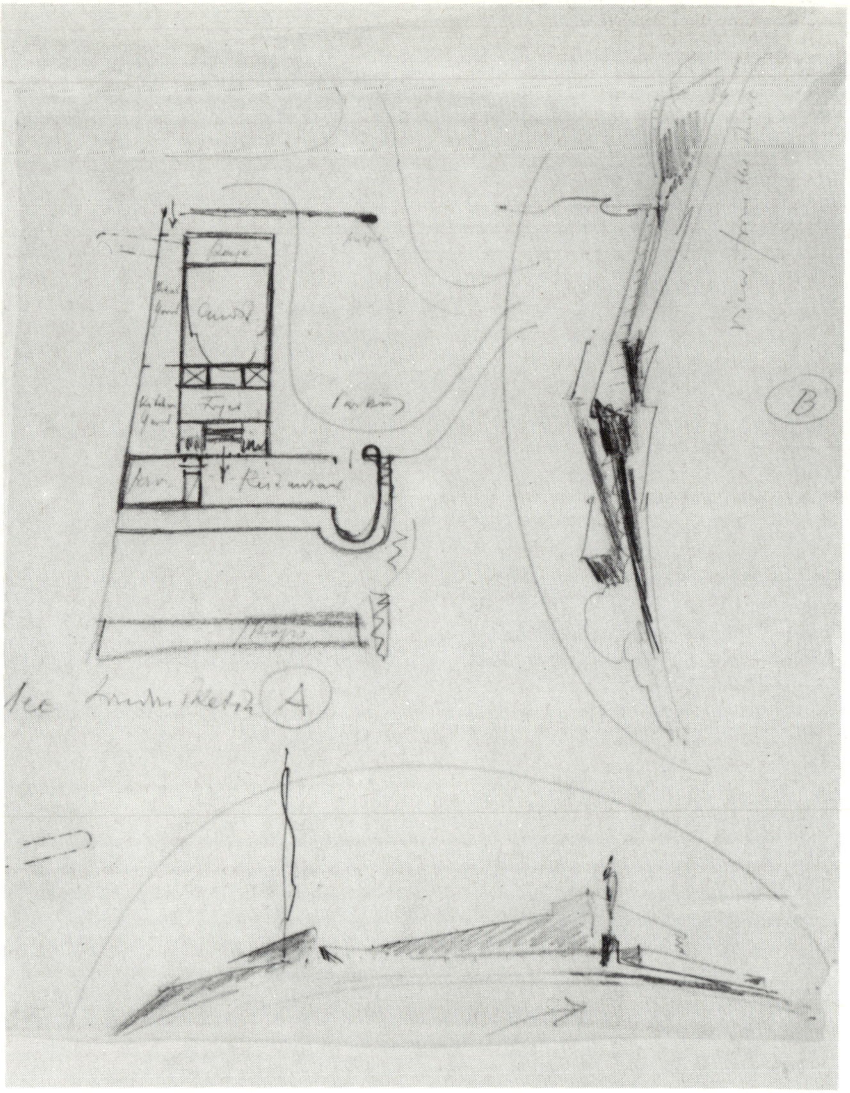

117. **Frank Lloyd Wright** (1867 or 1869-1959)
Design for *All Steel houses*, Los Angeles, 1937
Pencil on tracing paper (380 x 465)
Provenance: as for no. 106.

Frank Lloyd Wright's project for a hundred all-steel houses was never built. Designed at the time that he was working on two of his most imaginative schemes, Falling Water and the Johnson Wax building, the years 1936-7 marked the start of Wright's 'second' career.

Wright's perspective (associated drawings are published in Drexler, op.cit., pp. 141-44) shows his design for a house using twelve inch steel channels, steel panels and steel components. The house (with part of another) is viewed from a high level and the leading lines of the design are emphasised by heavily weighted pencil lines. When looking at the perspective, the eye is taken by the diagonal of the perimeter wall to the right where it is stopped by a clump of trees, one of which breaks through the enclosing line drawn across the top. From the right, the eye travels to the left focusing on the ocean indicated by closely spaced horizontal lines that thin out to suggest the hills below. This ruled device was borrowed from Japanese prints and used by Wright all through his life. The vines and other plants cascading over walls are again, very characteristic of Wright's drawings.

The drawing is inscribed by Wright: *The All Steel – houses – To Russell Hitchcock From FLlW.* Professor Henry-Russell Hitchcock's *In the Nature of Materials, 1887-1941: the Buildings of Frank Lloyd Wright* is the best known book on Wright. It was published in 1942, the year that Wright was offered the RIBA's Royal Gold Medal. Accepting it, Wright cabled

YOU PROPOSE A GREAT HONOR I ACCEPT GRATIFIED THAT DURING THIS TERRIFIC WAR ENGLAND CAN THINK OF HONORING AN ARCHITECT A CULTURE LIKE THAT CAN NEVER LOSE.

118. **Rudolph M. Schindler** (1887-1958)
Design for a beach house for Rupert R. Ryan, 1937
Print with crayon added (350 x 310)
Provenance: presented by Mrs P. Schindler, 1968.
Born in Vienna, Schindler trained both as an engineer and, (under Otto Wagner) as an architect. Encouraged by Adolf Loos he went to America in 1914, working for Frank Lloyd Wright (from 1917) for whom he supervised the construction of the Hollyhock house in Los Angeles. Here he stayed to set up his own practice, designing some highly individual houses of which the best known is the Lovell beach house, 1925-6.

Schindler's unrealised design for a beach house for R.R. Ryan (the location is not known) is in the De Stijl aesthetic that characterised much of his work in the 1920s and '30s. Schindler's drawing for it (in fact, a print with crayon added) emphasises the crucial factors of his design, that is, site, form, system and materials. The wooded site on a Californian hillside overlooking the ocean is crayoned-in with strong browns and greens that emphasise both the topography and 'the basic color character of its setting'. The billowing sea is drawn in the manner of a Japanese print. The interpenetrating volumes of the house are strongly outlined with the smooth, stucco surface left white. Vertical slab supports and inner walls are distinguished by diagonal lines indicating, probably, shuttered concrete. Blue shading and shadows, tonally adjusted, suggest the strong Californian sun. The vertically ruled crayon lines of sky and landscape serve to emphasise the floating horizontality of the building. A vine-covered trellis, cascading plants and the monogram acknowledge a lingering debt to Frank Lloyd Wright. Here, Schindler's draughtsmanship powerfully conveys the 'disturbing and contrary elements' of his architecture.
Lit: E. McCoy, *Five Californian Architects*, 1960, pp. 149-93; D. Gebhard, *The Architecture of R.M. Schindler*, exhibition catalogue, Santa Barbara, 1967 *passim*.; D. Gebhard, *Schindler*, 1971 *passim*.

119. **Charles Henry Holden** (1875-1960)
Design for Senate House, University of London, Bloomsbury, London drawn by Raymond Myerscough-Walker (1908-1984), 1936
Pen, watercolour & chinese white on coloured paper (535 x 750)
Provenance: presented by Adams, Holden & Pearson, 1984.
Holden's monumental new building for the University of London was built in 1933-37. He exhibited this unusual and dramatic drawing of it at the Royal Academy in 1936 under the title 'London University – Nocturne'. It was unusual in showing a building by night, floodlit from below, and was not only a very accomplished exercise in lighting and shadows but took the architectural drawing as near to photography as it could go. In the '30s, with the delight in every aspect of the new technology and in particular with neon lighting and glass, architects often chose to present their buildings in photographs which showed them floodlit by night.

Myerscough-Walker was one of the best architectural draughtsmen of the '30s. Gavin Stamp has well described his career and character in the catalogue of a recent exhibition of his work at the Architectural Association. 'His technique, which he described in his book *The Perspectivist*, was unusual: accurate in three-dimensional delineation but rich and thick in painterly style. Myerscough-Walker used body colour rather than thin washes and experimented with series of glazes. He developed his distinctive style under the influence of two teachers at the Architectural Association, John Holmes and Walpole Champneys. But another quality of his work, a certain mannerism in draughtsmanship, seems to derive from his familiarity with contemporary painting. In the thirties in Chelsea he knew English painters like Sutherland and he was much influenced by Surrealism. His style was quite distinct, with strange trees and dark, cloud-filled skies; he added drama and distinction to otherwise pedestrian representation of buildings'.

Lit: G. Stamp, *The Great Perspectivists*, 1982, fig. 178; *Raymond Myerscough-Walker. Architect and Perspectivist*, exhibition catalogue Architectural Association, London, 1984.

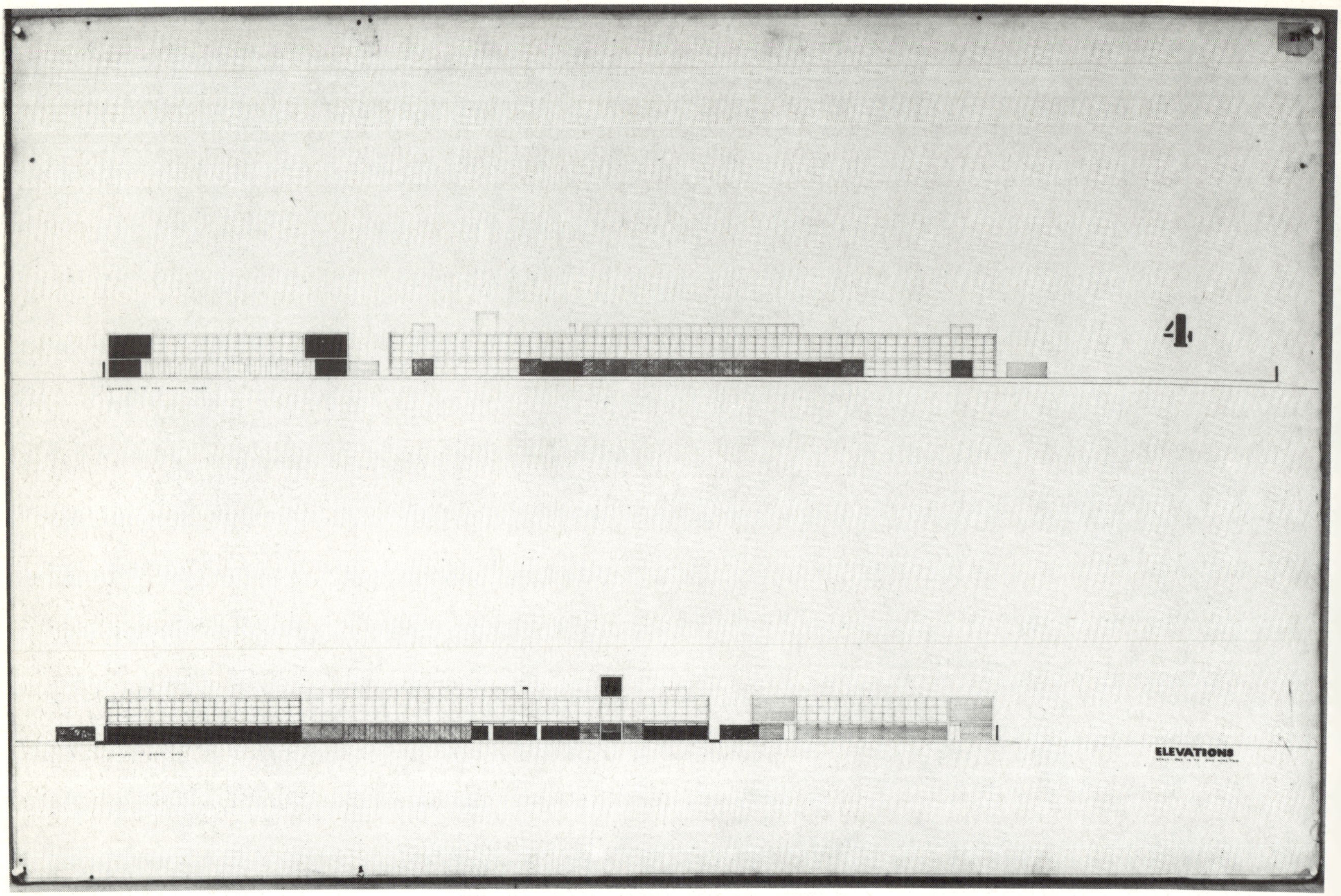

120. **Alison** (born 1928) **& Peter** (born 1923) **Smithson**
Competition design for Hunstanton School, Norfolk, 1950
Graphos pen, pen & chinese ink, brush, with packing-crate stencil (690 x 1030)
Provenance: presented by the architects on indefinite loan, 1966.
This sheet of elevations is one of a set entered by the Smithsons in the competition for Hunstanton School. After leaving the School of Architecture at Durham University, they joined the LCC Schools Division in 1949, working long hours on the competition in their spare time. They won first prize in May 1950 and the assessor, Denis Clarke-Hall noted that 'the elevations were very carefully worked out and the drawings beautifully prepared and presented'.

Hunstanton School has a formal and symmetrical layout and was inspired by Mies van der Rohe's campus buildings for the Illinois Institute of Technology. It has come to be seen as the first 'Brutalist' building, the word 'Brutalist' being defined by Reyner Banham as referring to a 'modern architecture of the pure forms then current, especially the work of Mies van der Rohe'; the exposed materials and services added a more literal meaning to the term. In its elegance, sheer simplicity and innovatory welded steel structure it has been one of the most influential buildings in Britain.

The elevations were fastidiously drawn by both architects. Peter first drew the main frame of the structure with a Graphos pen; Alison then added the hatching with an old-fashioned drawing pen, using watered-down chinese ink. The larger areas of ink were put in with a brush, the stippled areas (which are reminiscent of Mies drawings) being cut away with a razor blade. The lettering was designed by Alison and blocked in with chinese ink, the smaller lettering was printed with a mapping pen. The packing-crate stencil, '4', was bought in Italy and was the only mechanical aid used in the drawing. All the dark and hatched areas indicate brick, the blackest panels being the ones that project the furthest forward.

Both architects have said that as students they admired the drawings of Le Corbusier, which they saw in the volumes of the *Oeuvres Completes* in their university library, and Mies's drawings, some of which were published in Philip Johnson's book on Mies in 1947, and in the *Architects' Journal.* Peter particulaly liked Asplund's drawings which he had seen in *Byggmästeren* and in Stockholm where he went in the summer of 1947 for his fifth year thesis on Asplund's Woodland Crematorium.

Lit: *Architects' Journal*, CX1, 1950, p. 576-577; CXVIII, 1953, pp. 323-328; CXX, 1954, pp.341-352; *Architectural Design*, XXIII, 1953, pp. 238-248; R. Banham, *The New Brutalism* 1966.

121. **Sir Hugh Casson** (born 1910)
Design for the Coronation Decorations in Whitehall, 1953
Pen & watercolour (350 x 320)
Provenance: presented by the architect, 1967.
The Coronation was a great national celebration and was welcomed as the herald of a new Golden 'Elizabethan' Age. This optimism had first manifested itself at the 1951 Festival of Britain, where the austerity of pre-war international modernism had been abandoned in favour of decoration and pattern.

The tradition of providing temporary decoration on such occasions goes back to the Roman Empire, and at times of greater prosperity or extravagance consisted of complex architectural structures (*see* no. 17 Gerbier's design for 'Loyalty Restored', 1661). The City of Westminster appointed Casson – Director of Architecture for the Festival of Britain – to design the street decorations along the Royal route. This widely published perspective shows a Trophy designed by Christopher Ironside upon a structure by Casson, and illustrates the twentieth century's appreciation of the 'sketch'. In this characteristic watercolour Casson has used various stylistic devices to convey the idea of a drawing executed at speed – the figures and trees, for instance.

Lit: *Architects' Journal*, CXVII, 1953, p. 734; *Builder*, CLXXXIV, 1953, p. 824.

122. **Sir Basil Spence** (1907-1976)
Design for the *Modified Porch* at the Cathedral of Saint Michael, Coventry, Warwickshire, 1957
Pencil & coloured chalks, in a white painted contemporary frame (570 x 770)
Provenance: presented by the architect, 1963.
On 14th November 1940 the old Cathedral was largely destroyed. A competition for a new building was held in 1950 and was won by Basil Spence on 15th August 1951. The design, when made known, was decried by the moderns as not modern enough and by the traditionalists as too modern – 'a concrete disgrace'. These initial controversies are now over, and since its consecration in 1962, thousands have visited the Cathedral and still continue to do so. Spence himself was awarded the Order of Merit (an honour he shares with Sir Edwin Lutyens) and was probably Britain's best known architect in the 1960s and 70s. The Cathedral has great popular appeal – an appeal that Pevsner has called 'true, spiritual functionalism'. This was no doubt due to Spence's approach to architecture which was not intellectual but emotional; he seemed to think himself into an appropriate state of feeling about each work he was engaged on.

His drawings have a similar emotional dash about them. Unlike many architects, he made all the presentation elevations and perspectives himself, in black or coloured chalks, although he did once employ Lawrence Wright to make an early perspective of Coventry when he was pressed for time. 'Painting' was listed as one of his hobbies, but rather unusually he also made design sketches in oil. He made 'four interiors and one exterior' of Coventry when he was on holiday in Spain in late 1951 so that he could visualize the Cathedral.

This perspective shows his revised design for the porch which was inspired by the porch at Gerona which he had seen in 1951 after the competition. On the left are the remains of the old Cathedral, on the right Epstein's bronze figures of St Michael and Lucifer. It is a most accomplished rendering, both of three-dimensional form and of the textures of the local pinky-grey sandstone. It is spontaneously executed in chalk over a careful pencil skeleton; even the exact dating, *10 Feb 1957* gives the impression that it has been dashed off – on the spot.
Lit: *Architectural Review*, CX1, 1952, pp. 3-7; B. Spence, *Phoenix at Coventry*, 1962; N. Pevsner & A. Wedgwood, *Warwickshire*, 1966, pp. 249-259.

A3. **Jorn Utzon** (born 1918)
Design model demonstrating the spherical roof system of the Sydney Opera House, 1961
Wood & resin (890 high x 295 wide x 100 deep)
Provenance: presented by the architect, 1978.
Jorn Utzon's fame rests essentially upon just one building, the Sydney Opera House, which he did not even complete; he won the competition in 1956, but resigned as architect ten years later leaving the glass walls and interior to be completed by Hall, Todd & Littlemore. The building was opened in 1973. Its most striking feature is the roof, which Utzon considered of particular importance because the site meant that the building could be seen from all angles, including from above; the series of vaulted shapes also copes unobtrusively with the problem of incorporating a stage tower, which is so often a conspicuous single element. The design of the shells (so called because it was originally hoped that membrane action alone would support the roof structure) presented great problems for the structural engineers, Ove Arup and Partners; the final decision was not achieved until 1963, after six years work. The solution arrived at was to take the shape of the four main shells from just one sphere, 246ft (75m) in radius; this not only, to Utzon's mind, meant that they were in harmony with each other, but also greatly simplified construction, as it meant that the concrete ribs which form the framework of the shells, were all identical (although of different length) and could, therefore, be mass produced. These ribs were then covered with 'tile lids' precast chevron-shaped panels, covered with extruded ceramic tiles, the aim being to prevent the surface being smooth, dull and uninspiring. There were, in all, some 4,000 of these tile lids, weighing up to three tons each, covered with a total of 1,300,000 tiles.
Lit: *Architectural Design*, XXXV, 1965, pp. 133-142; *Architecture in Australia*, LIV, 1965, pp. 72-92; *Architect & Building News*, CCXXXI, 1967, pp. 17-24; *Arup Journal*, VIII no.3, 1973 (special issue).

123. **Foster Associates**
Design for the glass retention system, Willis Faber & Dumas building, Ipswich, Suffolk, 1973
Pen & transfer on tracing paper (620 x 860)
Provenance: presented on indefinite loan by Foster Associates, 1976.

The site of the Willis Faber & Dumas building was acquired piecemeal, so a design was evolved that could be adapted to expand with it. Glass was chosen for the external walling as it allowed a degree of flexibility.

This early drawing dates from before the involvement of Pilkington Brothers. It is an exploratory design by Foster Associates for a clamp to hold the glass panels together. The clamp has been drawn to a slightly unusual scale: ten times full size. Wash or hatching has been replaced by 'dry-adhesive' paper, variously polka-dotted to indicate different materials.

Lit: *Architectural Review*, CLVIII, 1975, pp. 131-153.

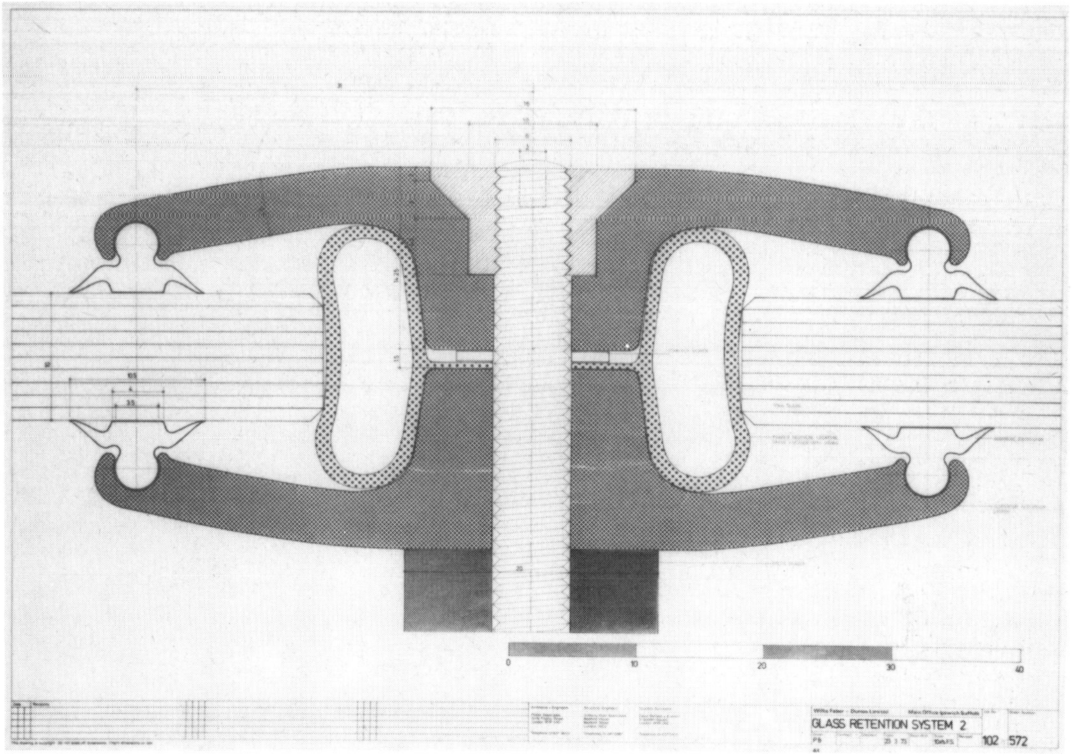

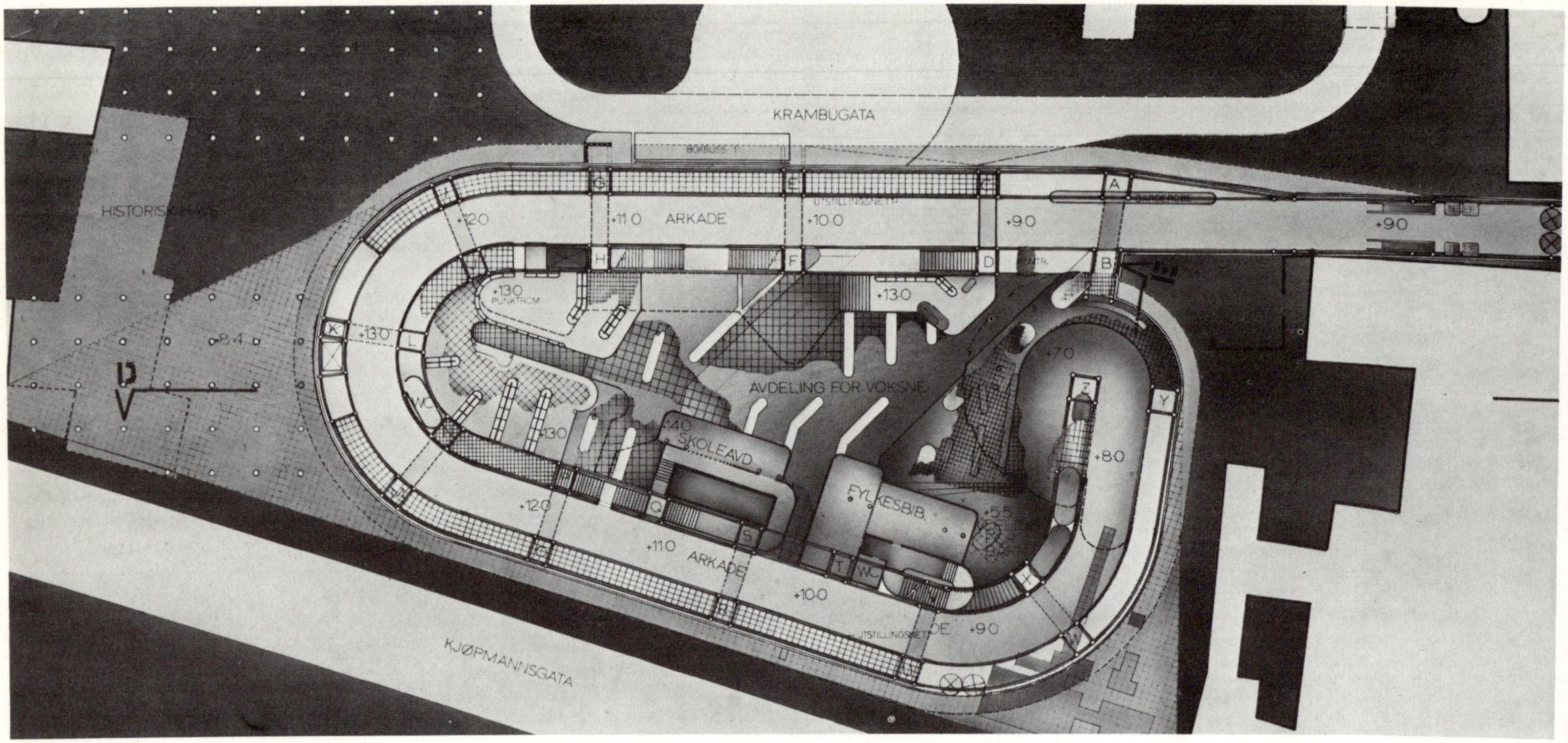

124. **Peter Cook** (born 1936) **& Christine Hawley** (born 1949)
Competition design for Trondheim City Library, Norway, 1977
Print, air-brushes with Dr Martin's inks
(605 x 1230)
Provenance: lent by the architects, 1984.

The architects felt that Trondheim, one of the most northern cities in the world, needed a 'place where people could find an easy excuse to loiter creatively in a conditioned environment'; they therefore provided what they have called an 'internal landscape'. The plan is the most informative drawing in their competition set. It shows, in pale blue and pink, the principal structure and thoroughfare of the building, an arcade which winds around the lending library in the central space. The outer side of the arcade carries the dead book storage, the inner the public facilities; the individual departmental buildings form separate units within the central space.

The drawing is also a skilful example of modern drafting methods. It was first drawn with a Rapidograph on tracing paper and lettered with stencils; then photographically enlarged and dry-mounted. The architects (who both worked on this drawing) then air-brushed the plan with five colours, using Dr Martin's inks, often overlaying onè colour on another and achieving very subtle effects. The skill lies in the delicate and time consuming operation of cutting and applying the film to mask out different areas of the drawing and in merging one colour with another.

The architects have used applied Letracolour and Pentels diagrammatically on drawings since 1964. Their use of colour is now softer and more pictorial and they often combine watercolour and crayon with air-brushing.
Lit: *Architectural Design*, 1979, IXL, pp. 332-337.

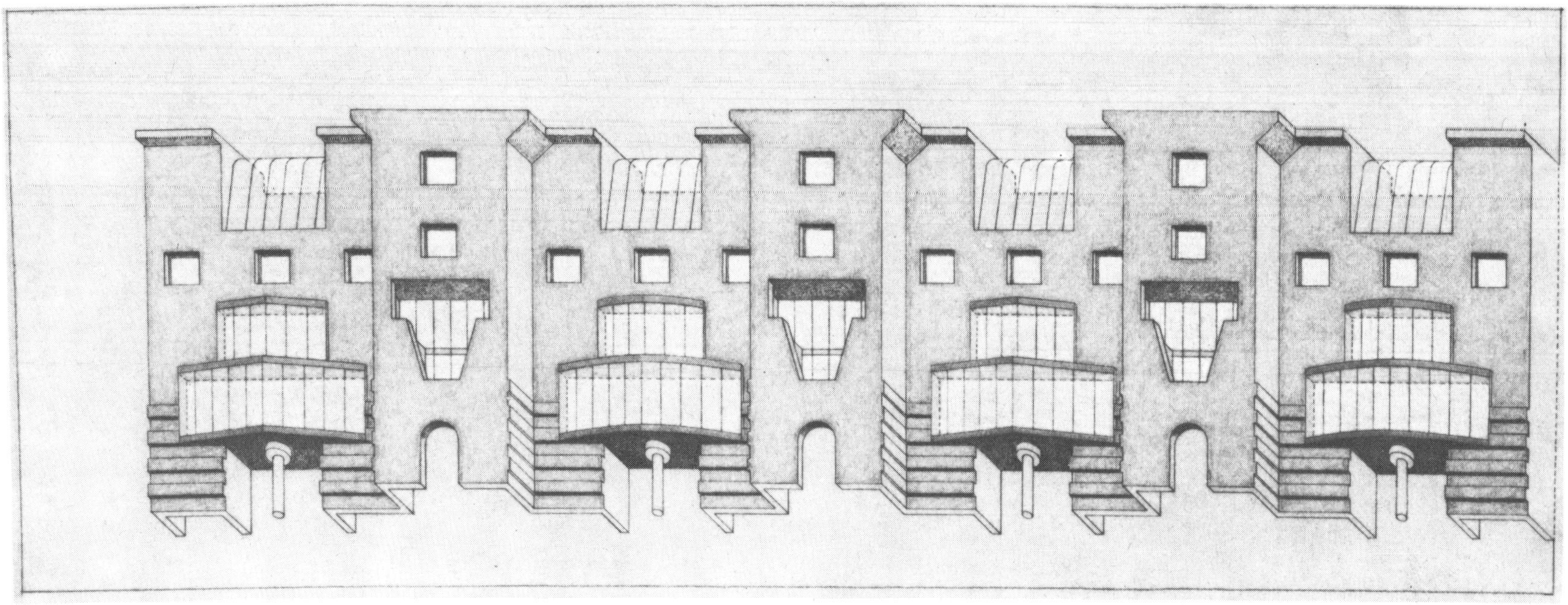

125. **James Stirling** (born 1926)
Competition designs for eleven town houses in E. 67th Street, New York, 1978
Pencil & coloured crayon on tracing paper;
Short elevation (190 x 180), 'up-view' axonometric (245 x 390)
Provenance: lent by the architect, 1984.

The requirement of Sheldon Solow, architect and developer, was for the design of eleven luxury town houses (some of which could be apartments), the whole to be five storeys high and built over an existing underground garage. It was a limited competition between three architects and Stirling's design was not chosen.

Using the existing structural bay of 18 feet and the New York Town house as his model, Stirling invented two types: an 18ft wide house on five storeys and a 36 foot wide two-storey apartment over a three-storey house. He also provided for a small front garden set behind railings, which is a feature of this part of New York. The 'up-view' axonometric – or 'mole's-eye view' as Sir John Summerson has called it – is a standard method of presentation in the Stirling office and was spectacularly used to present his design for the Florey building at Queen's College in 1966. It is used here as one of several three-dimensional studies made specifically to study the proportions of the composition, rather than for the client, and accurately conveys the alternating backwards and forwards movement of the street façade, with its sophisticated secondary rhythm of alternating rounded and angled bays.

Up until the mid 1970s Stirling chose to present his designs by fastidious ruled line perspectives or axonometrics. The latter gave the effect – as Banham has noted – of 'expository mechanical cut-away drawings of complex machinery', the former are reminiscent of nineteenth century perspectives by Schinkel or Choisy, although they do not actively seek to present an historical effect. Since the late 1970s, and particularly in his sets of presentation designs for the Stuttgart National Gallery, 1979, and for the Tate Gallery, 1980, Stirling has turned to 'up-view frontals' made in crayon and pencil which have more in common with contemporary paintings of the last decade.

Coloured pencils and wax crayons are now the vital equipment of any architectural office. The reasons for the change to colour and to a more informal and artistic effect are hard to determine. In the last decade there has been a renewed interest in the history of architecture and in architectural drawing; the architectural magazines have regularly published drawings in colour and those by Stirling and Michael Graves have had considerable influence. There have been many more exhibitions of architectural drawings, notably the Beaux Arts exhibition in New York in 1975. Books on drawings by Wright and le Corbusier have appeared, both of whom used coloured crayons. Stirling himself, however, has been quick to point out that he used crayon to colour the elevations of his design for flats at Ham Common in 1955.

Lit: *James Stirling*, exhibition catalogue, RIBA Heinz Gallery, 1974; *International Architect*, 1981, No. 5, I, Issue 5, pp. 27-35.

126. **Arup Associates**
Design for the IBM Head Office, North Harbour, Portsmouth, Hampshire, drawn by James Burland, 1981
Rotring pens on tracing paper, on a grey paper backing, with Letraset lettering (2070 x 630)
Provenance: lent by the architects, 1984.

Set in the middle of a large site on reclaimed land in Portsmouth's North Harbour, IBM's UK Headquarters form a huge complex which is very like a small town. The first three phases of building were completed in 1976-77. This drawing shows part of Phase 4, which consists of four separate office blocks, whose stepped façades provide roof terraces, linked by a barrel-vaulted glazed arcade which threads together all the buildings on site.

Arup Associates were formed in 1963 as a multi-disciplinary practice, 'a partnership of architects, engineers and quantity surveyors, who undertake the total design of buildings'. The office has its own model-making department and generally prefers models to perspectives when it comes to presenting a design to the client. It was made 'after the event' as an art drawing,both for exhibition at the Royal Academy (1981) and for the client, who has a copy, and naturally absorbed many hours of office time.

It is a 'sectional-elevation', compiled from several sheets of existing working drawings, and shows how the cut-away section of the arcade breaks into the side elevation of one of the office blocks. The fine pen draughtsmanship seems to capture the qualitites of steel and glass and concrete, and the shading is drawn by hand – the only mechanical aid being the 'Letraset' lettering. The draughtsman has mentioned his own admiration for old–fashioned engineering drawings and for Piranesi's etching technique; this drawing could certainly hold its own with any made in the past.
Lit: *Architects' Journal*, 1981, p. 931; 'IBM Flagship', *Architectural Review*, CLXXIV, 1983, pp. 46-57.

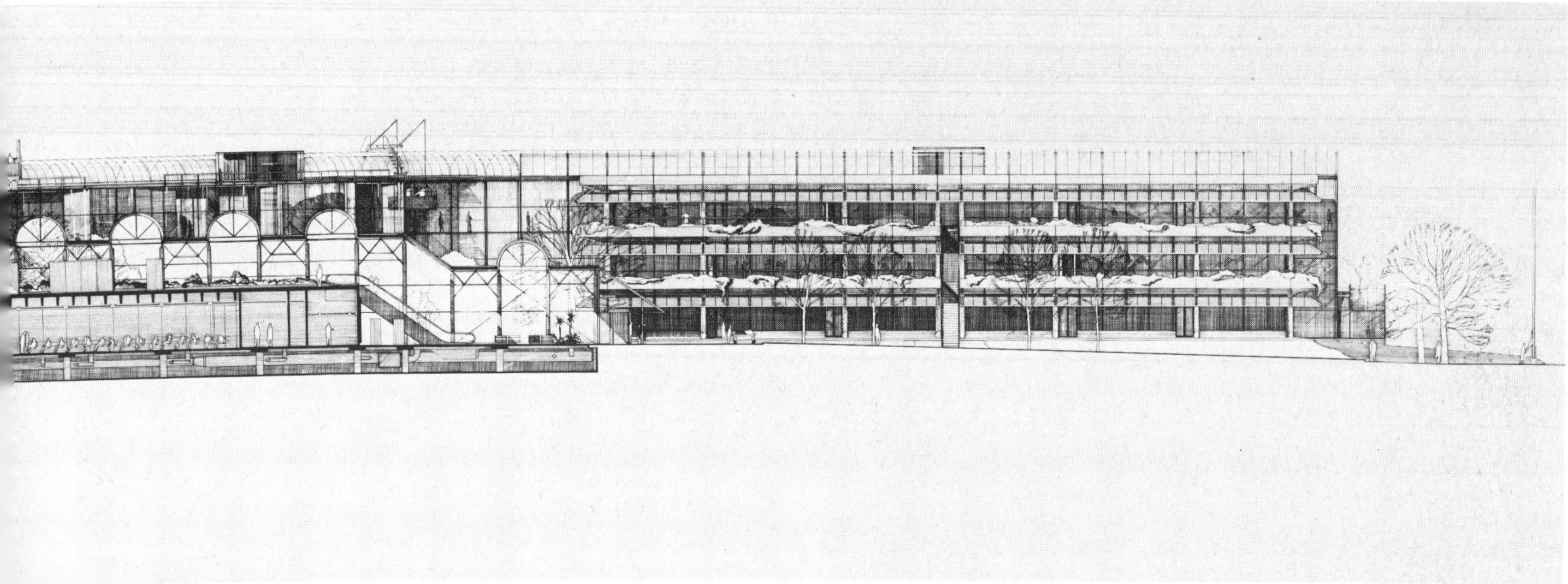

127. **Aldo Rossi** (born 1931)
'Venezia analoga', 1981
Print with oil/crayon & varnish added (605 x 710)
Provenance: presented by the architect, 1984.
The composition features Rossi's Teatro del Mondo, designed as part of an exhibition on architecture and theatre held in Venice in 1979. It was built upon a pontoon and followed a Venetian tradition of temporary floating theatres dating back to the sixteenth century. Its form, however, owed less to these earlier examples than to the wooden light-houses of the northern coast of America. Symbolically, it represented the relationship between architecture and water that is a fundamental characteristic of Venice. Rossi wanted it to be built of wood, a material he associated with the theatre; it was actually constructed of timber-sheeting suspended on a scaffolding frame, a solution both economical and practical in terms of time.

The print is dated 1981 and constitutes a re-drawing of the design after its execution. Although composed of architectural elements – such as plan and elevation – these no longer fulfill their original functions. Here the practical language of architecture has been adapted to create a pleasing image and the architectural drawing has metamorphosed into an 'art' drawing. Its existence has become an end in inself.

Lit: *Architecture d'Aujourdhui* 1980 pp. 72-73; *Progressive Architecture*, LXI, 1980, pp. 64-65.
See colour plate page 32.

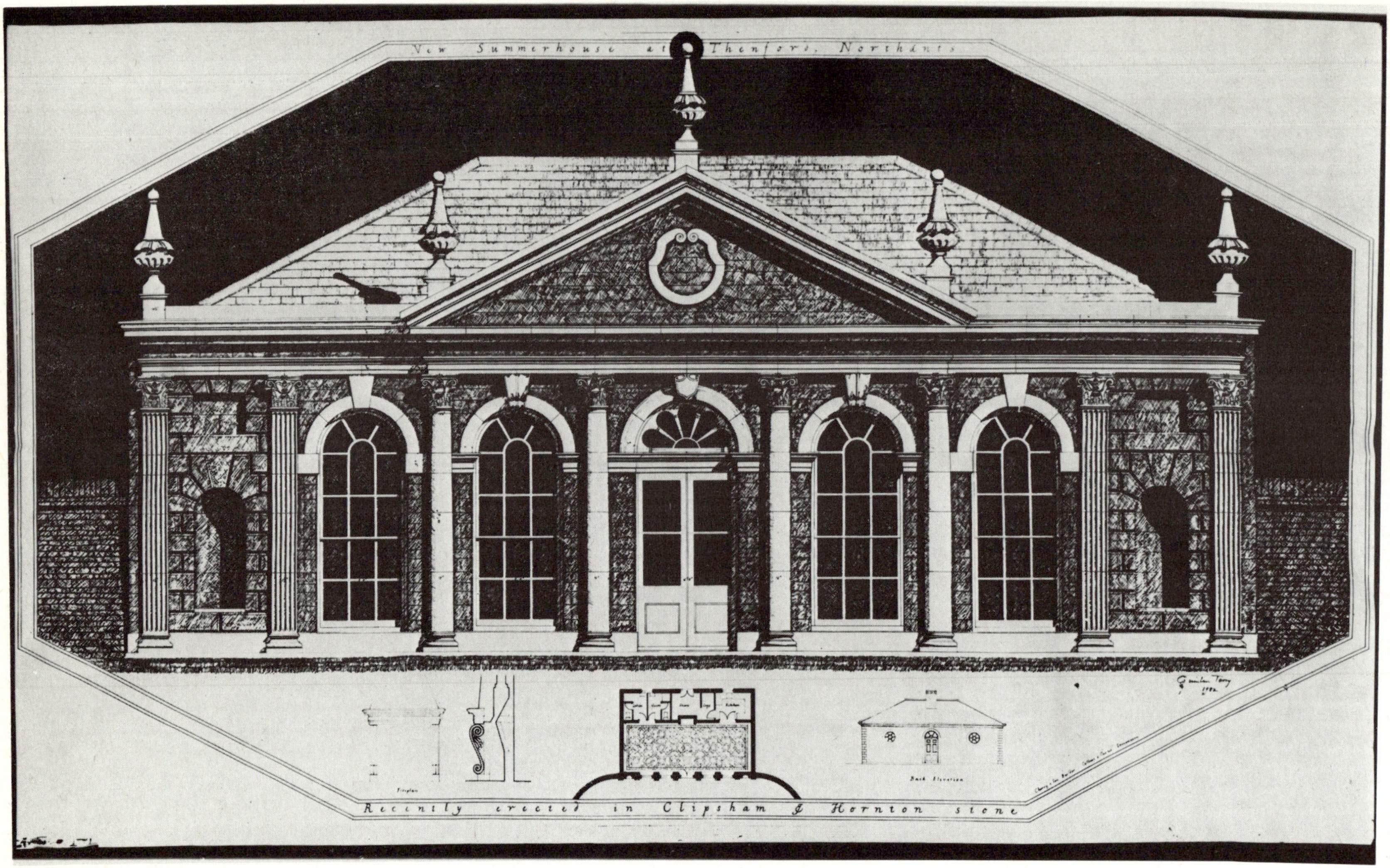

128. **Quinlan Terry** (born 1937)
Design for a *New Summerhouse at Thenford, Northants*, 1982
Pen & black & coloured inks on tracing paper, dry mounted (865 x 1420)
Many of the buildings that Quinlan Terry designs are recorded in the form of finished drawings made 'for their own sake'. The front elevation, with inset plan, back elevation and details of the fireplace, shown here, is one such drawing (exhibited at the Royal Academy 1982). It was drawn with ruling and mapping pen on tracing paper which was then dry-mounted, the heavier inking done after mounting. Terry uses thin tracing paper for finished drawings both because of its attractive smoothness and because his partner Raymond Erith (1904-1973) had always done so. An alternative medium to pen and ink employed by Quinlan Terry, and a highly unusual one for architectural drawings, is the linocut.
Lit: *Quinlan Terry*, (ed.) F. Russell, 1981, *passim*.

129. **Richard Rogers Partnership Ltd**
Design for a *cleaning crane* for Lloyd's Underwriters' new building, Leadenhall Street, City of London, 1984
Pen, mechanical tone & transfer over pencil on tracing paper, the edges bound (845 x 1185)
Provenance: lent by the architect, 1984.

Rogers's commission for the Lloyd's building was the result of an international limited competition organised in 1977-8 by the RIBA. The Beauborg Art Centre in Paris, also won in competition, is probably Rogers's best known building. Both the Beauborg and Lloyd's share the technologically innovative approach to design that characterises Rogers's work; and that makes him, with Norman Foster, the leading British exponents of so-called 'High-tech' architecture.

Shown here is an unfinished drawing for a crane to clean the external cladding of one of six 'satellite' towers. It is drawn to a scale of 1:20 with a 2H pencil on heavyweight tracing paper, inked in with a Faber Castell pen and with some mechanical tone added. Interestingly, the spiral stair, notoriously difficult to design and draw, is a 'transfer' achieved by drawing part of it to a larger scale (1:10), reducing it via a photocopying machine to an intermediate scale, then reducing it (1:20) on to adhesive film. The drawing is bound with a colour-coded (related to job) blue tape.

Essentially this is a design co-ordination drawing made so that the different elements can be read and appraised together. Not yet labelled or dimensioned, the next stage is a development of each element, first by the architect and then by the consulting engineer until (after checking and re-checking) it reaches its final destination, the steelwork sub-contractor. The drawing is in the hand of two architects and took about six to seven hours to make. Initially, the design was worked out in sketch form in a large, bound, ruled Cambridge notebook, one of hundreds in the office. Finished working drawings are usually on A0 size paper, pen is preferred to pencil since it is more legible and more durable. Freehand lettering is discouraged and a Rotring Scribe stencil machine or, conventional stencils, are used. At this stage, something like 10,000 drawings have been prepared by Rogers's office for the Lloyds's building, due for completion in December 1985.

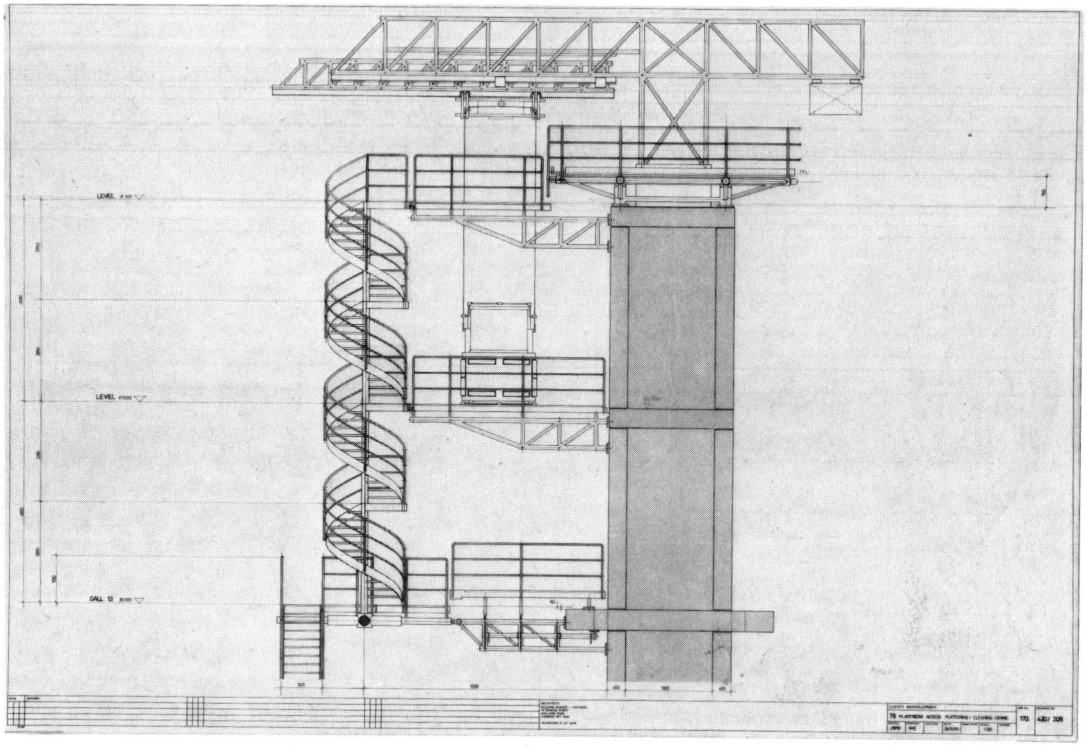

A4. **Carlo Scarpa** (1906-1978)
Model for the Brion Cemetery, San Vito near Asolo Italy, 1971
Wood, painted grey, gold (indicating water) & red base (595 x 595, maximum height 80)
Provenance: presented by the architect, 1974.
The design was comissioned by Onoria Brion, widow of a wealthy industralist, for an 'L' shaped site flanking the existing village cemetery. It is composed of a number of structures – including Chapel and family vault – the natures of which evolved gradually. The bridge that rises over the two sarcophagi was first conceived as an arch, based on the "arcosolium" found in early Christian catacombs; it was eventually to be built of reinforced concrete and decorated with mosaics in the Ventian tradition. One of Scarpa's aims was to show his fellow country-men that there was an alternative to the "mechanically stacked shoe-boxes" common to most Italian cemeteries.

Influenced by the park-like cemeteries of nineteenth century Chicago, he wanted to create a tranquil garden. The Brion Cemetery has been described as 'pure architecture' or 'architecture as poetry', functionalism not being the prime consideration; this corresponds to Scarpa's concept of the architect-artist.

Lit: *Architectural Review*, CLIV, 1973, pp. 393-396; *Progressive Architecture*, LXII, 1981, pp. 124-131; *Carlo Scarpa 1906 1978*, exhibition catalogue, Gallerie dell' Accademia in Venice, 1984.

A5. **Denys Lasdun** (born 1913)
Model of the National Theatre, with the IBM Central Marketing Centre alongside, South Bank, London, made by Philip I. Wood, 1982
Balsa wood, hardwood & cast metal (790 x 680 x 230)
Provenance: lent by the architect, 1984.
This model was made to record the unified design and relationship of two buildings, the National Theatre and the IBM building on the South Bank, a concept that was based on Lasdun's original scheme for the National Theatre and Opera House (1965) on the site in front of the Shell Centre. The finish and purpose of the model differs considerably from the rough working models used by the practice to explore every stage of the continuing and creative process of design. The practice has always been noted for its consistent use of models, which Lasdun believes are a closer guide to a spatial and architectural qualities of buildings than drawings. This particular record model expresses better than drawings the 'strata' and finely-textured concrete of the South Bank buildings; its elegance and craftsmanship make it a work of art in its own right.

Denys Lasdun currently leads the practice of Denys Lasdun Redhouse & Softley.

Lit: *A Language and a Theme: The Architecture of Denys Lasdun & Partners*, 1976; *Architecture in an Age of Scepticism – A Practitioners' Anthology compiled by Denys Lasdun.* 1984.

130. **Charles Mark Correa** (born 1930)
Design for the Vidham Bhavan, Bhopal, Central India, 1984
Pen on handmade paper (350 x 510)
Provenance: presented by the architect, 1984.
Norn in Hyderabad, Correa trained in the United States, returning to India in 1958 where he has lived and worked ever since.

The Vidham Bhavan is the new state Assembly for the Government of Madhya Pradesh; it is Correa's most recent scheme and is under construction now.

In 1984 Charles Correa was awarded the RIBA's Royal Gold Medal.

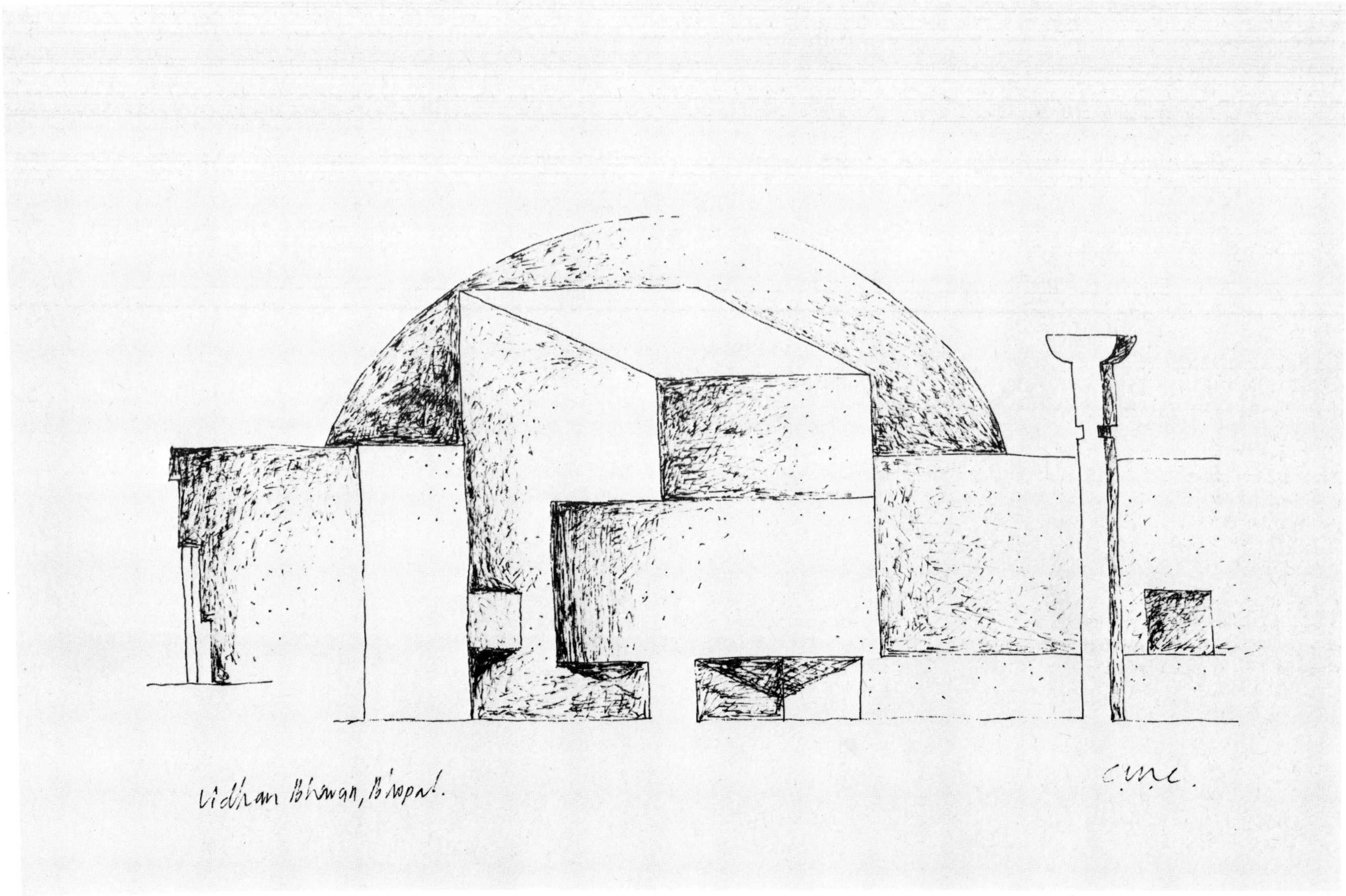
Vidhan Bhawan, Bhopal.
CMC.

Sources and further reading

A brief bibliography (*Lit.*) is given with the entry for each drawing. Further information on the drawings, buildings and architects discussed can be found in the following:-

Catalogue of the Drawings Collection of the R.I.B.A. (Farnborough and Amersham, 1969-83) General editor: Jill Lever. (Volumes available: A, B, C-F, G-K, L-N, O-R, S, T-Z (*in preparation*), Colen Campbell, Jacques Gentilhâtre, Inigo Jones & John Webb, Edwin Lutyens, J.B. Papworth, Pugin Family, Scott Family, Alfred Stevens, Antonio Visentini, C.F.A. Voysey, Wyatt Family.

RIBA Drawings Series (London and New York 1981-3) Volumes available: The Palladians (John Harris), The Great Perspectivists (Gavin Stamp), Architects' Designs for Furniture (Jill Lever), Architecture of the Arts and Crafts Movement (Margaret Richardson), The Thirties (David Dean).

The Buildings of England (Harmondsworth, 1957 to date) N. Pevsner & others. 50 volumes.

Colvin, H. *A Biographical Dictionary of British Architects 1600-1840* (2nd ed. London, 1978).

Index

The pages on which subjects are illustrated are given in italics.